IMAGES
of America

NORTH AMHERST AND CUSHMAN

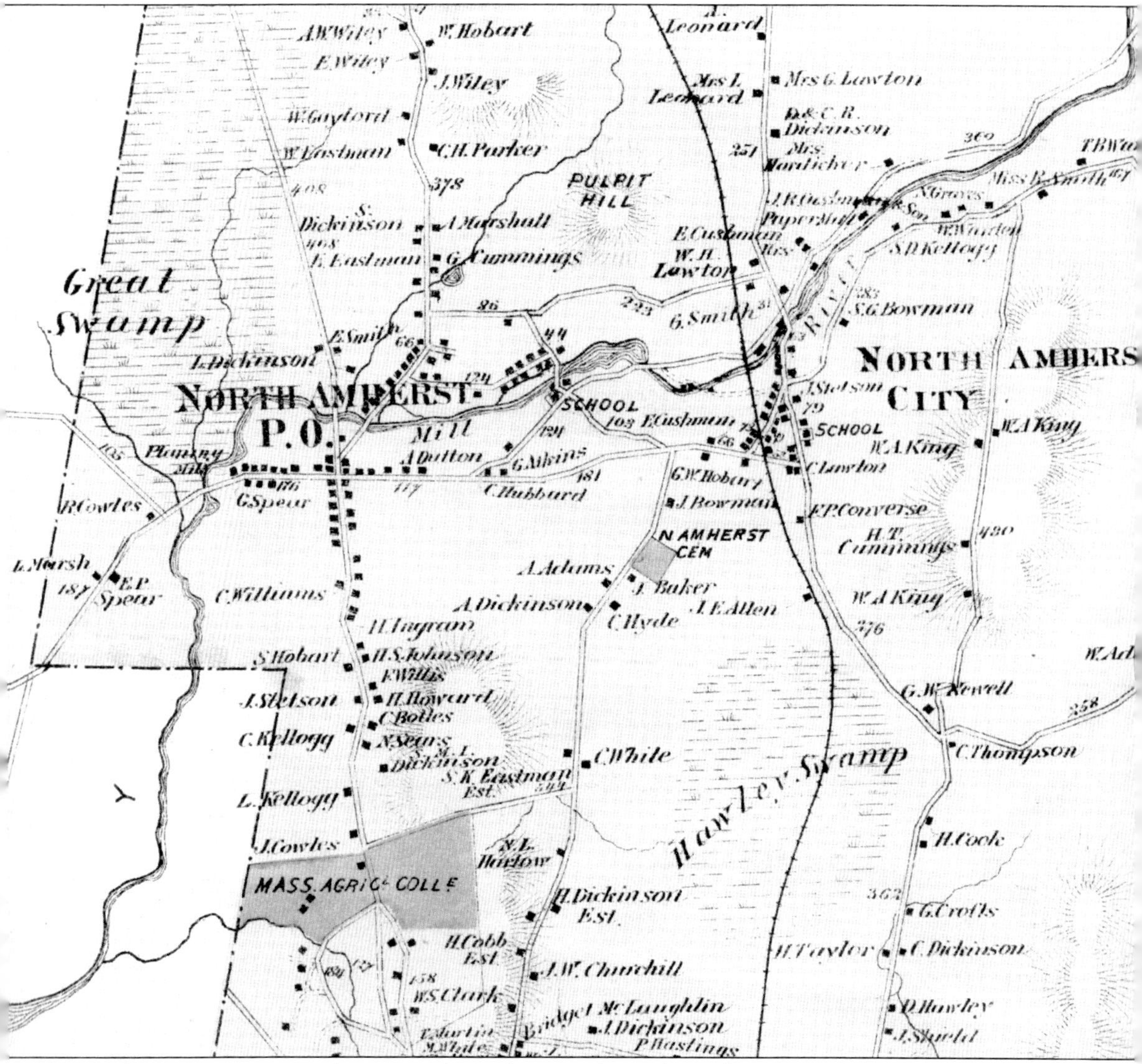

This F.W. Beers map shows North Amherst and North Amherst City, later called Cushman, in 1873. Note the Great Swamp in the northwest corner, the mills along Mill River, and the Massachusetts Agricultural College, now the University of Massachusetts Amherst. (Courtesy of the Jones Library Inc., Special Collections.)

On the Cover: Ransom Cowles sits with his son Albert and Albert's wife, Mary, outside this farmhouse, which is still located on the corner of Meadow Street and Russellville Road in Amherst. In the 1900 census, the occupation of Ransom Cowls, 81, who had farmed the same property for years, is listed as "Capitalist." (Courtesy of the Jones Library Inc., Special Collections.)

IMAGES
of America

NORTH AMHERST AND CUSHMAN

Patricia G. Holland and William N. Robinson

ARCADIA
PUBLISHING

ISBN 978-0-7385-9292-3

Published by Arcadia Publishing
Charleston, South Carolina

Printed in the United States of America

Library of Congress Control Number: 2012935145

For all general information, please contact Arcadia Publishing:
Telephone 843-853-2070
Fax 843-853-0044
E-mail sales@arcadiapublishing.com
For customer service and orders:
Toll-Free 1-888-313-2665

Visit us on the Internet at www.arcadiapublishing.com

To all the people of North Amherst and Cushman, past, present, and future.

Contents

Acknowledgments

Special thanks go to Tevis Kimball, curator of special collections at the Jones Library, the public library of Amherst, and her associate Kate Boyle, for all their help in finding images and information and for permission to publish the photos. Many of the photographs from the 1880s and 1890s in their collections were taken by the Howes Brothers of Ashfield, Massachusetts, who in the 1800s went all over western New England using glass plates on which to record images of houses, mills, and the people.

The excellent website of the Town of Amherst with its online historical town reports and the staff of the Planning Department were most helpful as well.

We thank Rob Cox, curator of special collections at the University of Massachusetts Amherst, for permission to publish images from the Bates Family Collection and the Robert Francis Collection. Dylan Gaffney of the Forbes Library in Northampton, Massachusetts, kindly found an important photograph from the files of the *Daily Hampshire Gazette*. Our gratitude also goes to the following people who gave us their recollections and let us reproduce images from their personal collections: Alton Acker, Janna L. Aldrich, Edna Ball, Eugene Battistoni, Lawrence Britt, Isabelle Callahan, Charlie Clark, Stewart T. Coffin, Sondra Corcoran, Louis and Hilda Greenbaum, Susan Holden, Ruth F. Hooke, Houghton and Judith Ingram, Cinda Jones, Ruth Owen Jones, Reed Kaynor, Pauline Lannon, Joseph Larson, Robert Leitch, Phyllis E. Longto, Mary Lucas, Joyce Matuszko, Richard Natthorst, Donald and Jean Pelkey,Victoria Pratt, Elizabeth Rolander, Judith Schaeffer, Paul and Leona Searle, Mary Szala, Marie Twohig, Shirley Whittemore, and Stanley and Beverly Ziomek.

The majority of the photographs are courtesy of the department of Special Collections and Archives at the Jones Library; all others are credited accordingly.

INTRODUCTION

North Amherst and Cushman are villages within Amherst, Massachusetts, a town of uplands and lowlands whose streams flow into the Connecticut River, which runs into the Atlantic Ocean. Those uplands and lowlands shaped how people have lived here.

500 million years ago, the land was in the southern hemisphere, below the equator, surrounded by volcanoes, and there was nothing living—no plants, or fish, or animals. Then, the continents slowly began banging into each other, and the Pelham Hills that border Amherst on the east were formed.

220 million years ago, all seven continents of the world were hitched together. Western Massachusetts looked like the rocky landscape between Colorado and California but with taller mountains and more volcanoes. Then the continents began to split off. Africa was the first. It began to pull away from North America to the south and east, leaving behind our broad Connecticut River Valley. This was the time of the dinosaurs.

15,000 years ago, in Amherst, the last glacier melted. Where the Connecticut River is now, there was instead a broad, long lake that geologists in the 19th century named Lake Hitchcock after Amherst College professor Edward Hitchcock. The water came nearly up to the ridge where East Pleasant Street is now. The steeple on the church in North Amherst would have been under the water. When the southern end of this big lake broke through, the water went down, and the lake narrowed into the Connecticut River.

8,000 years ago, people appeared. The lake bottom soil was excellent for farming. Fish and game were plentiful. Some of North Amherst was flat lake bottom with rich soil, and hillier parts had sandy soil left behind when the lake drained, along with great boulders and gravel pits.

In 1653, John Pynchon from Springfield, Massachusetts, bought the land from the local Nonotucks and Norwottucks, who kept hunting and fishing rights. Immigrants originally from England moved up from Connecticut to settle in Hadley in 1659. Hadley then included what are now the towns of Hatfield, South Hadley, and Amherst.

In 1703, Hadley's town fathers laid out the land for what later became Amherst, a long narrow site about nine miles north to south and three-and-a-half miles east to west. An official drew in two north-south roads on a map. What are now called South East and North East Streets were the roads to the east, and South Pleasant and East Pleasant Streets the one to the west, with North Pleasant Street branching off to the northwest.

Wars with Native Americans delayed settlement, but by 1731, a few families from Hadley and Hatfield lived in the new area. In 1734, the area was called the third precinct of Hadley. Because the site was so long, informal villages grew at its north and south extremes. There was a formal drawing of lots for Hadley and Hatfield residents in May 1742. On February 13, 1759, the Commonwealth of Massachusetts officially declared it an incorporated district, imposing the name Amherst; in 1775, it became a town. The town was enlarged by grants from Hadley in 1789, 1811, 1812, and 1814, mainly to the north and west of North Amherst. Farming was the main occupation, and the minister and several of the wealthiest landowners had slaves to help.

In North Amherst, the river that ran down from the hills of Shutesbury to the Connecticut River was the northern boundary of the town until 1789, when additional parcels were attached to the north. That river powered mills beginning in the 1700s. In Shutesbury the river is called Roaring Brook, in Cushman the Cushman Brook, and in Amherst the Mill River. By the 1800s, there was so much factory development that North Amherst's upstream neighbor to the east was called North Amherst City; it did not become Cushman until 1898, named after the most prosperous of the factory families.

In North Amherst, as in the rest of the town, a few people did not support the revolution against England, but others fought for it, some losing their lives. In 1786, supporters of Daniel Shays and his rebellion against farmers being jailed for debts caused by increased taxes headed through North Amherst and Cushman to make their protest. Land values began plummeting after the Civil War. Many local families moved west, and in the 1890s, immigrants, especially the Polish and Lithuanians, were able to purchase farms of their own. In their home countries at the time they were forbidden to own property.

A Congregational church was built in North Amherst in 1826, financed mainly by Oliver Dickinson, who lived across the street from its site in the center of the village. A memoir by its pastor George Cooke provides detailed information about the members during the time he served there, from 1838 to 1852. A Methodist Episcopal church began holding services in private homes in 1842 in North Amherst City and built a church building in 1844. It drew its largest numbers from the factory workers. It began to decline in the middle of the nineteenth century but was active again during the first half of the 1900s.

The Irish and French Canadians who began arriving in the 1840s were served by traveling clergy in the 1850s and 1860s. St. Brigid's Roman Catholic Church was organized in the center of Amherst in 1869, and the first building erected by 1871. The new church building was erected in 1925. In the 1930s and 1940s, Catholic services for North Amherst residents were held in a barn, the priest coming from the church in the center. Those of other faiths had to worship elsewhere, and many did not worship in a church at all.

Schools were created in both North Amherst and Cushman in the 1700s, as was the North Amherst Cemetery.

In 1946, a local journalist, Warren R. Brown, published a column on the names used colloquially for different parts of the area. The center of North Amherst was called "The Corner." Meadow Street was called "Westville," as most of the houses were at the west end. Cushman was "North Amherst City," its residents "Cityites." They called North Amherst Center "West Street" and the people "West Streeters." Factory Hollow was "Factory Holler." "The Patch" was the few factory workers' homes near the Cushman Bridge on State Street.

At present, North Amherst, including Cushman, is a single census-designated place in the town of Amherst with a population of 6,819 at the 2010 census. Both North Amherst Center and Cushman are historic districts listed in the National Register of Historic Places. North Amherst is also home to two co-housing communities: Pioneer Valley and Pine Street Cohousing.

The journey begins at the top of Montague Road, then down to the center of North Amherst, and to Meadow Street and Sunderland Road. The tour continues along the Mill River, where all the mills and factories used to be, then into Cushman, formerly North Amherst City, and all around Cushman Village. It will pick up along Market Hill Road and the Flat Hills, coming down to North East Street. The last stage of the journey will be north along East Pleasant Street, west on Pine Street, and finally North Pleasant Street, before returning to the center of North Amherst.

One

Montague Road

In the 1800s, Montague Road was known as West Street and was the northern section of the road that ran all the way to Amherst's southern border. Before the trees grew up, at the top of the hill where Amherst borders Leverett, there used to be a panoramic view southward over all of Amherst. Farms lined both sides of the road.

At the age of 72, George Cooke, a retired pastor of the North Amherst Congregational Church, recalled his years there between 1838 and 1852 and gave an overview:

> Entering Amherst from "Long-Plain" in Leverett, one finds himself on an eminence from which, in a wondrously beautiful panorama here bursting upon the view, may be seen the larger part not only of this parish but of the entire town, nestling in a scene of rural beauty rarely equaled. . . . The houses quietly repose at well selected and most convenient points, on either side of this long street, flanked by huge barns with their proper retinue of small supplementary "out-buildings,"—the whole forming a faithful picture of domestic peace, content, comfort, industry, well-doing & well-wishing.

Photographs from the end of the 1800s portray a contrasting image of harder times. By the end of the nineteenth century, West Road was called Leverett Street, meaning the road to the town of Leverett, and in 1938, Amherst's planning board changed the name to Montague Road in part to distinguish it from the Leverett Road in Cushman. In 1945, it became state highway 63 and was named the Rev. Patrick E. Carey Highway after a priest at St. John's Church in Millers Falls to the north.

At the top of the hill and the northern border of Amherst is old Plumtrees Road, leading west toward Sunderland, where the early 19th-century painter Erastus Salisbury Field lived. The street addresses used here are modern. Numbers were not assigned to houses until 1937 for the center of North Amherst, and even in 1957, the houses beyond Pulpit Hill Road had no numbers. People picked up their mail at the post office, as many do today.

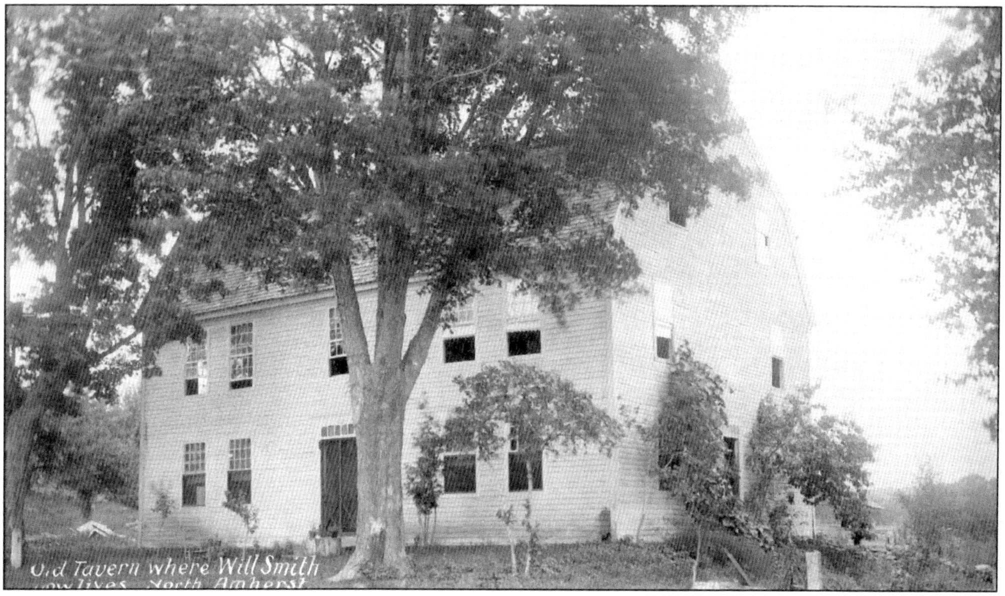

A tavern used to be at 483 Montague Road, on the east side. It was later the home of Will Smith and then Chester Dickinson. The tavern was later torn down, but the enormous 1700s barn behind the building still remains, and the land is still farmed.

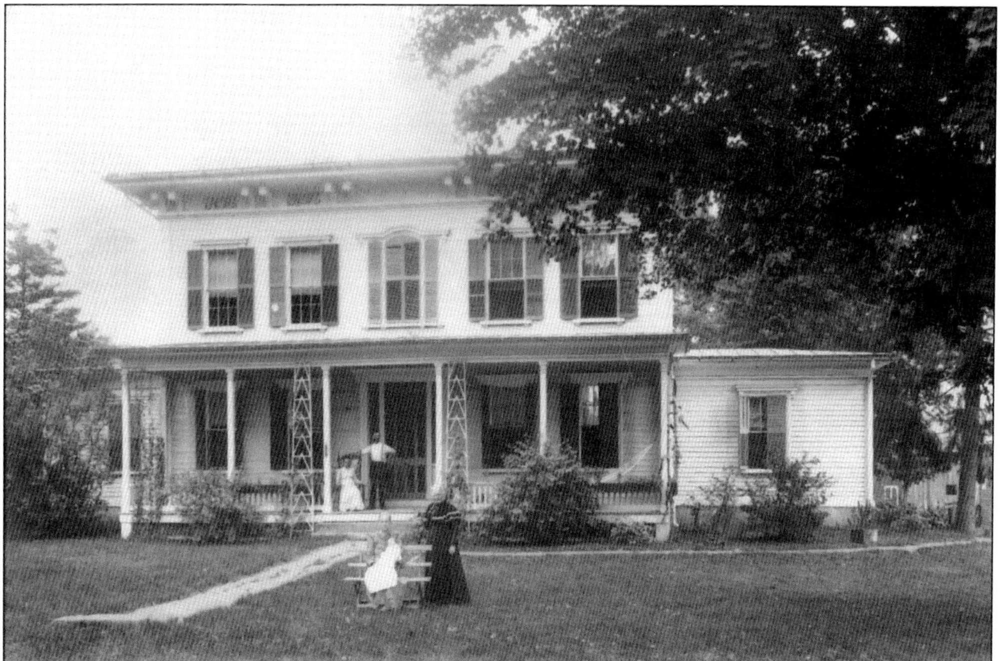

Farther south on the same side of the road was the family home of Ansel E. Marshall in the 1890s. David Maxon bought the house later and designed a golf course on his land; it was built in 1963. The Cherry Hill Golf Course is now run by the Town of Amherst.

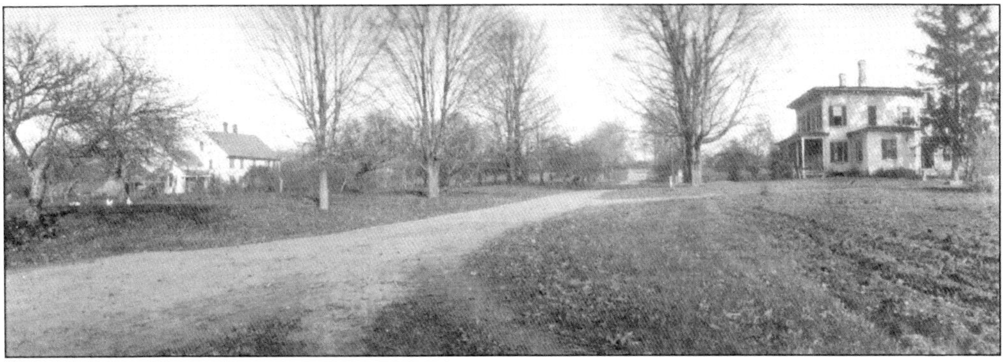

Above, looking north on Montague Road, the Marshall home is on the right, or east side, of the road. Below, looking west, is the farmhouse of Herbert S. Dickinson with its cider mill. People drank cider because the water was not pure, but as George Cooke noted, its value was "all thrown out of gear when somebody discovered that it was an alcoholic drink and demonstrated that the cider-drunkard was just the crossest and most inveterate of the class." The temperance movement had arrived, though there is no evidence it carried much weight in North Amherst.

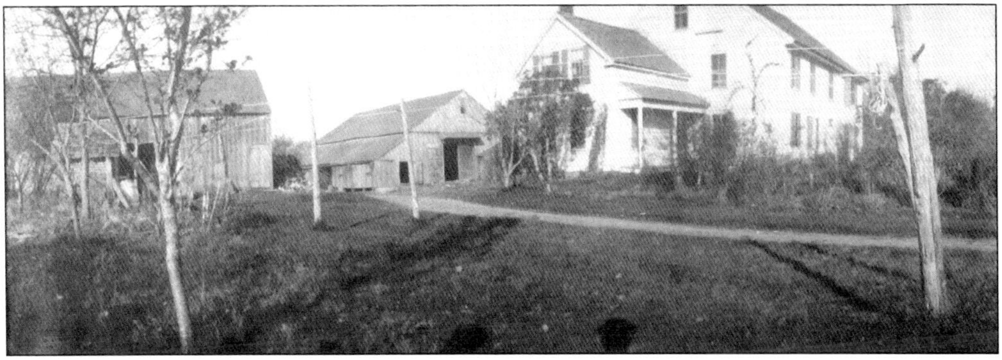

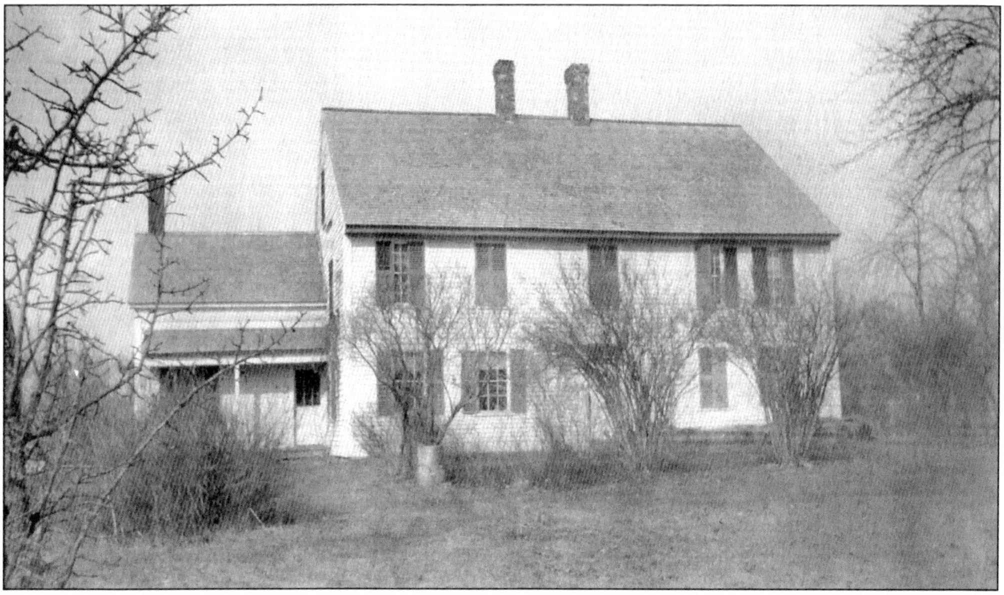

Here is the Herbert Dickinson farm and barns. Below, the clan has gathered for Thanksgiving; the year is unknown. From left to right are (first row) two foster sons of Clayton and Emily Bartlett; (second row, seated) Hattie Kellogg, Alice Dickinson Chandler, Mary Dickinson King, Herbert Samuel Dickinson, Abbie Dickinson Bartlett, and Emilyetta Dickinson King; (third row, standing) Myron Pettingill, Edward King, Julia Wood, Melia Wood, Nellie Ford, Edith Chandler Pettingill, Edna Pettingill, Florence King, Clayton Bartlett, Emily Bartlett, and B. Franklin Kellogg.

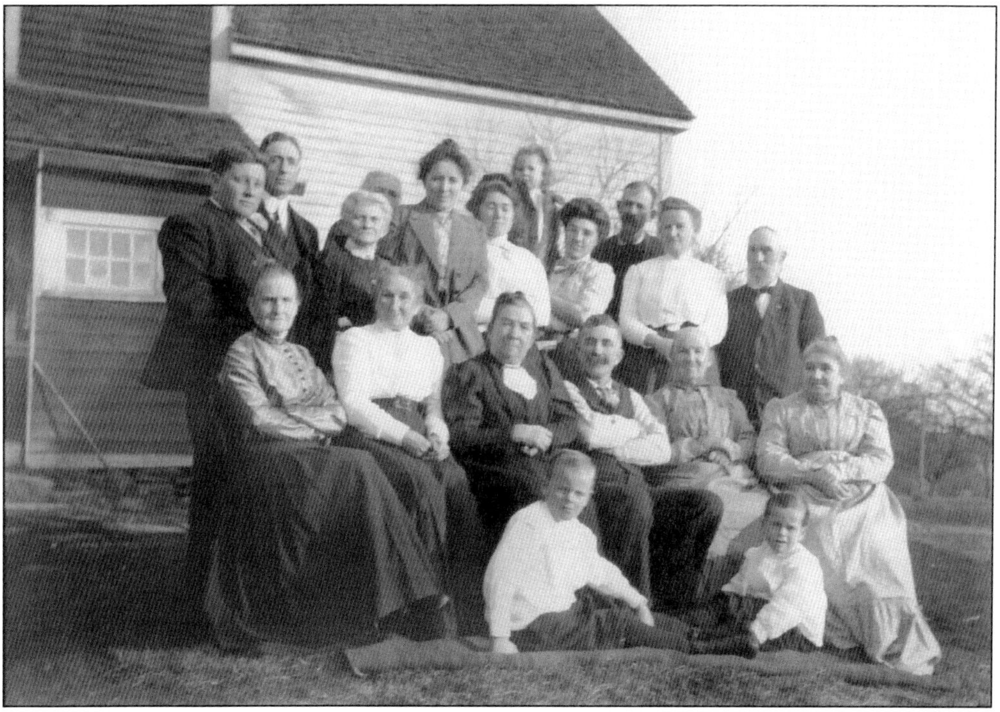

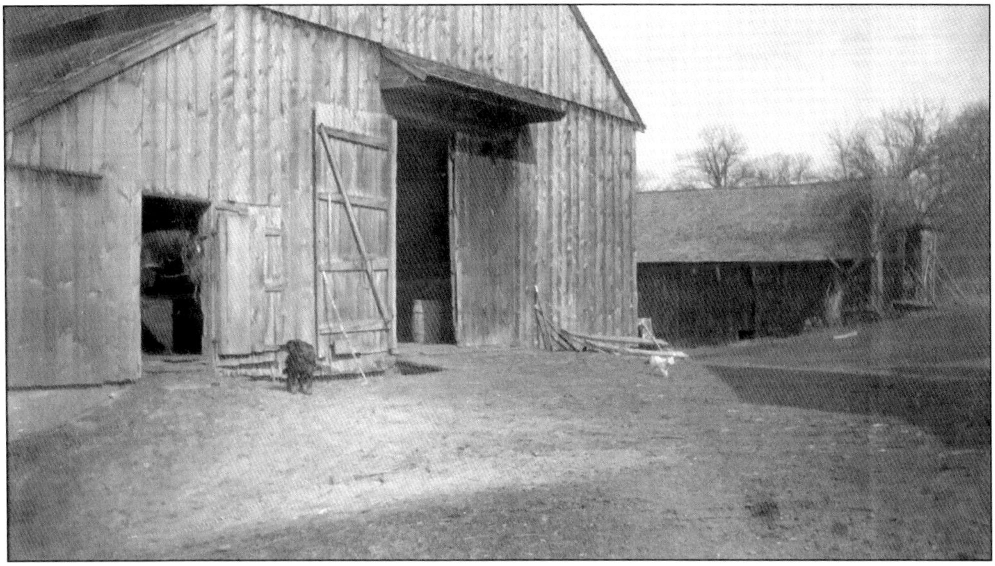

In the back of the Dickinson house is a large cider mill. George Cooke described the mill as a "sort of open shed with a large upright screw in the centre, also a shaft not so high, having within the 'hopper', strips of wood inserted so as to leave an inch or two of space between them at their apex, and meeting at their base, to act as crushers of the apple. A beam attached to the shaft, sometimes, and sometimes to the big screw,—to the end of this beam a horse attached who travelled around in a circle supplying the power both for the grinding and the pressing." Below, a later generation took over the house. The names written on the back of the 1884 photograph, probably right to left, are Aunt Fidelia, Aunt Alzinia Dickinson, Abbie Dickinson Bartlett, Cora Bartlett, Lewis Bartlett & Collie, Herbert S. Dickinson, Clayton Bartlett.

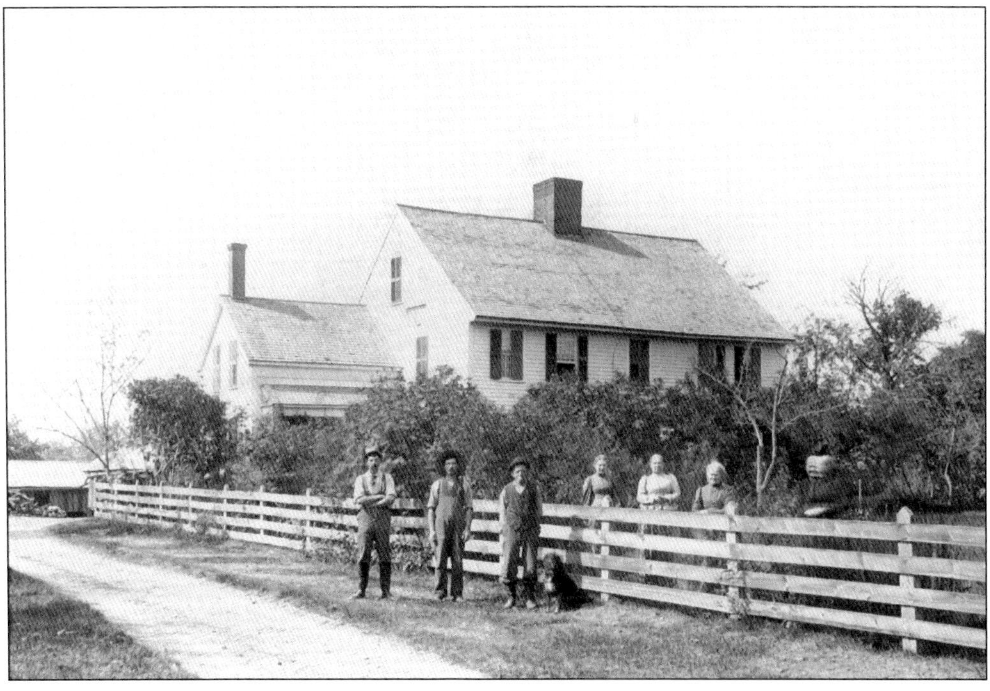

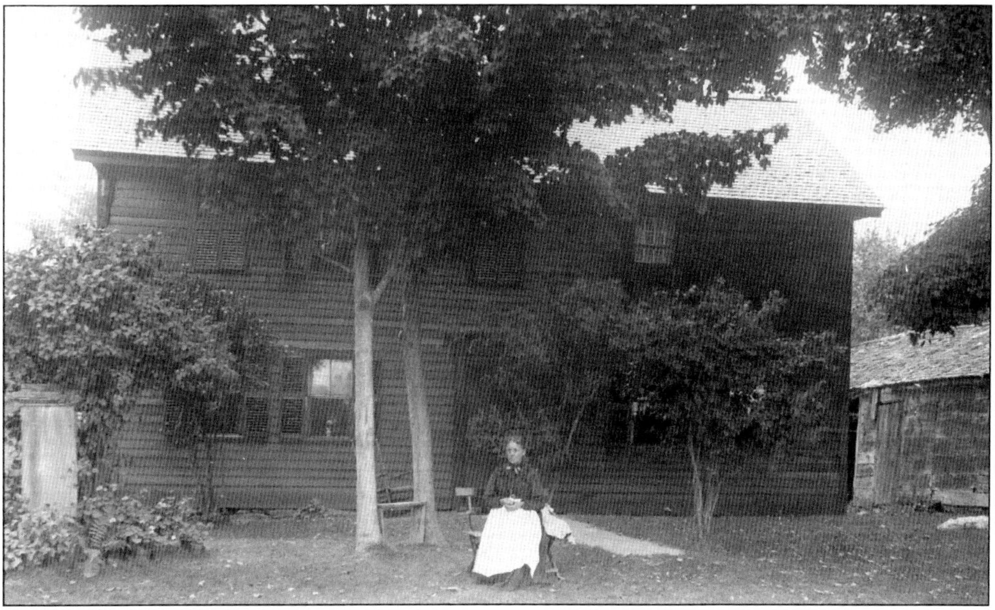

One of the very oldest houses in Amherst dates from 1737. In 1748, Noah Wright, an affluent citizen from Northampton, Massachusetts, probably upgraded the house, given its stylish workmanship, and a century later, in 1850, Baxter Eastman paid $2,000 to buy the 25-acre farm from Chester Dickinson. It stayed in the Eastman family until 1974. The new owners, Louis and Hilda Greenbaum, moved the house well back from the highway. Above is a photograph of Baxter Eastman's wife, Marietta, in front of the house about 1870, transformed with a second floor addition. Below is the house about 1880. (Both courtesy of Louis and Hilda Greenbaum.)

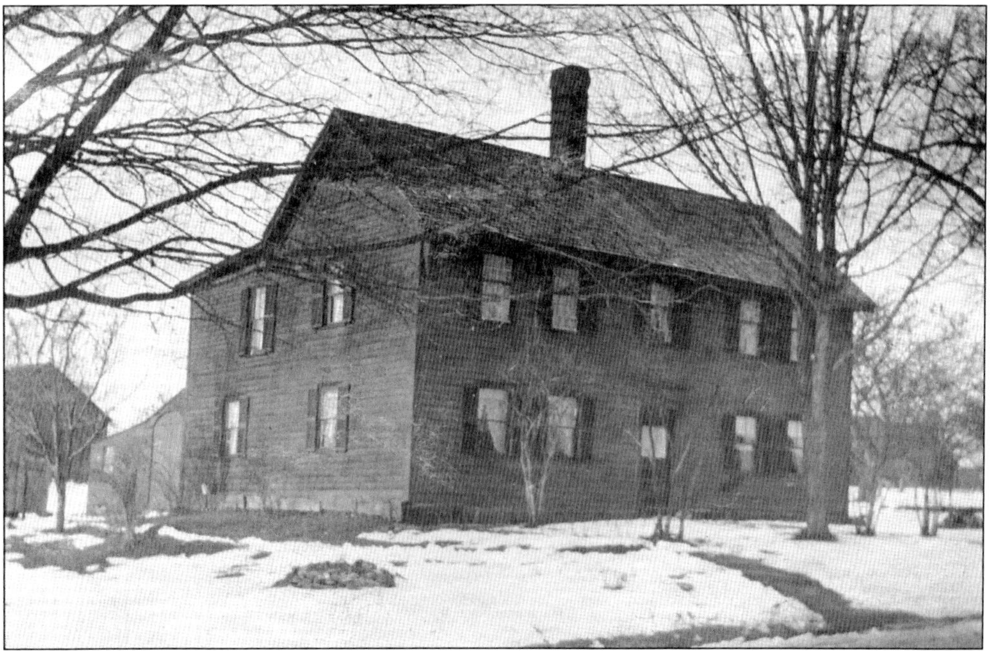

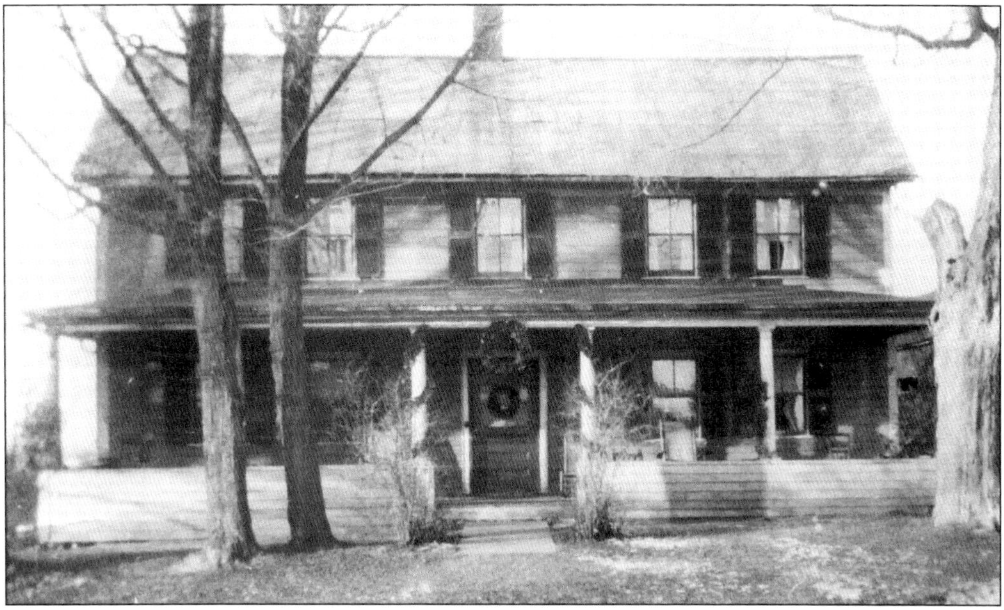

A brother of Baxter Eastman had an illustrious career. Zebina Eastman, born in Amherst on September 8, 1815, was part of the antislavery movement. In 1838, at the age of 21, he moved to Illinois where he edited several antislavery newspapers starting with the *Genius of Universal Emancipation*. He married in 1840 and had a family. He became the personal and political friend of Abraham Lincoln, who made him consul at Bristol, England, which position he held from 1861 to 1869. He then moved back to Illinois in 1870 and died in 1883. The house, above, has a new front porch and Christmas decorations in 1895. According to Margot Rand, the wife of Amherst historian Frank Prentice Rand, the poet Robert Frost said this house had his favorite barn in Amherst. (Both courtesy of Louis and Hilda Greenbaum.)

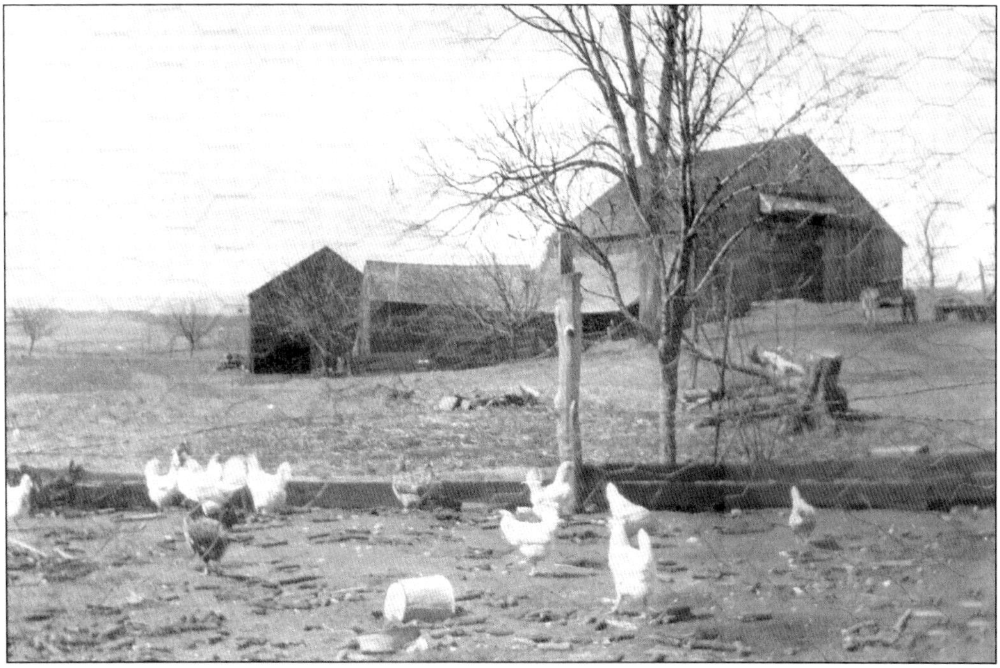

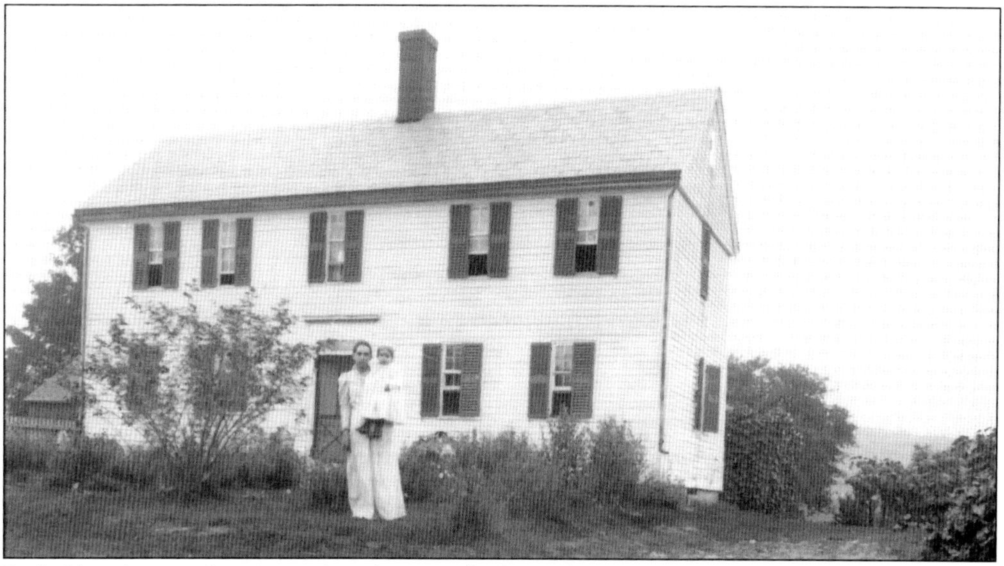

Probably taken in the 1890s, this photograph shows the house at 293 Montague Road, to the south. The house is still there. The unidentified young mother in her long dress with her baby looks very somber.

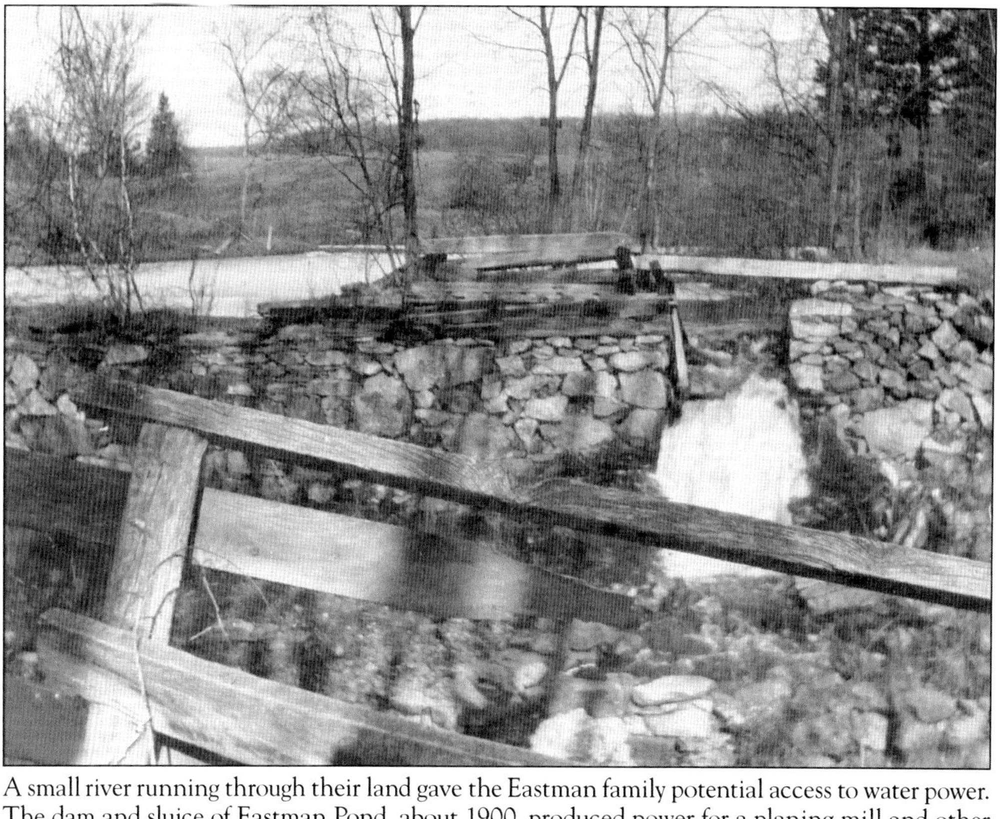

A small river running through their land gave the Eastman family potential access to water power. The dam and sluice of Eastman Pond, about 1900, produced power for a planing mill and other uses over the years. Those who were children in the 1940s and 1950s remember skating there in the winter; the Eastman Brook still flows. (Courtesy of Louis and Hilda Greenbaum.)

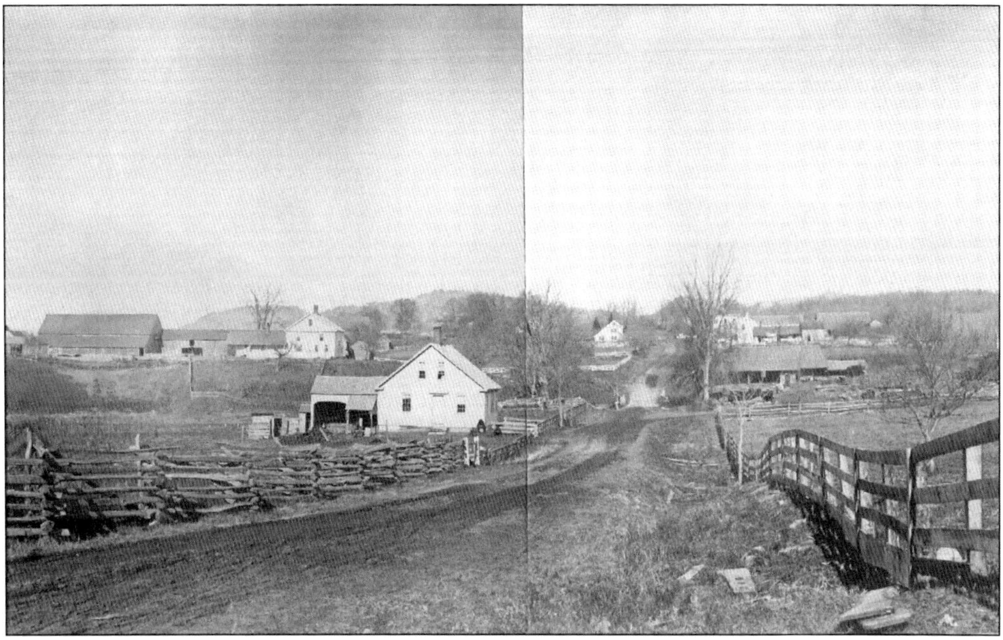

Montague Road is pictured in 1861, facing north. The house in the foreground on the left is across from Pulpit Hill Road. In the distance on the left side of the road is the Baxter Eastman saltbox at 298 Montague Road. The Austin Eastman farm is on the left. The photograph was ordered by Zebina Eastman to take with him to England. (Courtesy of Louis and Hilda Greenbaum.)

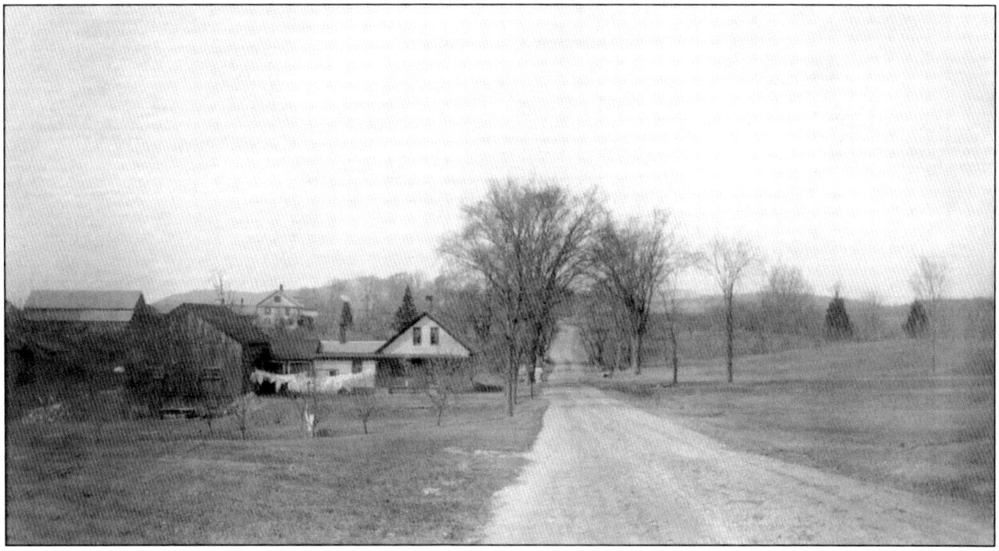

Nearly 40 years later, this view was taken from the same location. The fences and the mill are gone. Stanley Mitchell of North Amherst bought the farm at top left in the 1890s. He was from Lithuania; his name was anglicized. For years he kept geese on a pond along Sunderland Road. When asked why, he answered, "Why do you hang pictures on your walls?"

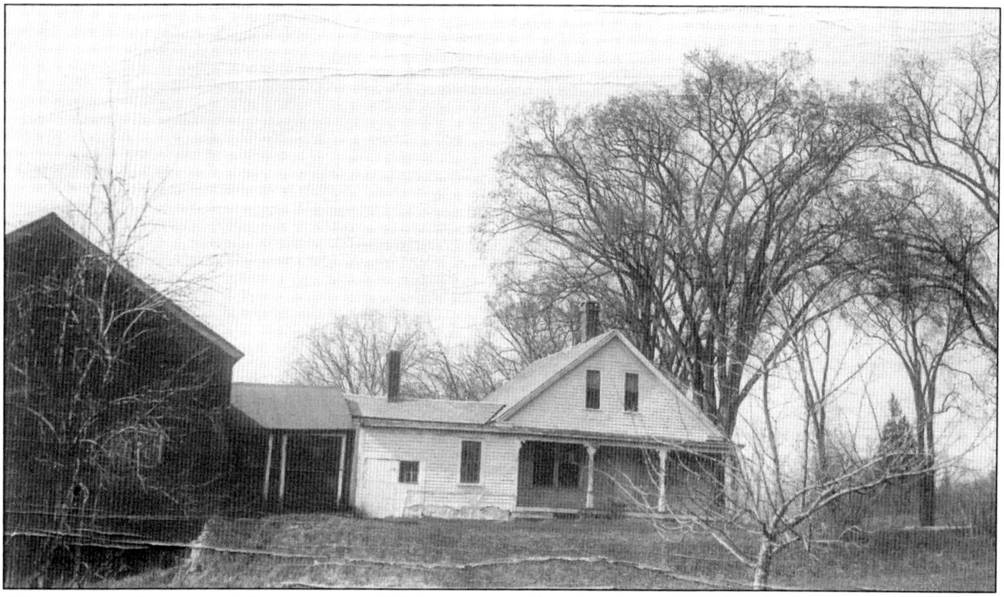

Above is a side view of the house at 208 Montague Road taken in 1933. This is the house shown on the left in the views of Montague Road on the previous page. Edna Ball and her husband lived there as a young couple in that year. (Courtesy of Edna Ball.)

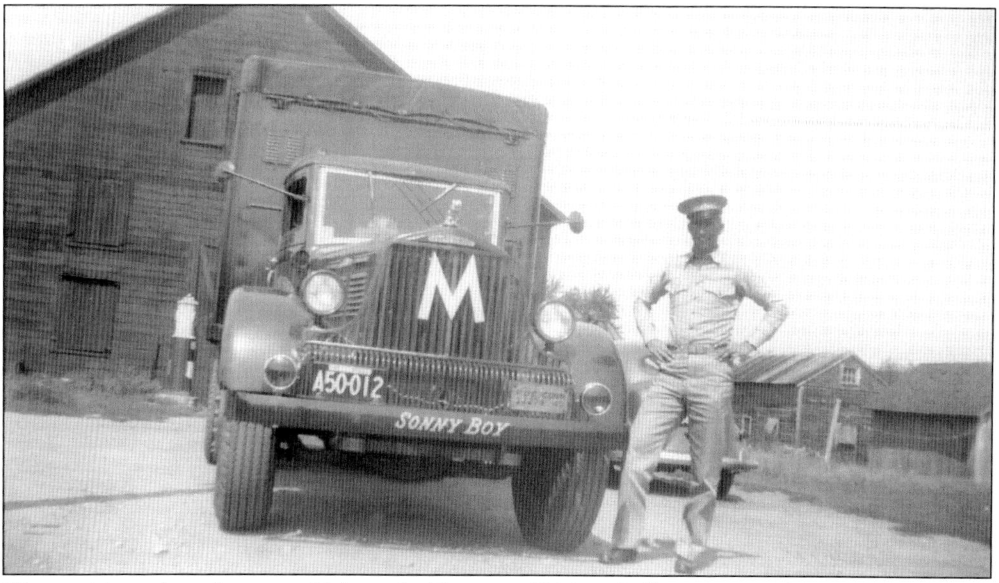

Chester Matuszko, who started Matuszko Farms in 1934 on Ball Lane, on a farm once owned by the Ball family just off Montague Road, expanded into the trucking business and formed Matuszko Trucking Inc. His brother and son continued the business after Chet died in 1974. (Courtesy of Joyce Matuszko.)

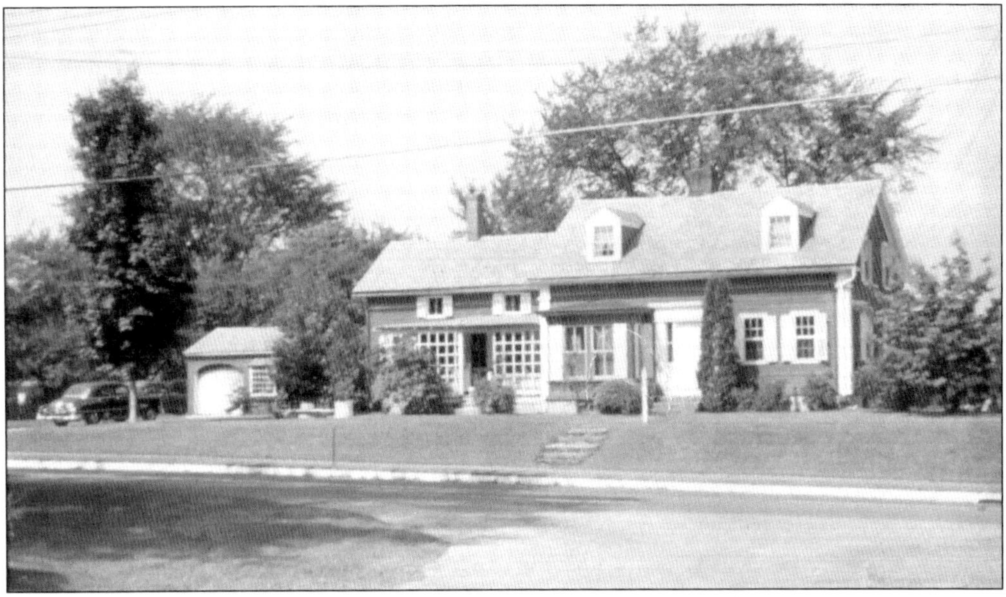

This house at 180 Montague Road was owned in 1860 by Henry Haskins, a carpenter. In 1947, when the town put in a sewer line, that house and neighboring ones were moved back 50 feet. In 1958, Stanley Ziomek bought the house and with his wife, Beverly, raised their five boys there. Stanley grew up on Meadow Street; he was head of the department of public works and the leader of the baseball little league. (Courtesy of Stanley and Beverly Ziomek.)

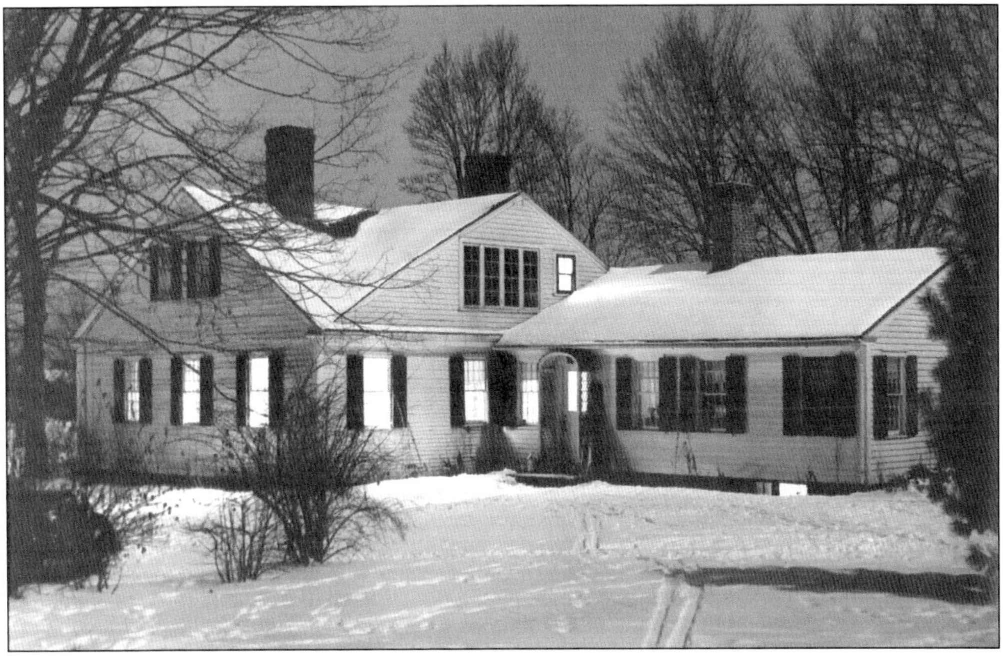

This house at 167 Montague Road was built in the 1820s and still stands. George Cooke wrote about it when it was the home of Sylvester Dickinson in the 1840s and noted the unusual names of the Dickinson children: Avalmy Evander, Levander Valette, and Ophelia Mundane. Reverend Cooke's parents came to live there in 1848; his father called it "The Pink House" and so it was known over a century later. (Photograph by Robert Coffin, courtesy of Janna L. Aldrich.)

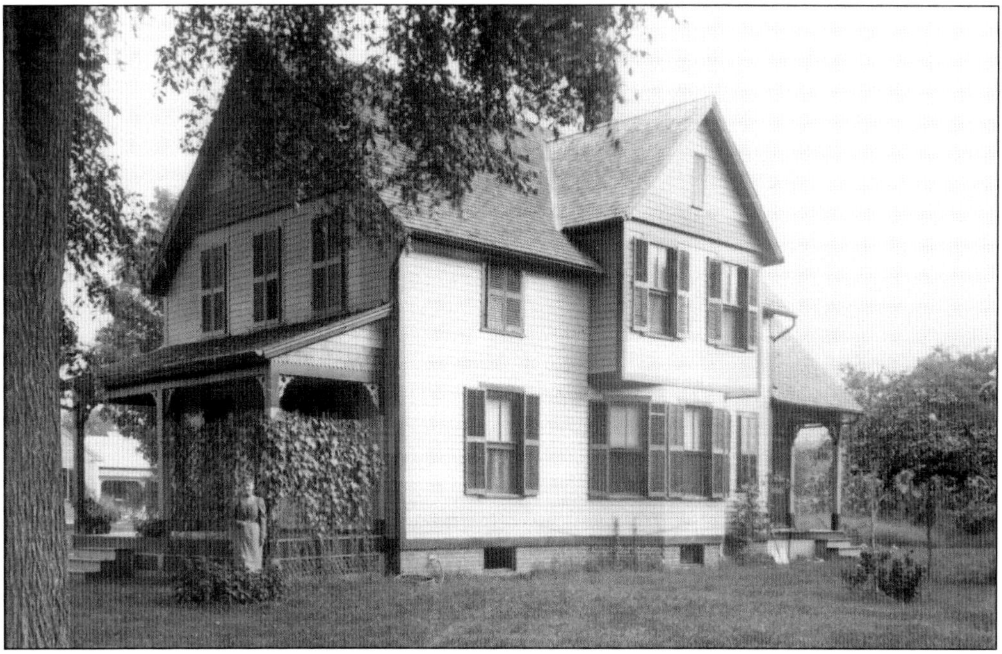

The Howes Brothers photograph above shows the house still at 159 Montague Road. Harlan Asa "Ace" Wood, a house painter, pictured below, lived across the street at 150 Montague Road in the 1950s. He and his wife, Mildred, had a guesthouse there at the time. He used to be a motorman on the street railway system that his neighbor Walter Cowls built. Ace Wood started work in 1903, first repairing the tracks and then running the trolley cars. He usually worked with Edward Hobart. On the level, a trolley car could reach 40 to 50 miles per hour. One night, the two of them raced the trolley car from the Notch at the south end of Amherst, through the center, and into the barn at North Amherst in a record-setting 20 minutes. Below, Wood holds a rare Currier and Ives print, "The Sleigh Race."

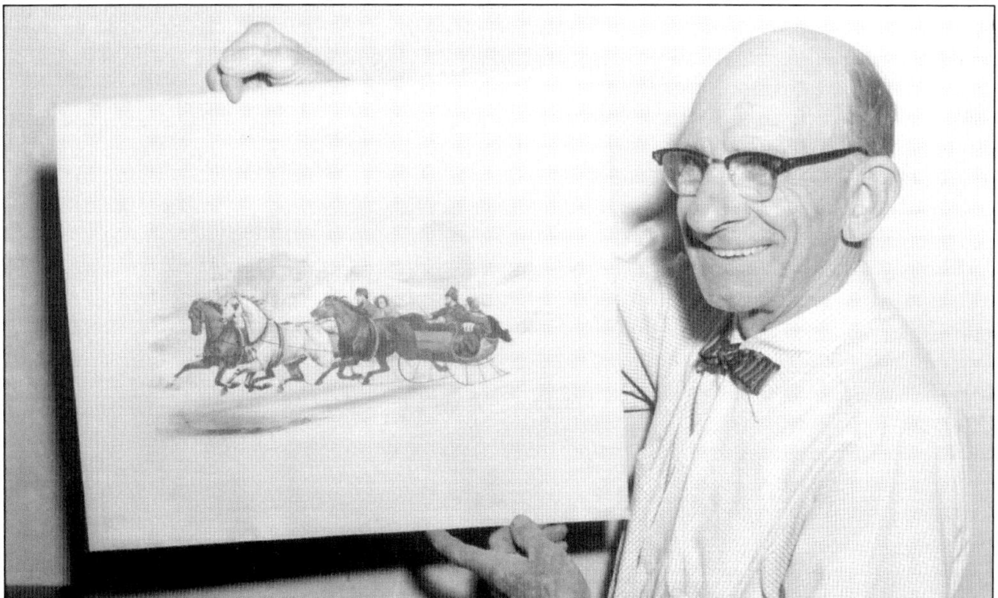

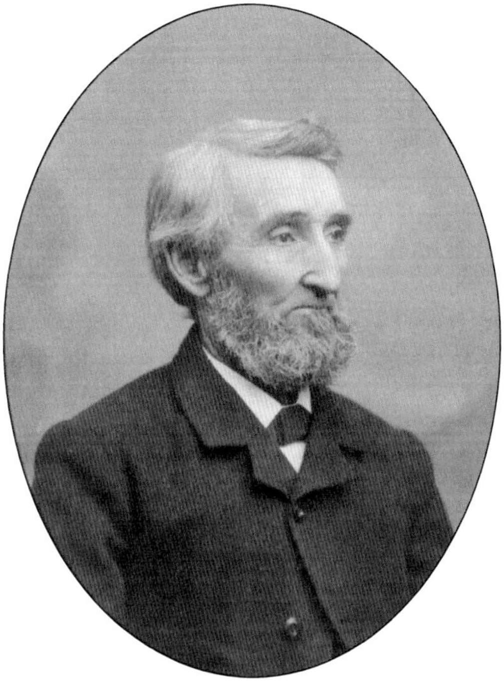

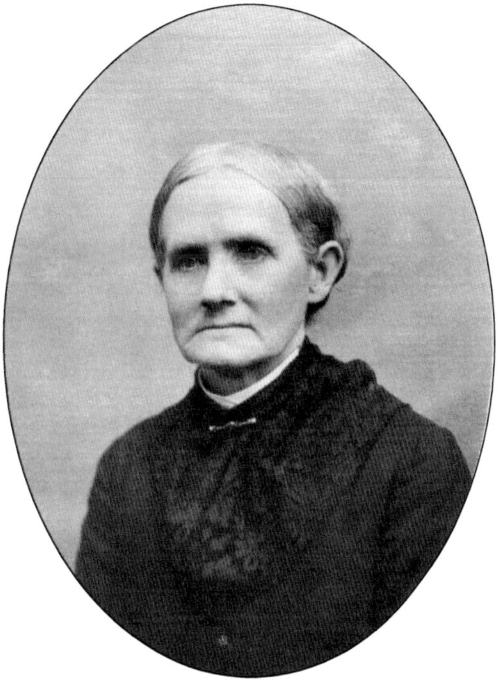

134 Montague Road, built in 1768 by David Cowls on land settled by his father, Jonathan Cowls, in 1741, was later the home of Jonathan Cowls (above left, 1822–1902) and his wife, Sarah M. (Dickinson) Cowls (above right, 1828–1901). As of 2012, the home has housed nine generations of the Cowls family, which still uses the homestead as a business office. Walter Dickinson Cowls (right, 1852–1928) continued the family's timberland management, lumber manufacturing, and land development businesses, as well as its farming enterprises. In the 1890s, he developed the Amherst and Sunderland Street Railway System, and housed the trolley cars in a former onion barn on Cowls Road. The trolley ran from 1897 to 1928 and connected people all over the area. Cowls was a state representative from 1912 to 1914. (Courtesy of Ruth Owen Jones.)

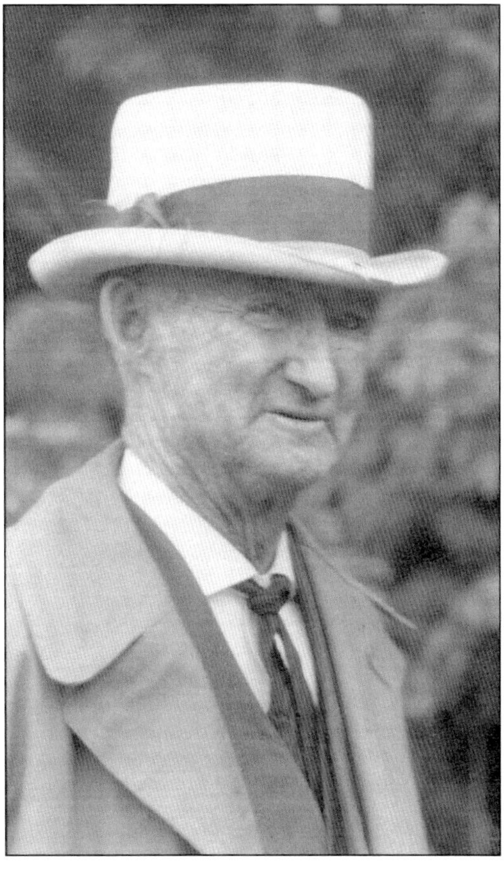

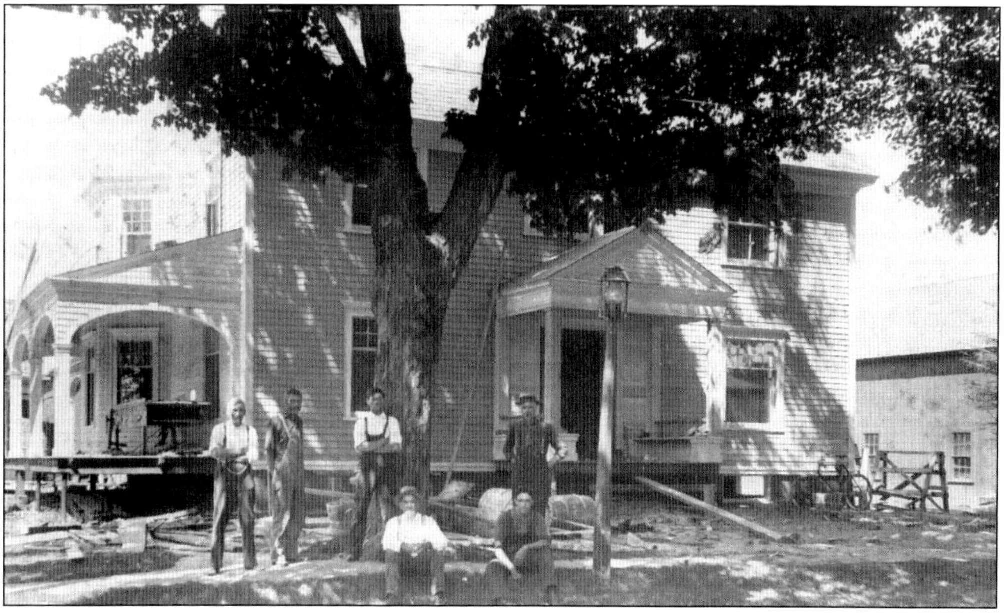

In 1898, Walter D. Cowls converted the family's saltbox at 134 Montague Road into a colonial that featured a glassed-in porch to serve as a weatherproof community trolley stop. His homestead features the same woodwork as the North Amherst Library. (Courtesy of Ruth Owen Jones.)

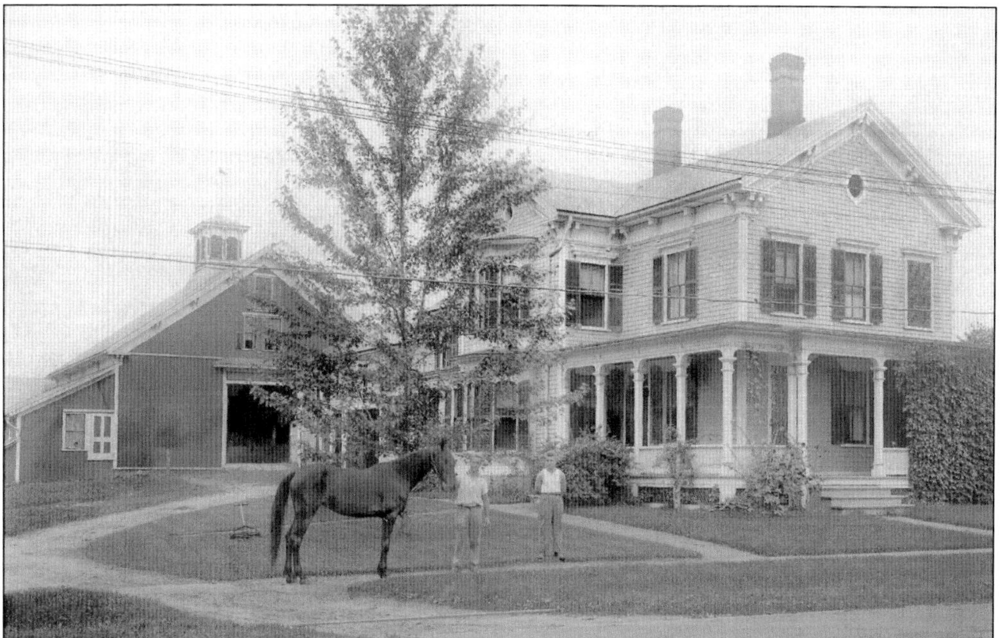

Next door was the elegant home owned by four generations of Hobarts. Edmund Hobart carried on a lumbering business. His sons Frank and Clarence concentrated on farming, tobacco, onions, and dairy. They pastured their cows in a low-lying field where the Mill River recreation area is now, herding them across the street through a path between the houses at 115 and 125 Montague Road, which then turned behind the houses at 115 and 105 Montague Road, and led down into the field.

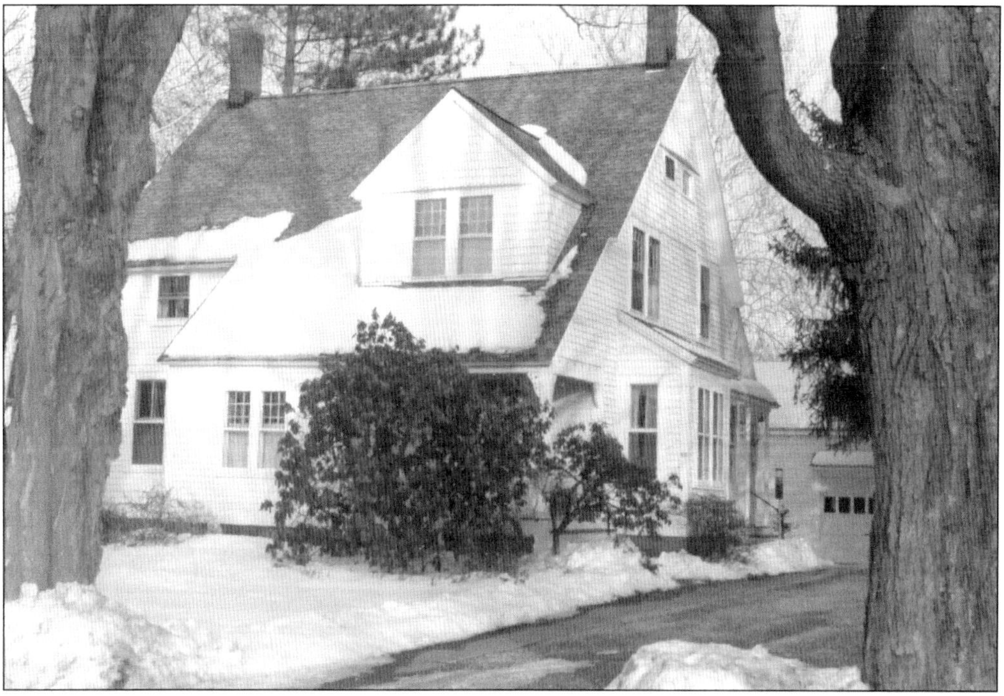

Across the street, at 105 Montague Road, a house designed by Roswell Putnam was built in 1888. Eugene O. Puffer, who had it built, belonged to the prosperous family who owned much land and the gristmill down the street. He was one of the millers. The new house was built on the foundation of a much older, saltbox-style house, owned by Eleazar Cowls. Below, a sidewalk maple died in the fall of 1992 and had to be cut down. Patricia Holland stands next to the logs the single tree produced. (Both courtesy of Robert Winne.)

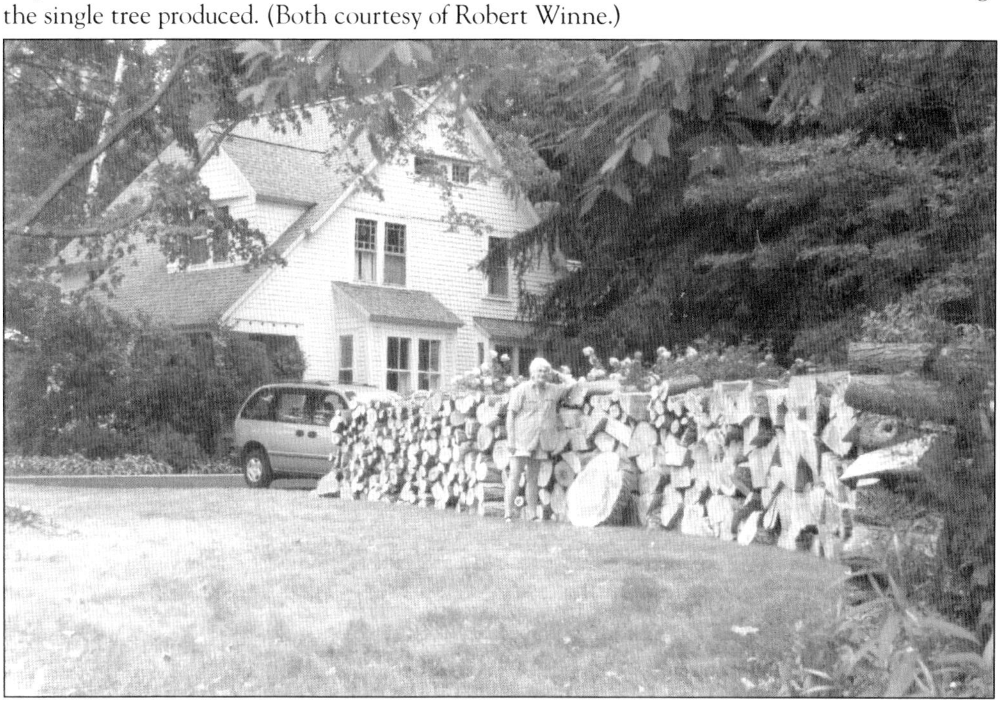

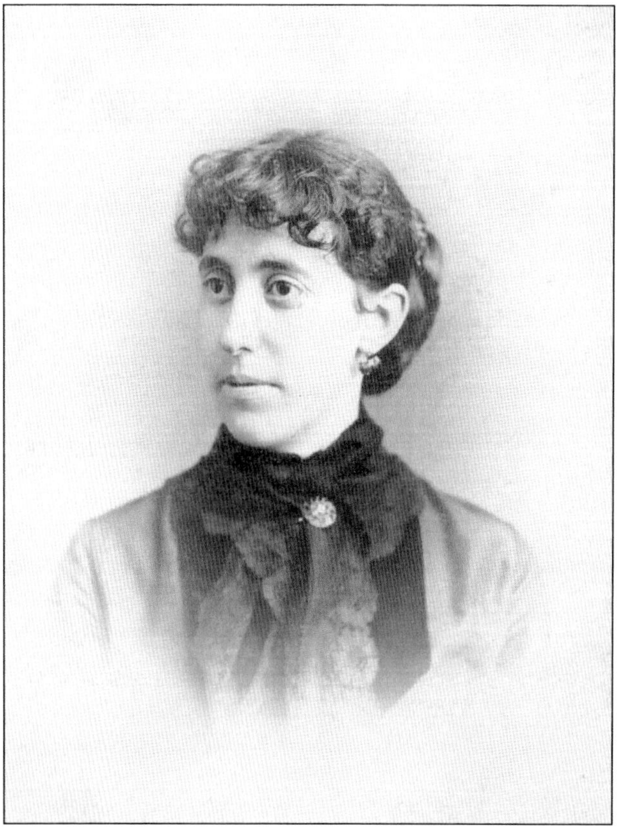

Eugene O. Puffer was married to Ida E. Cushman (pictured). After he died in 1919, Ida in 1929 married Charles Sumner Howe, whose first wife had grown up in the house next door at 115 Montague Road. Howe had retired as president of the Case School of Applied Science in Cleveland, Ohio. They were each in their early 70s, and they enjoyed a long wedding trip. Ida died in 1938; her husband died the following year.

In 1970, the meadow where the Hobarts used to pasture their cows became a town-owned recreation area, thanks to a donation from Stephen Puffer. Among those at the groundbreaking ceremony for Mill River Park in April 1973 are Stanley Ziomek, Nancy Dill, Don Johnson, and Stephen Puffer.

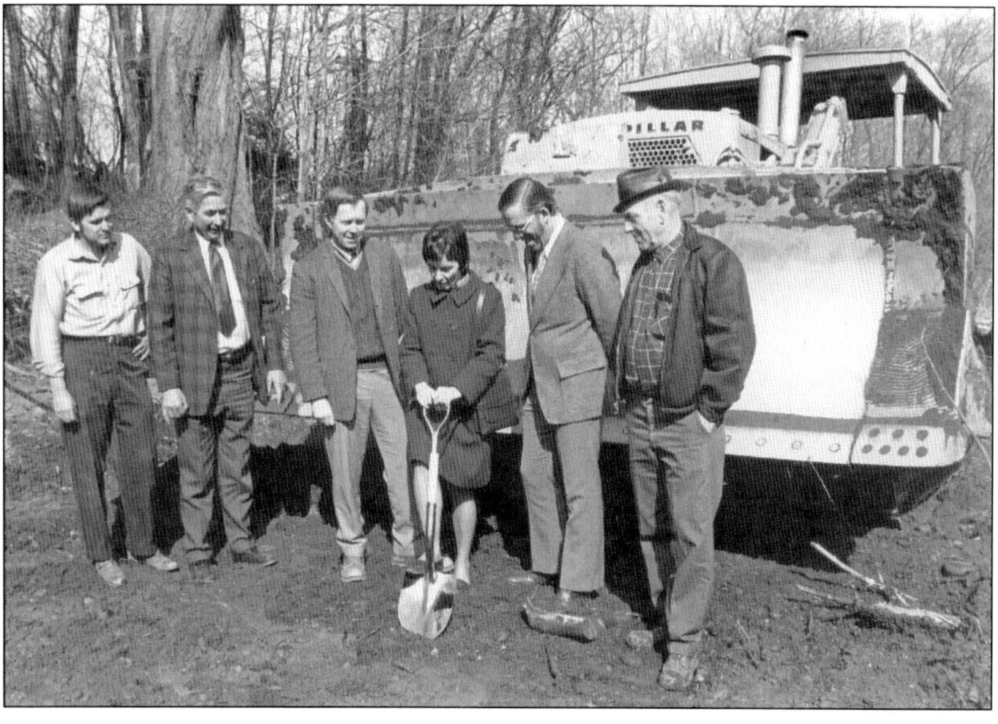

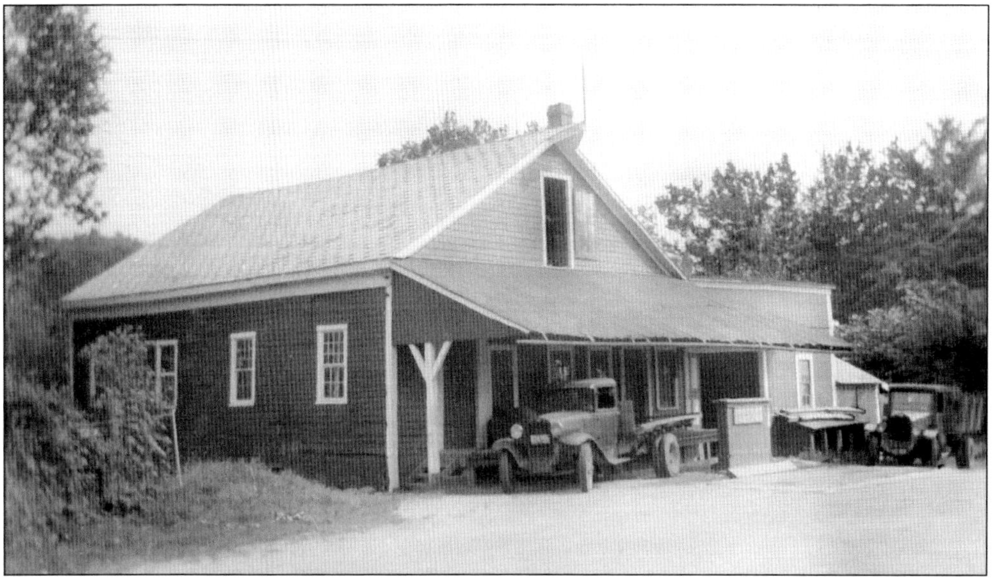

The red gristmill on Montague Road was built in 1838; it ran from 1844 to 1934. A canal off the Mill River brought water to the mill. The canal ran along the north side of a field that is now the Mill River Park, then south right next to Montague Road; the water exited into the downstream river near the Mill River bridge. The millstone was shipped from France and brought overland by ox teams from New London, Connecticut. The mill signified the beginning of the Puffer family's prosperity in town. The family lived across the street. Stephen Puffer (1914–2011) was an entrepreneur who worked in his father's ice works, owned and drove school busses, ran a construction business, directed the public works department for the town of Amherst, and built apartment complexes. (Above, courtesy of Victoria Pratt; below, photograph by Robert Coffin, courtesy of Stewart Coffin.)

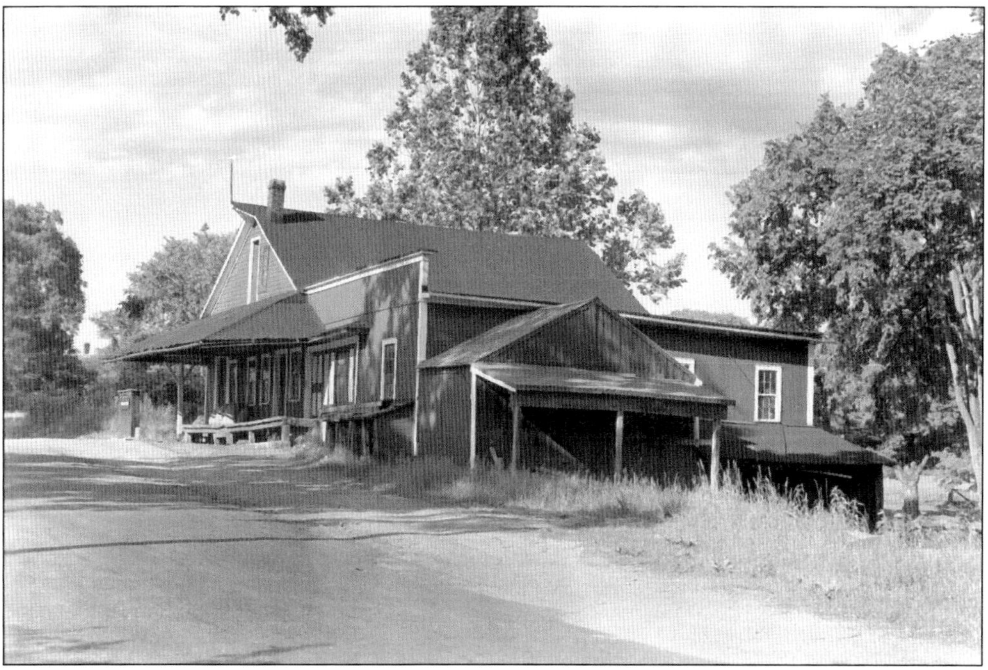

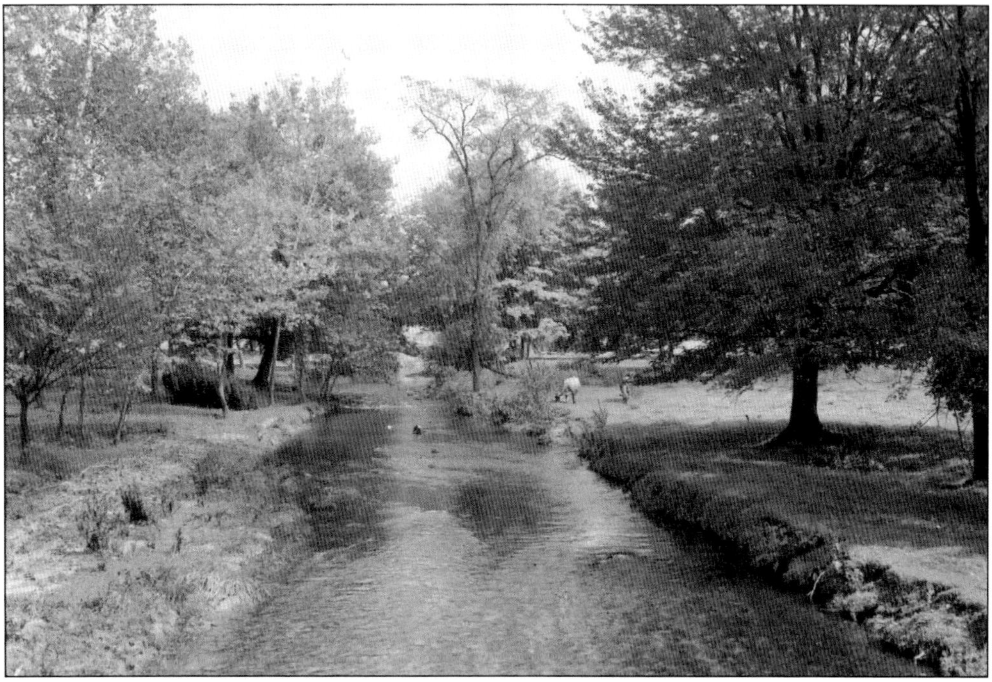

This view of the Mill River just below the gristmill shows Hobart's cows. Local people also recall how Hobart would plow the sidewalks with a horse. (Photograph by Robert Coffin, courtesy of Stewart Coffin.)

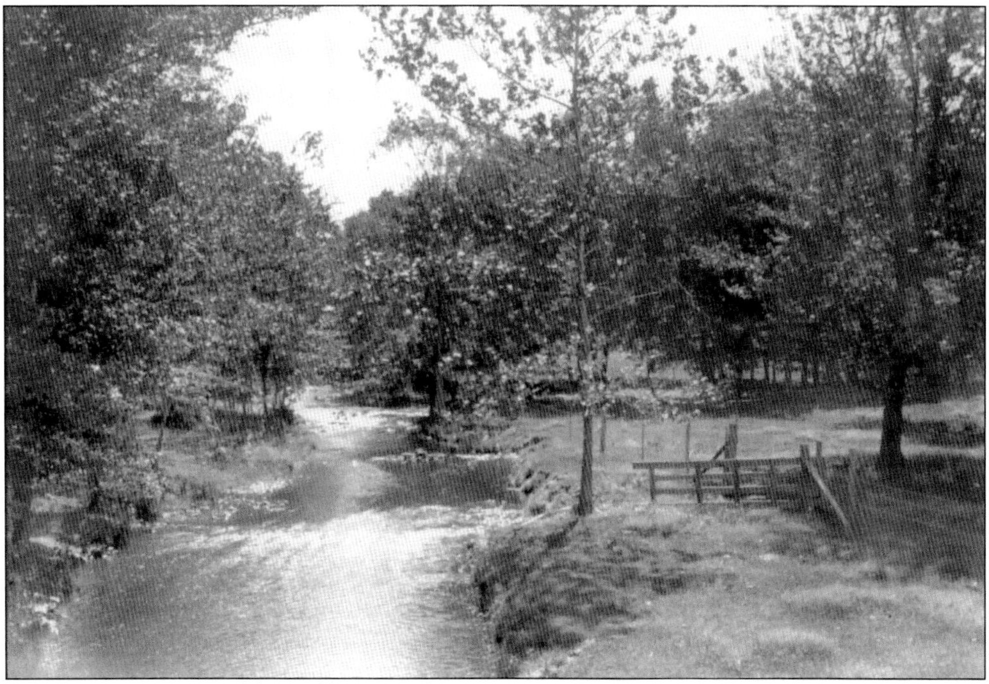

This is another view of the Mill River. This area was a popular spot for picnics. Ducks are often in the water, and sometimes a great blue heron can be seen catching fish. The Mill River Park now runs along the north side of the river, and people enjoy strolling alongside it.

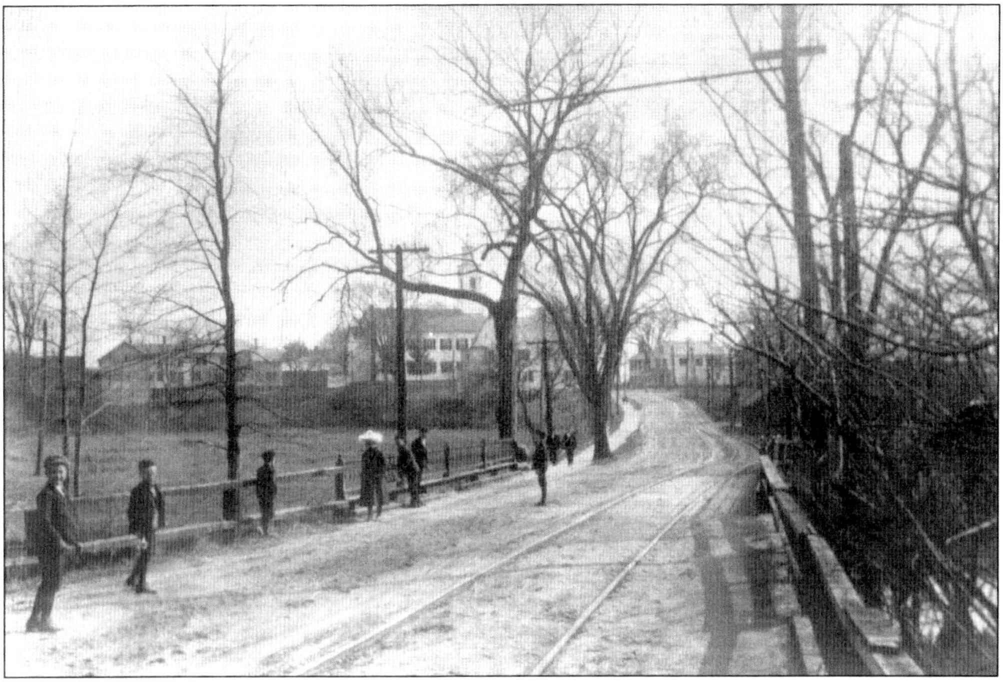

The early 1890s photograph above shows Montague Road heading toward the center of North Amherst. The North Congregational Church and its Parish House are on the left, trolley tracks are in the road, and three buildings are on the right, looking like one. From left to right, the three buildings are the Cowles house (now the Black Walnut Inn), the tiny North Amherst Library, and a woodshop. Pictured below in 1993, two houses on the west side of Montague Road were probably built in the late 1890s. (Courtesy of Robert Winne.)

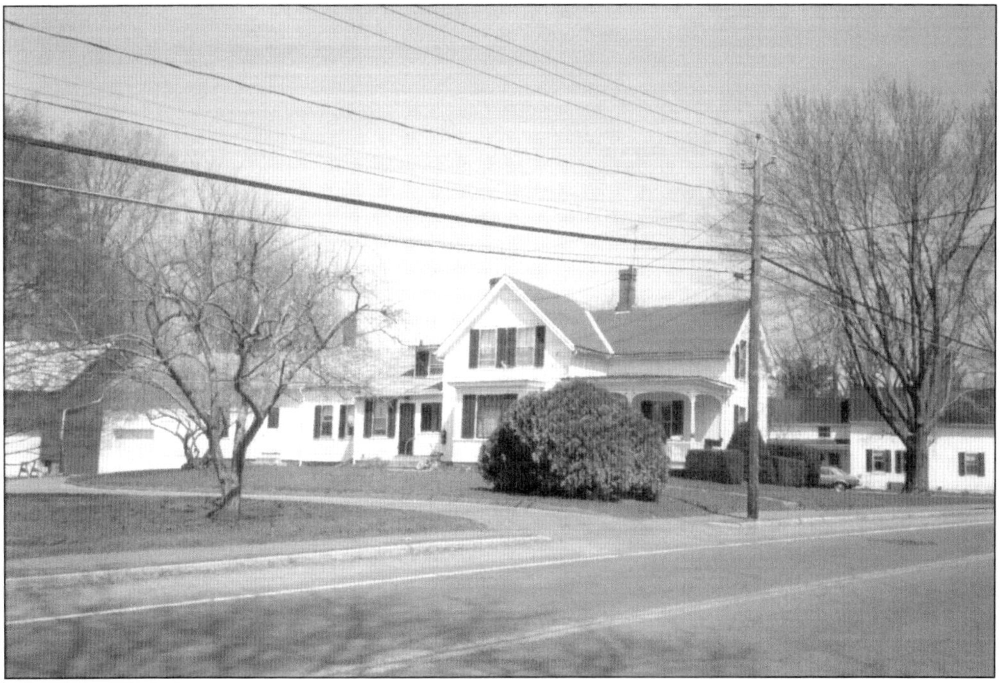

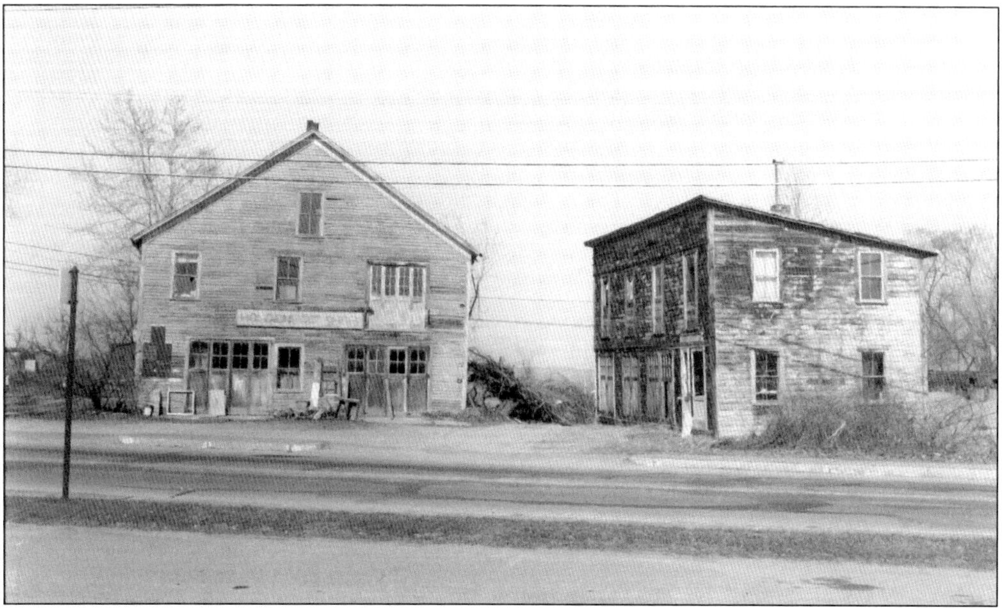

On the right side, approaching the village, a woodshop owned by H. Elmer Holden is pictured in 1969, just before it was torn down. Holden made many of the window sashes and doors for the buildings in the area. His father, a glazier, worked there too. Those who were children in the 1930s and 1940s remember picking up pieces of free scrap lumber from a bin outside the shop. (Courtesy of Susan Holden.)

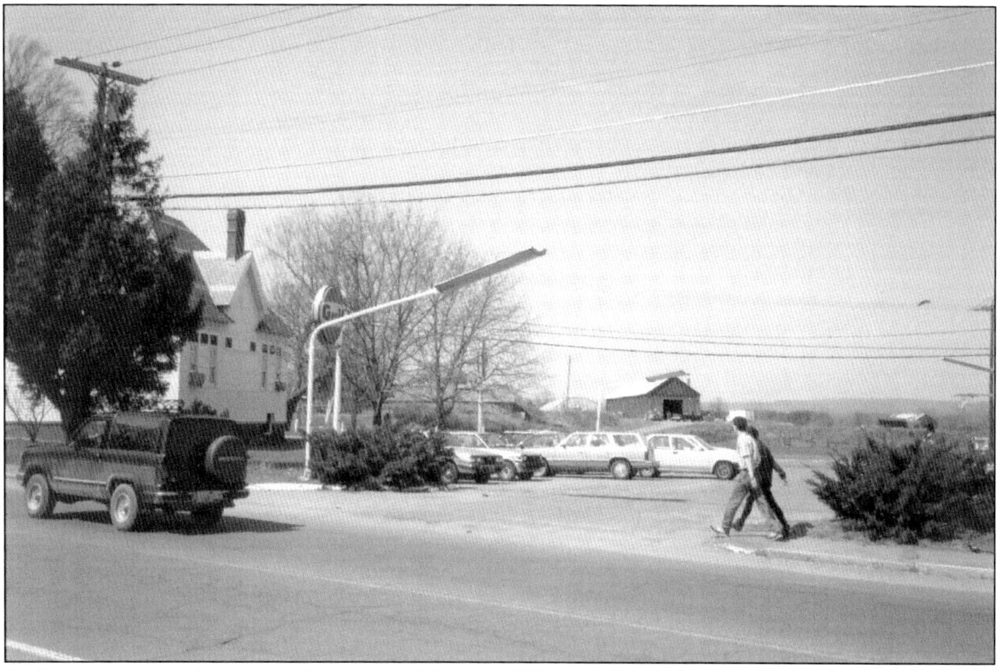

A Gulf station took over the location of the woodshop in the 1970s. In the background are the barns of Joseph Swartz's farm, where the family used to grow tobacco and onions. Joe Swartz developed a hydroponic farm in a large greenhouse and with his wife, Sarah, started a farmer's market. (Courtesy of Robert Winne.)

Two

North Amherst Center, Meadow Street, and Sunderland Road

Coming down Montague Road from the north, one enters a five-way intersection of streets. In horse and buggy days, the traffic presented little problem. One old photograph even shows a tree planted near the middle of the crossroads. With the arrival of cars and apartment buildings on Meadow Street, that intersection has become more and more dangerous, and planners scratch their heads trying to figure out how to turn it into a simpler four-way crossing. Still, it continues to be the center of town. The public library, built in 1893, is on one corner; next, a building that used to be a school; a house that used to be a store; the Black Walnut Inn that used to be a house; an old house that used to be an inn and is now offices; and the North Congregational Church, sold in 2012 to the Zion Korean Church. The church was built in 1826; up until then, people had to travel about three miles to a church either in center Amherst or in East Amherst. At a time when Unitarianism was coming into play, the 59 parish members remained committed to *Westminster Assembly's Shorter Catechism*. The first school in North Amherst was built in 1771 and another in 1796. When the church built its parish hall in 1842, the school was there. Then, in 1870, the town built a solid brick school in North Amherst Center. Around the end of the 1800s, there was an increase in the population of Polish and Lithuanian immigrants, and the town added on to the rear of the building. In 1970, the school closed. By 1977, the old school housed the Amherst Survival Center, providing clothing and lunch for those in need. It also housed an arts center and later, a Head Start program. Across the street is the North Amherst Library. Farther down on Sunderland Road, there used to be farms and then mostly family houses with trees lining the road. In the 1930s, many families had businesses operating out of their home.

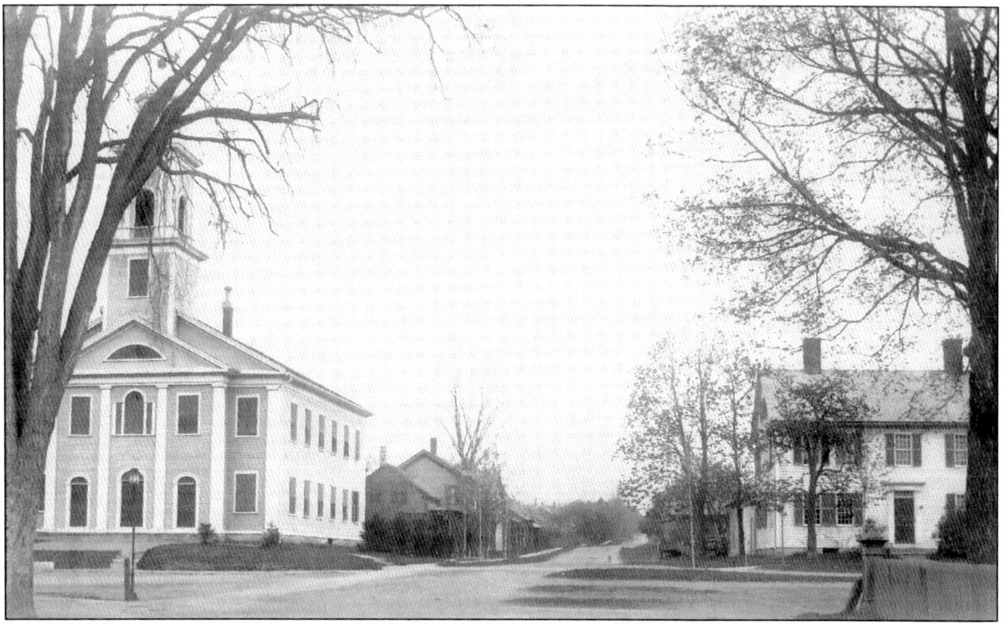

The photographs on this page show the center of North Amherst from the intersection of the five streets. Looking east on Pine Street in the 1890s, the North Congregational Church is on the left, and the Bates Inn is on the right.

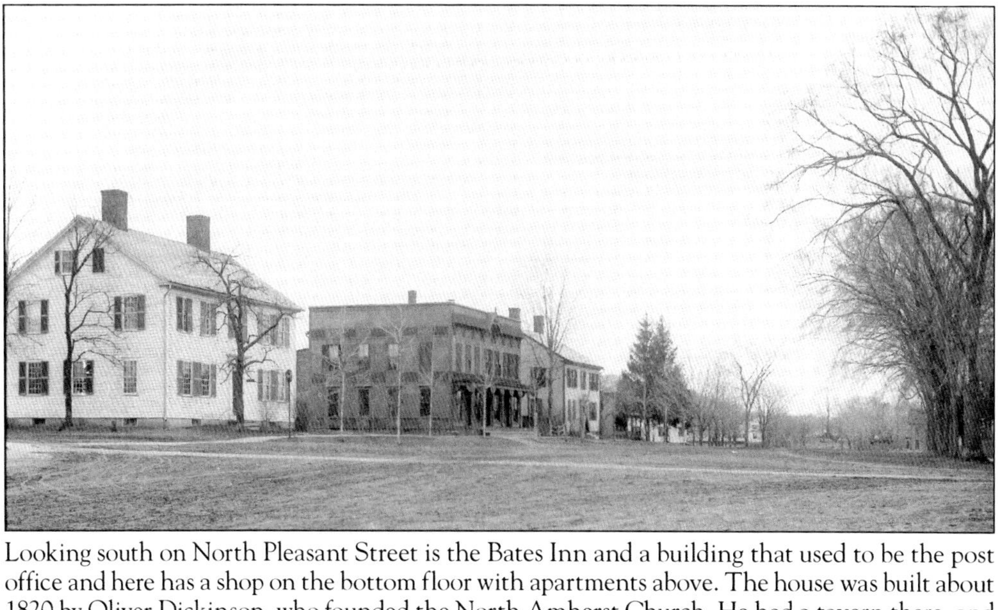

Looking south on North Pleasant Street is the Bates Inn and a building that used to be the post office and here has a shop on the bottom floor with apartments above. The house was built about 1820 by Oliver Dickinson, who founded the North Amherst Church. He had a tavern there, and later, the Bates family established their inn.

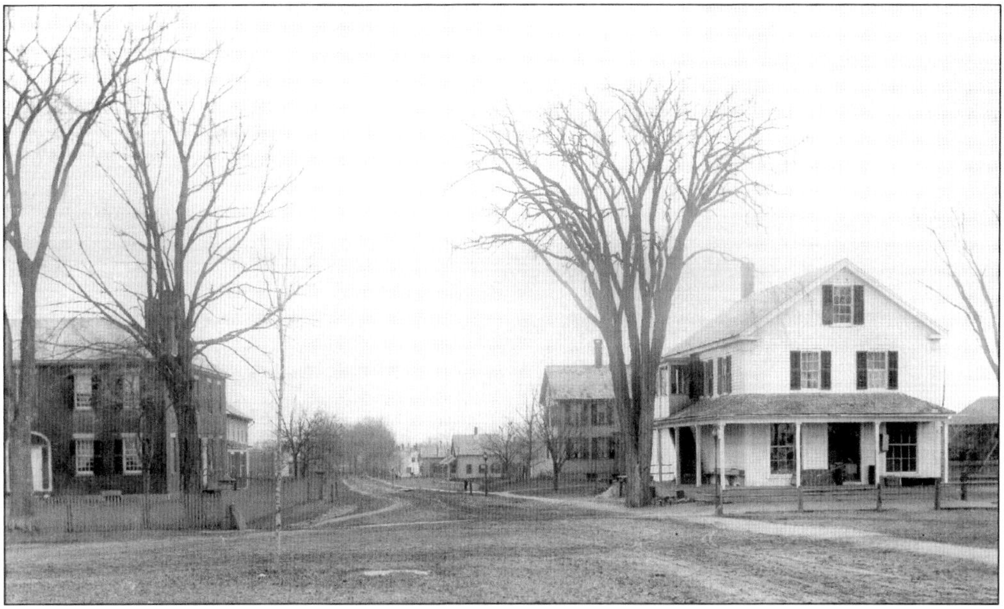

Looking toward the west is a postcard view of Meadow Street in the early 1900s, showing the big brick Cowles house on the left and on the right a house with a store. At this time the owner was probably Frank N. Dickinson. In 1897, he advertised groceries, hardware, crockery, and cigars.

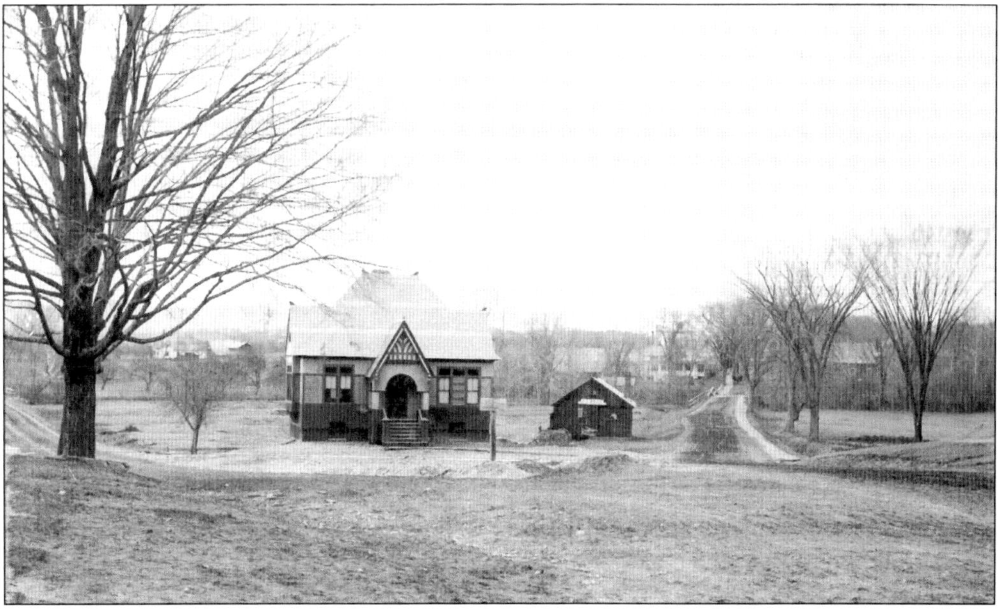

This 1893 photograph, looking north, shows the brand new North Amherst Library nestled between Sunderland Road on the left and Montague Road. The library was organized in 1869 by a group of men who included veterans of the Civil War, which had ended four years earlier. Before this building was erected, the library was housed first in the post office and later in the nearby school.

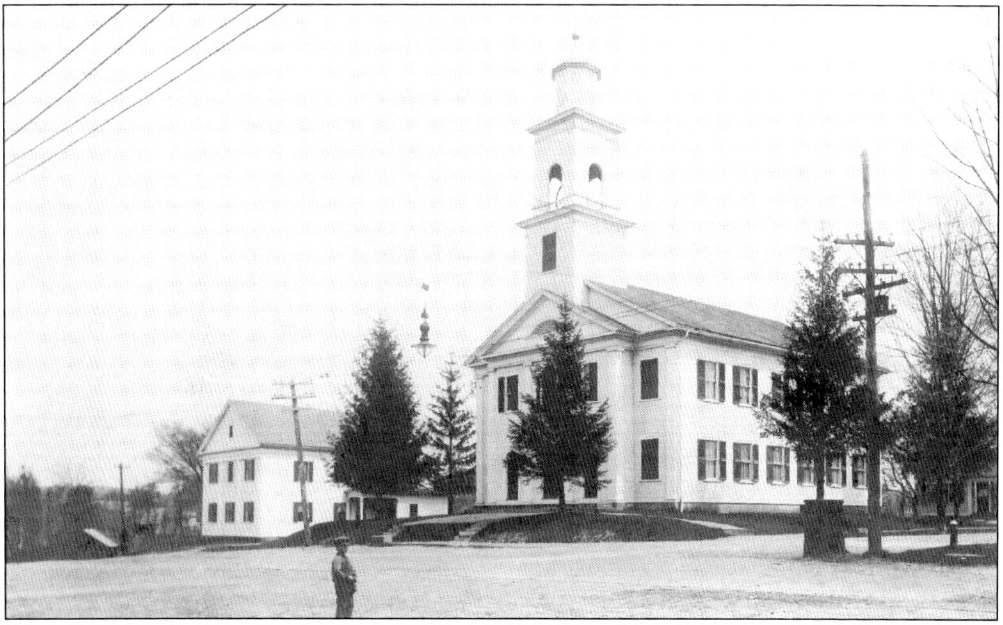

Oliver Dickinson, who financed construction of the church in 1826, demanded no pews could be sold to African Americans. But then, the first pastor, William Hunt, started the Anti-Slavery Society in Amherst in 1833, and that rule was rescinded. Still, blacks, along with older children, sat up in the balcony. In 1842, the next pastor, George Cooke, designed the Parish Hall next door to serve as a school and a public meeting place. (Courtesy of Cinda Jones.)

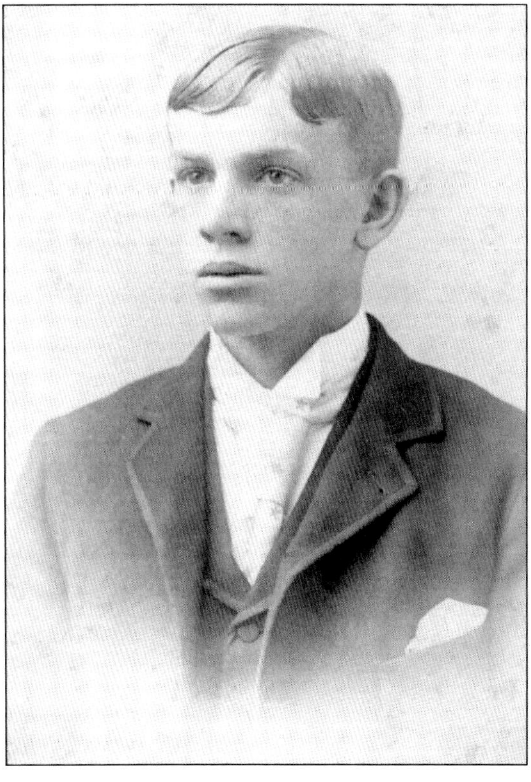

George Fisher became the pastor in 1852 and soon brought in 179 new members. Among them was 19-year-old Ellen Kellogg. Elders accused Reverend Fisher, who was married to an invalid, of inappropriate attention to Ellen. He resigned, giving a blunt defense of himself. His wife died eight months later, and he married Ellen. They moved away but later returned and became generous contributors to the church and library.

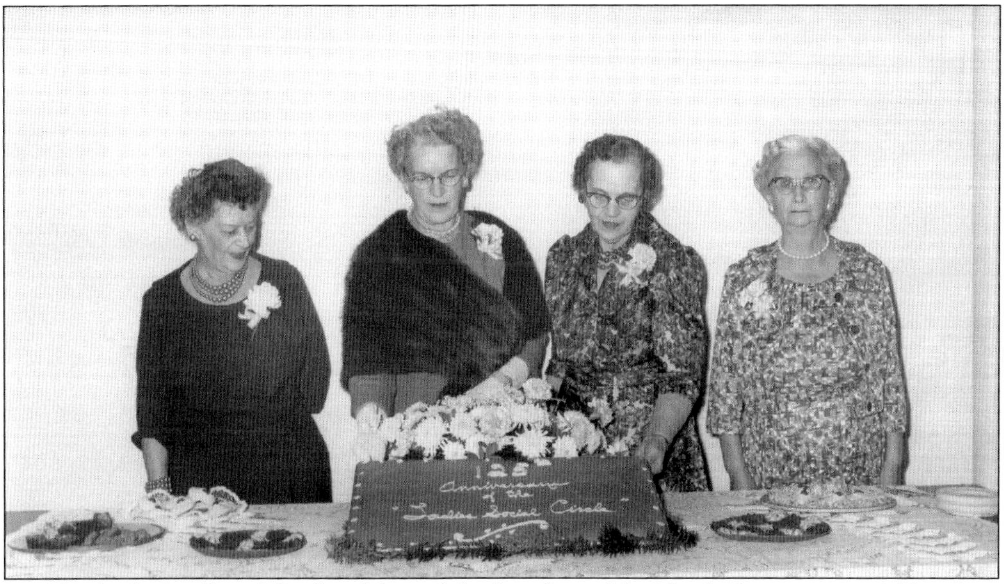

In 1951, the Ladies Social Circle celebrated the founding of the North Congregational Church in 1826. From left to right are Dorothy Haven, Marion Southwick, Ella Hobart, and Grace Burnett. (Courtesy of Houghton and Judith Ingram.)

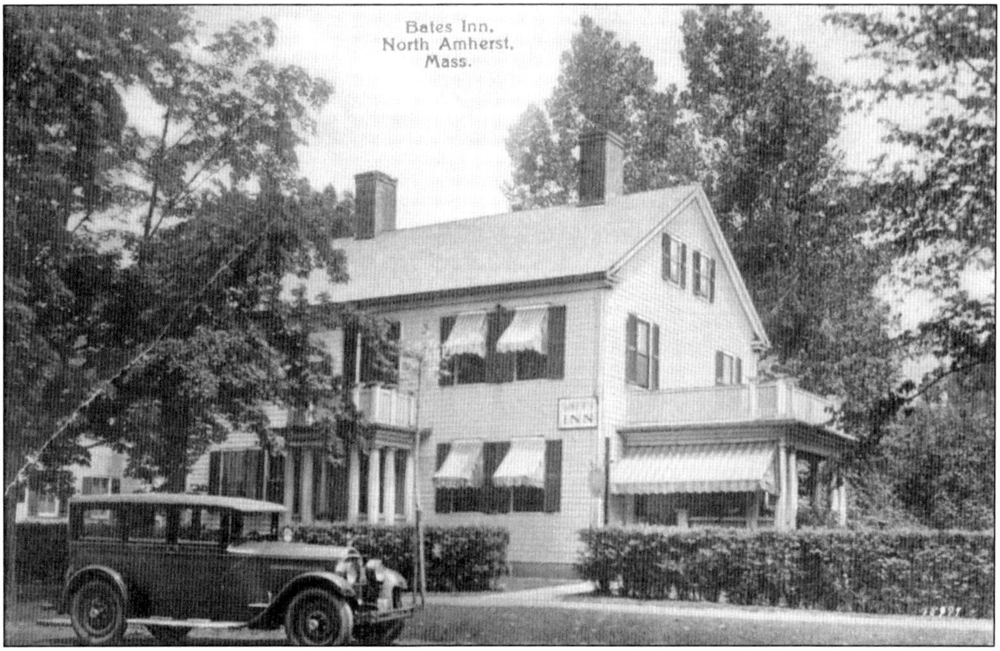

This 1920s postcard shows the Bates Inn on Pine Street, formerly the home and tavern of Oliver Dickinson, probably built around 1800. In 1917, William Bates, a trolley operator, bought the house. The car pictured here belonged to Charles Howe, who rented a room at 105 Montague Road during the summer and dined at the inn. He eventually married his landlady. (Courtesy of Patricia Holland.)

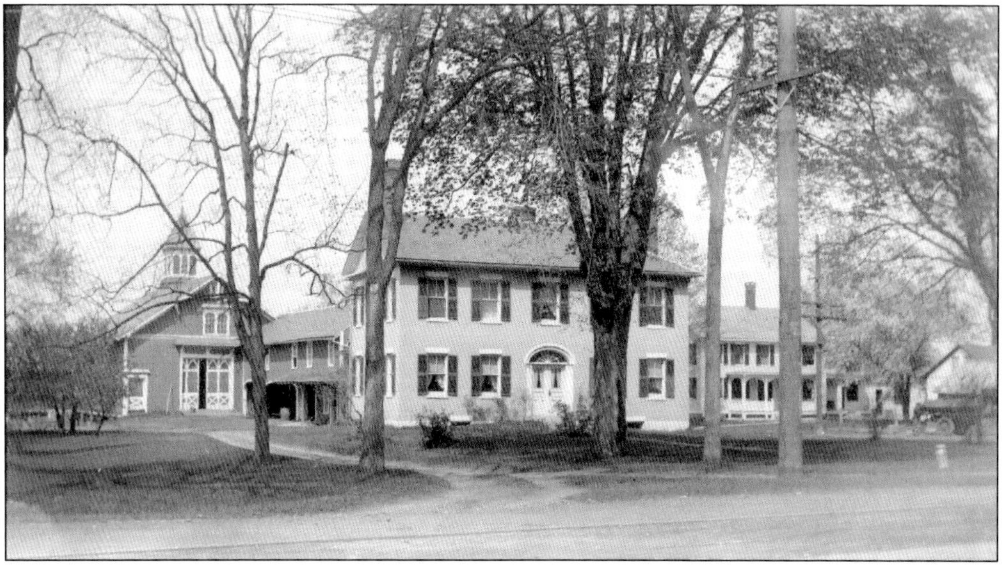

Across the intersection in the southwest corner was this big brick house, now the Black Walnut Inn. Joseph Cowles, born in 1777, built the house in 1821 using bricks made on the premises. The Cowles were related to the Cowls family on Montague Road but added an "e" to the name.

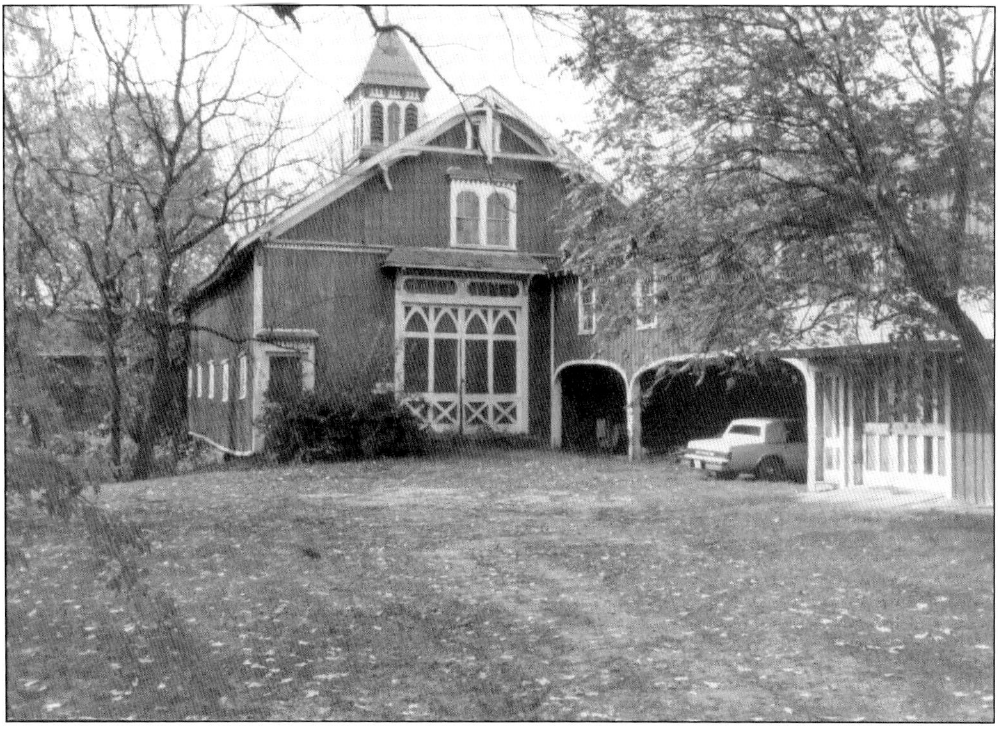

Joseph's son Clinton and grandson Almon Edward Cowles built the barn in 1876 and added the cupola. John Stetson took over the Cowles house and land in the 1890s and invited his niece and her husband, Clara and Allen G. Clark, to live there and grow onions and tobacco. The Clarks' daughter, Louise, married Scott Anderson, operated a gift shop, and lived in the house until 1991. She used to give local children rides in her cart drawn by a donkey. (Courtesy of Marie Twohig.)

Estella Cowles grew up in the house and worked as the librarian at the North Amherst Library for 12 years, overseeing a collection of about 1,700 books and journals. In 1895, she resigned and went to Portland, Oregon, to marry a classmate who worked for the railroad there.

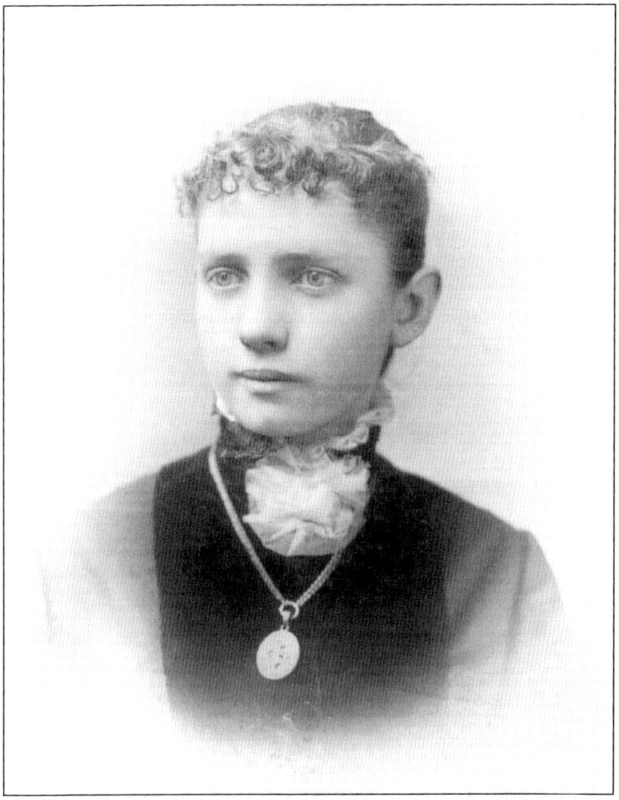

The photograph below of the center of North Amherst was taken from the top of the cupola on the Clark farm. Visible are the church, the roofs of the Clarks' house on the right, and the building that housed a general store on the left. (Courtesy of Marie Twohig.)

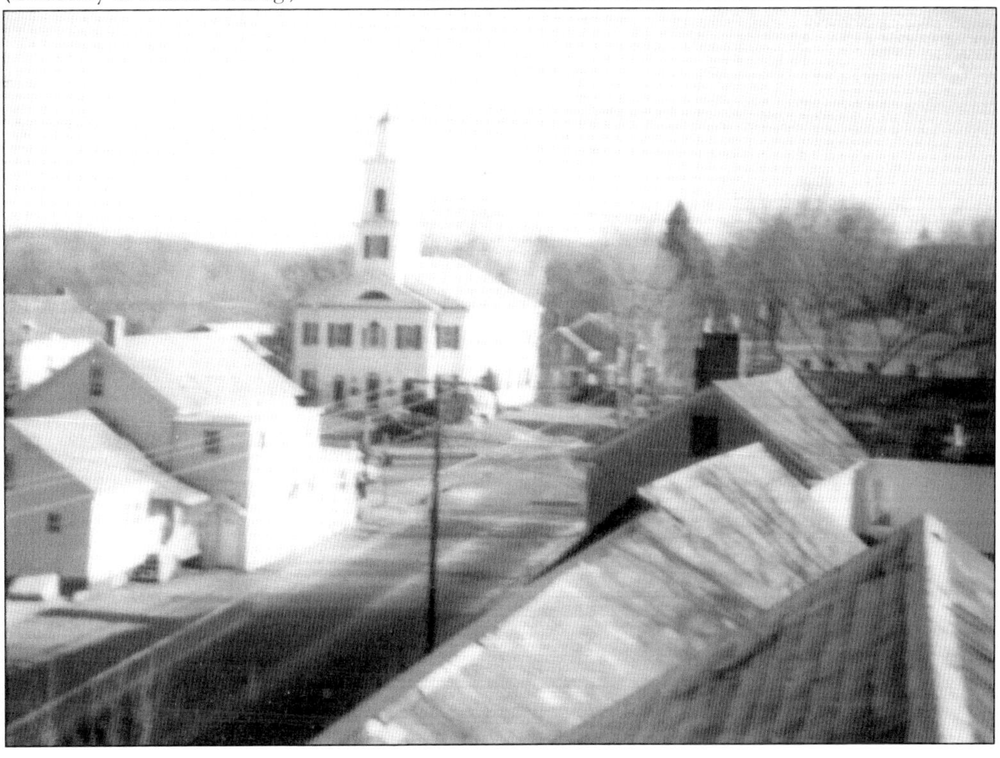

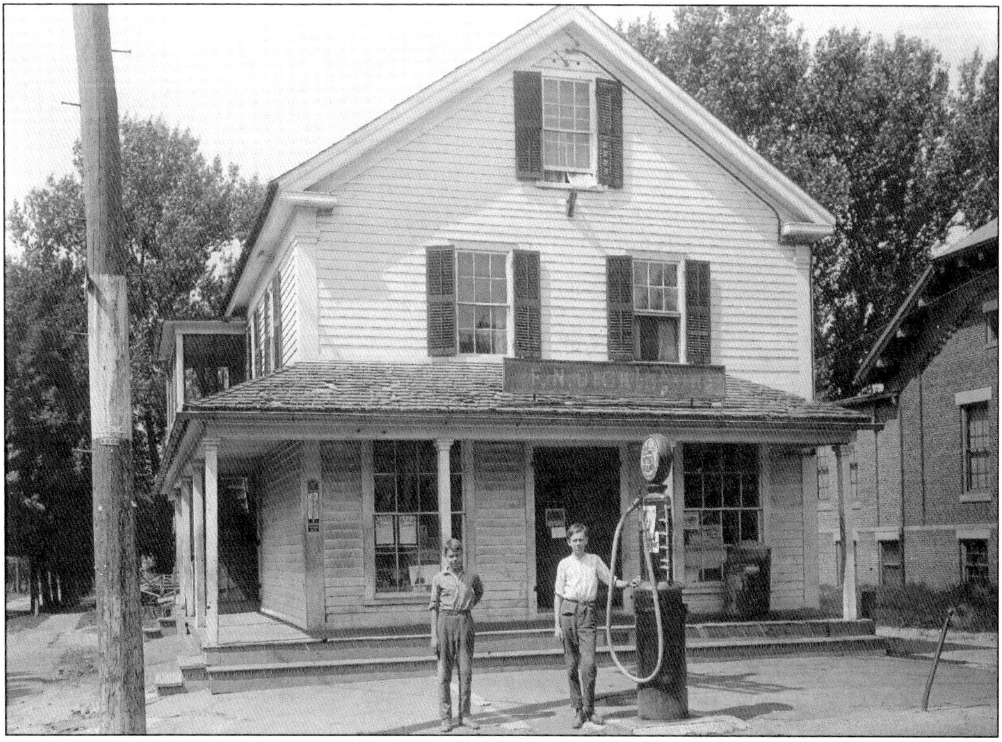

On the northwest corner of the intersection was a house probably built by Israel Billings, a blacksmith. In the early 1800s, the house was occupied by the first minister of the church, William Hunt. Later, it was a shop. Frank N. Dickinson and his son Edward ran it for years, followed by the Bates family, the Humphrey family, Daniel Ottinger, and, starting in 1960, the Chester Watroba family. Standing by the gas pumps are Raymond Bates and Earl Ottinger.

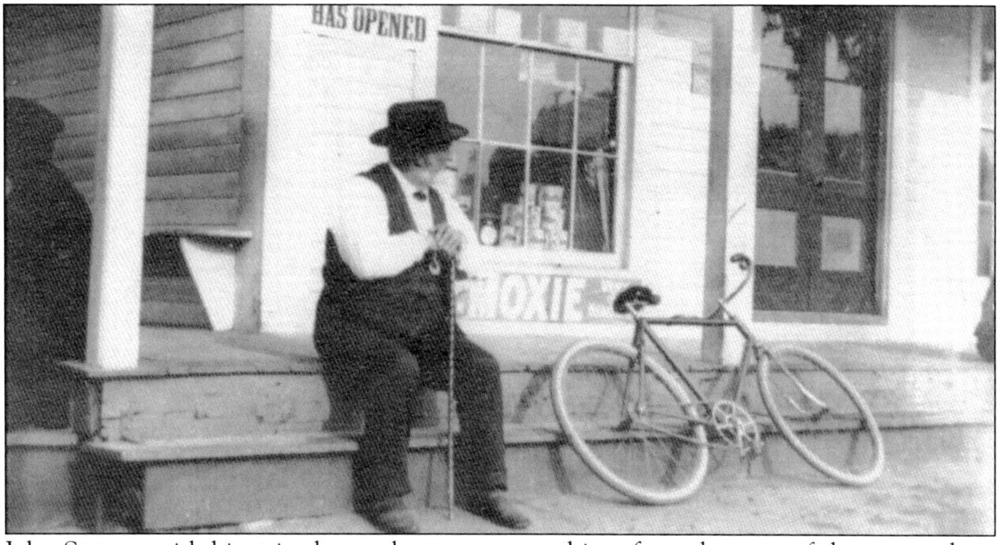

John Stetson, with his striped cane, kept an eye on things from the steps of the corner shop. Bicycles were a standard form of early transportation, coming in during the 1880s and encouraging the placement of macadam over the dirt roads. Moxie was a popular drink especially in the 1920s, first produced in Maine in the late 1800s; it contained gentian root.

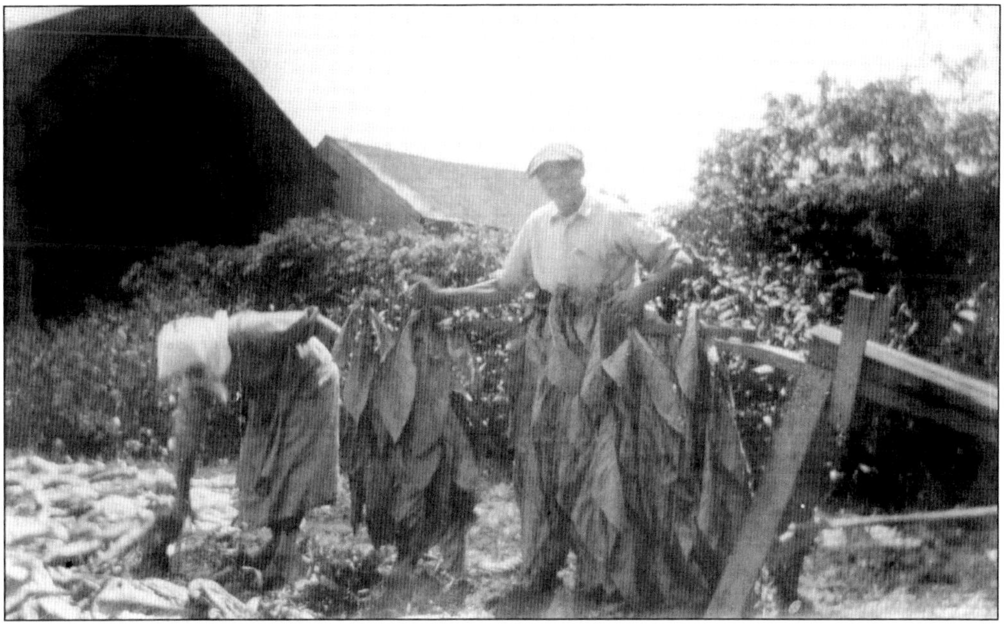

Heading west down Meadow Street toward Hadley is 11 Meadow Street. This large farm was once owned by the Cowles family and later several generations of the Swartz family. John Swartz came at the start of the 1900s from Poland and met his wife, Anastasia Baj, in America. She came from Poland at the age of 14 in 1909. The two are shown above picking tobacco. Their daughter Mary Szala recalls how strict they were, and how they refused to let her start school in the first grade because she was needed at home to help with the younger children. Below, Anastasia "Babci" Swartz, Sister Jolenta, and the Swartz children and grandchildren have a party by their house. (Both courtesy of Mary Szala.)

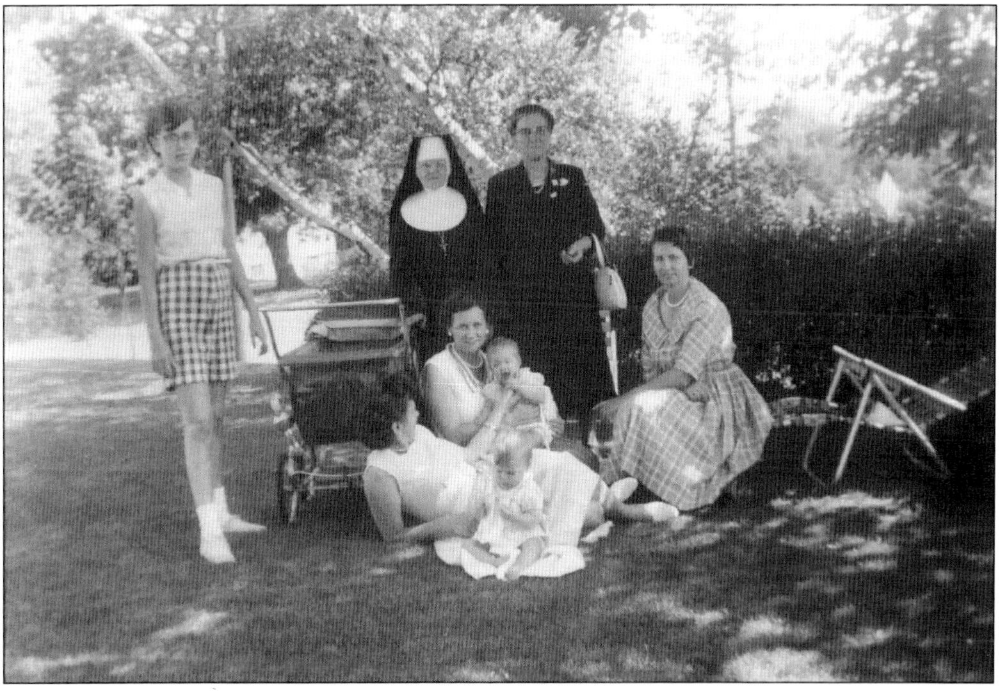

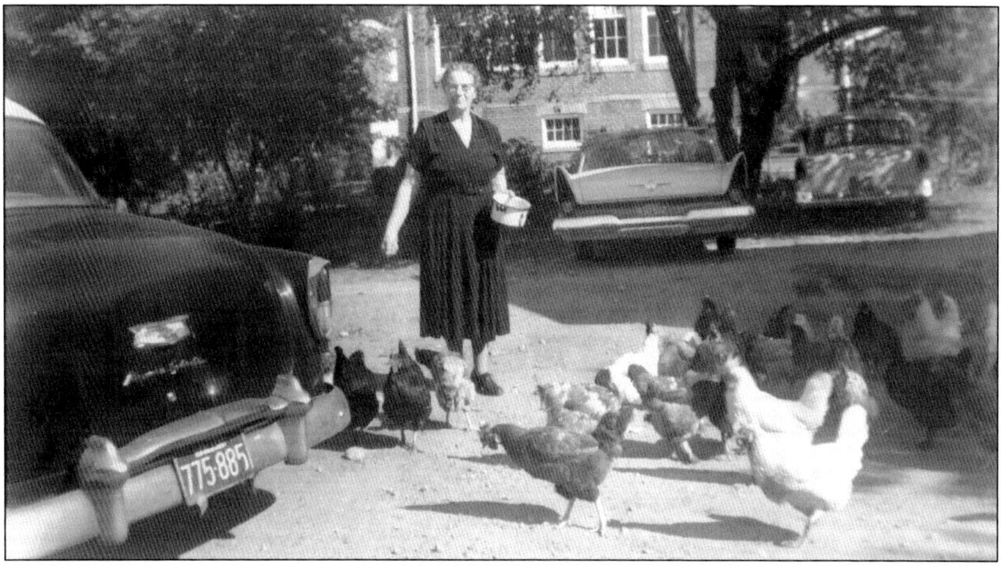

Pictured above in 1960, Babci (meaning grandmother) Swartz loved her chickens. She died in 1986. In the background is the North Amherst School. The 1970s photograph below shows the traditional way of harvesting cucumbers during the steamy summer months. Teenagers, boys and girls, lay face down on old mattresses putting the cukes into baskets, the cucumber picker pulled by a tractor. It was hot, sticky work. In May and June, asparagus was another large crop that teenagers would pick and put the stalks in bunches. In mid-summer, the boys picked tobacco in the tents outside, and the girls sewed the leaves in the sheds. They also hoed corn and weeded onions. Isabelle Callahan also remembers collecting milkweed pods for navy flotilla jackets. (Both courtesy of Mary Szala.)

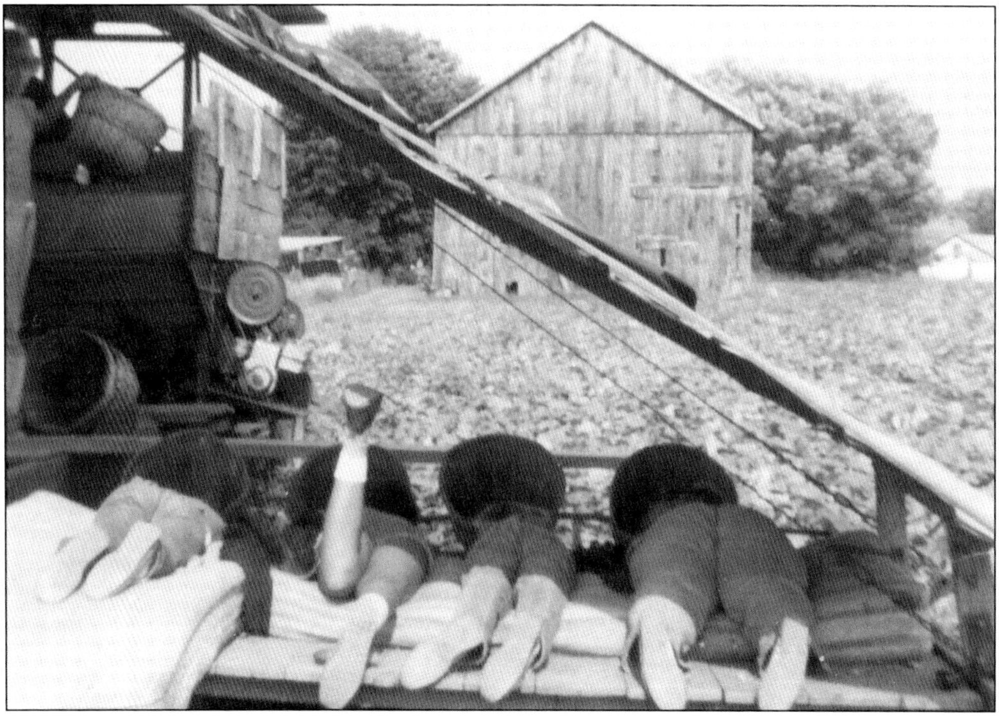

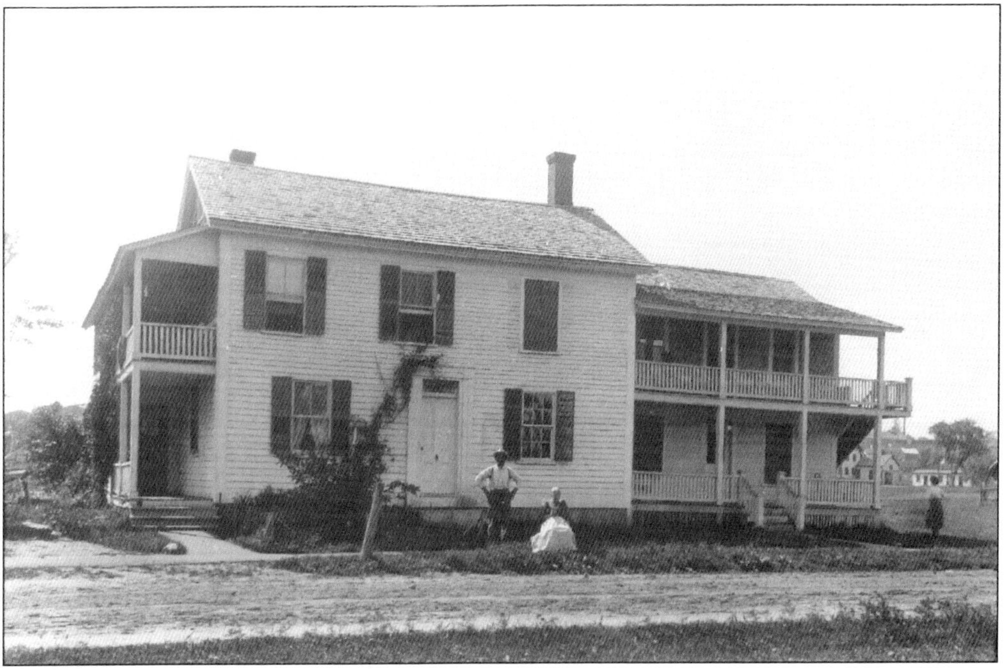

The 1890s photograph above shows a house at 111 Meadow Street with an addition for many rooms. It probably used to hold factory workers in the 1800s and later, and was owned by Ernie Paulin, a barber at the university. In 1955, the state began work on the north-south Route 116 highway that cuts across Meadow Street. Beyond what is now the highway, there was a planing mill in the mid-1800s, drawing power from the Mill River. As the photograph below shows, the land here was low and apt to flood. The 1873 map on page 2 of this book indicates this spot as the southern end of the Great Swamp.

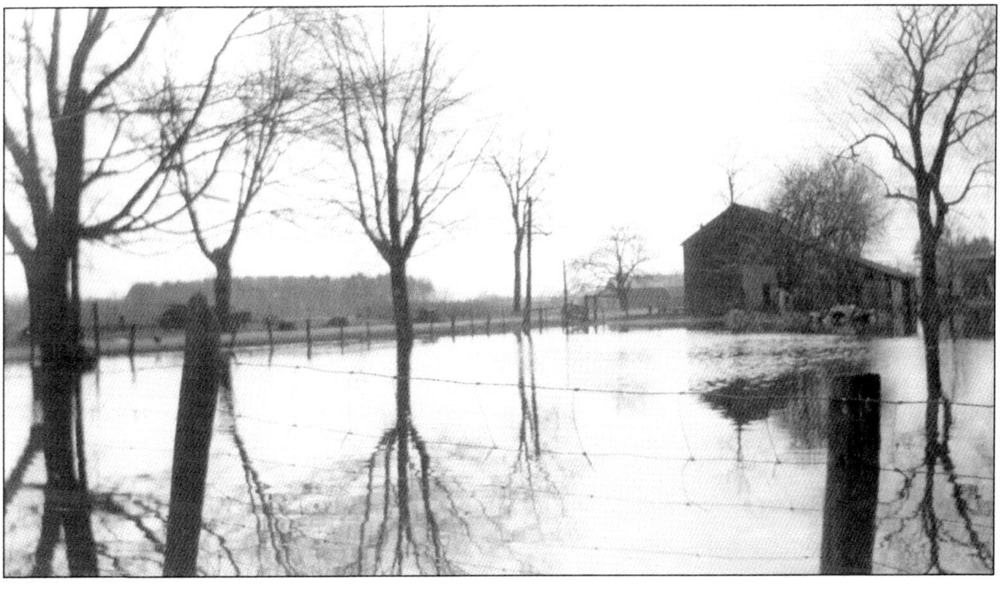

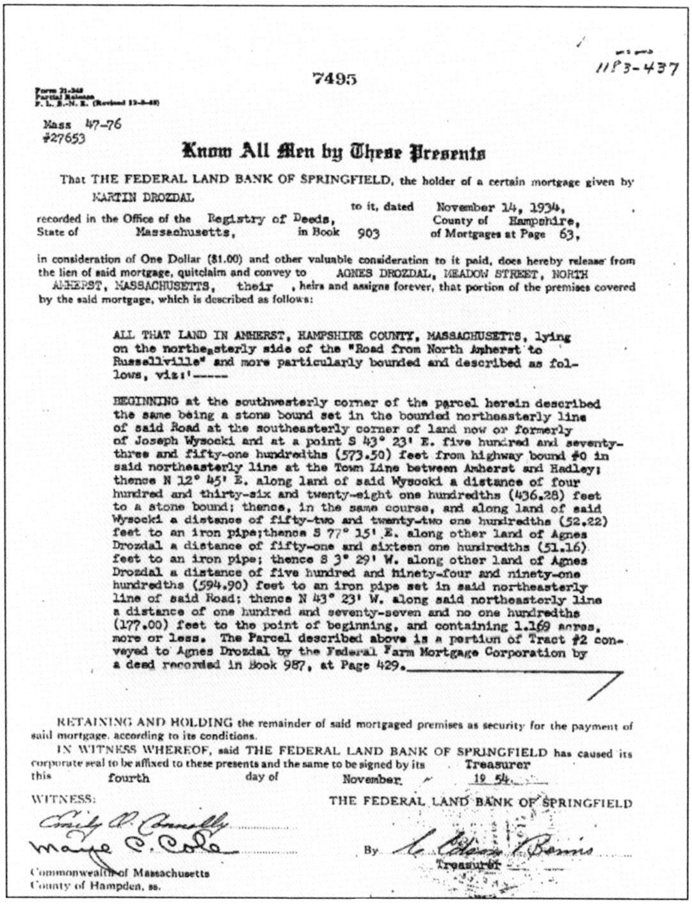

1183-437

7495

Form 21-348
Partial Release
F. L. B.-N. E. (Revised 12-8-48)

Mass 47-76
#27653

Know All Men by These Presents

That THE FEDERAL LAND BANK OF SPRINGFIELD, the holder of a certain mortgage given by MARTIN DROZDAL to it, dated November 14, 1934, recorded in the Office of the Registry of Deeds, County of Hampshire, State of Massachusetts, in Book 903 of Mortgages at Page 63,

in consideration of One Dollar ($1.00) and other valuable consideration to it paid, does hereby release from the lien of said mortgage, quitclaim and convey to AGNES DROZDAL, MEADOW STREET, NORTH AMHERST, MASSACHUSETTS, their, heirs and assigns forever, that portion of the premises covered by the said mortgage, which is described as follows:

ALL THAT LAND IN AMHERST, HAMPSHIRE COUNTY, MASSACHUSETTS, lying on the northeasterly side of the "Road from North Amherst to Russellville" and more particularly bounded and described as follows, viz:'-----

BEGINNING at the southwesterly corner of the parcel herein described the same being a stone bound set in the bounded northeasterly line of said Road at the southeasterly corner of land now or formerly of Joseph Wysocki and at a point S 43° 23' E. five hundred and seventy-three and fifty-one hundredths (573.50) feet from highway bound #0 in said northeasterly line at the Town Line between Amherst and Hadley; thence N 12° 45' E. along land of said Wysocki a distance of four hundred and thirty-six and twenty-eight one hundredths (436.28) feet to a stone bound; thence, in the same course, and along land of said Wysocki a distance of fifty-two and twenty-two one hundredths (52.22) feet to an iron pipe;thence S 77° 15' E. along other land of Agnes Drozdal a distance of fifty-one and sixteen one hundredths (51.16) feet to an iron pipe; thence S 3° 29' W. along other land of Agnes Drozdal a distance of five hundred and ninety-four and ninety-one hundredths (594.90) feet to an iron pipe set in said northeasterly line of said Road; thence N 43° 23' W. along said northeasterly line a distance of one hundred and seventy-seven and no one hundredths (177.00) feet to the point of beginning, and containing 1.169 acres, more or less. The Parcel described above is a portion of Tract #2 conveyed to Agnes Drozdal by the Federal Farm Mortgage Corporation by a deed recorded in Book 987, at Page 429.

RETAINING AND HOLDING the remainder of said mortgaged premises as security for the payment of said mortgage, according to its conditions.

IN WITNESS WHEREOF, said THE FEDERAL LAND BANK OF SPRINGFIELD has caused its corporate seal to be affixed to these presents and the same to be signed by its Treasurer this fourth day of November, 1954.

WITNESS: Emily A. Connolly
Marye C. Cole

THE FEDERAL LAND BANK OF SPRINGFIELD
By C. Oleson Bemis
Treasurer

Commonwealth of Massachusetts
County of Hampden, ss.

This is the release of the mortgage for the house of Agnes Drozdal on Meadow Street, which formerly belonged to Ransom Cowls. That house is pictured on the cover of this book. Below, farther along, this four-bedroom house at 253 Meadow Street was built in 1810. This area is flat, prime farming land, the original bottom of the ancient Lake Hitchcock, with deep, rich soil. The family shown here in the 1890s may be Caroline Spear, age 81 in 1900, her daughter Mary J. Spear, age 48 in 1900, and Earle L. Milliken, age 51 in 1900.

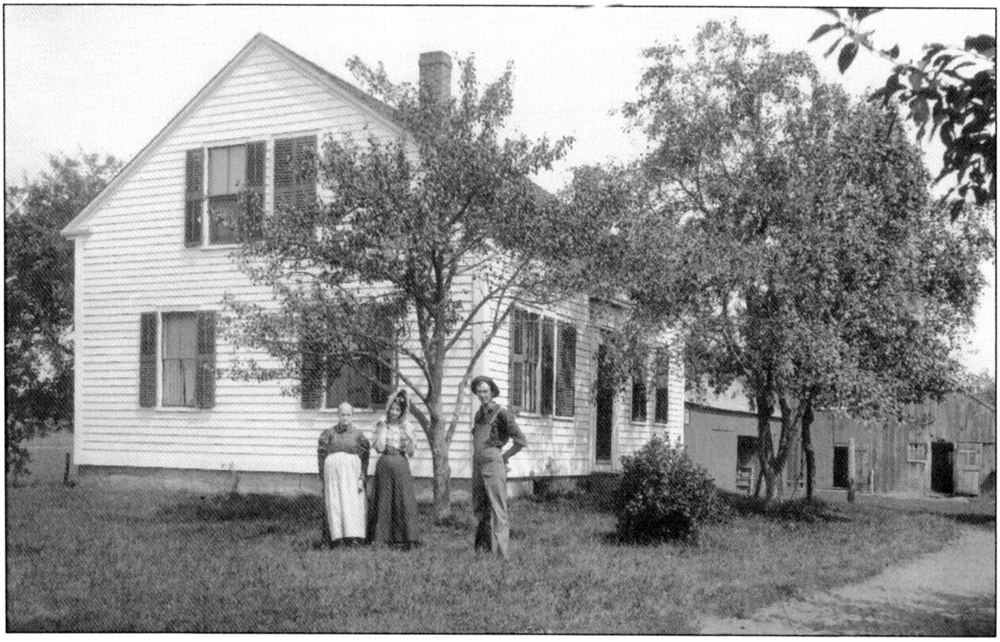

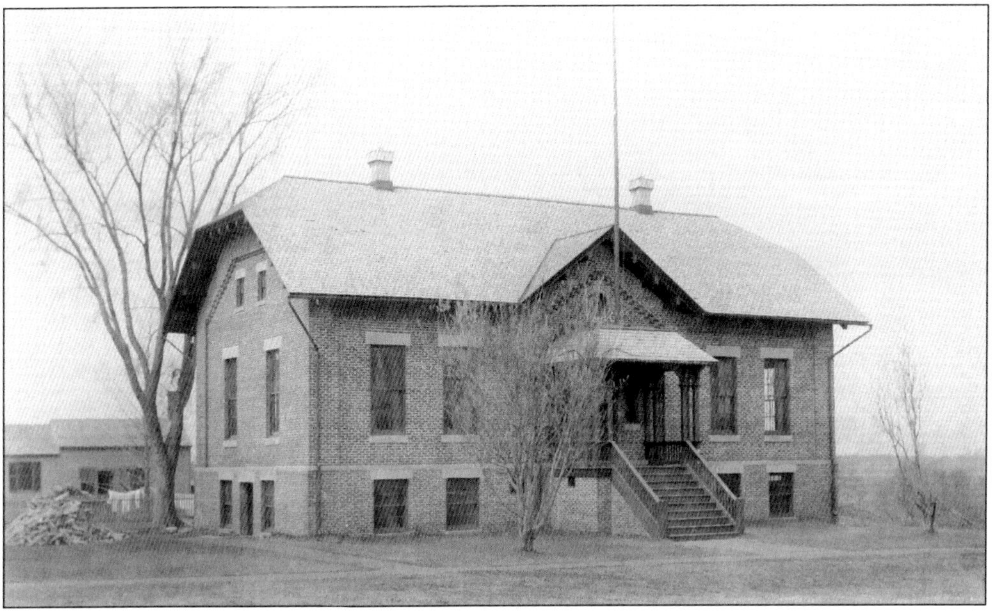

This view of the North Amherst School when it was new in 1871 shows its elegant brickwork and the laundry on the Cowles family line behind. There were two rooms, each holding four grades. A massive heating system used one register to heat the whole building and keep the children's lunches warm. Around the end of the 1800s, there was an increase in the population of Polish and Lithuanian immigrants, and the school population went up. Below, the students are shown in an undated photograph. The woman at the top left is probably the teacher.

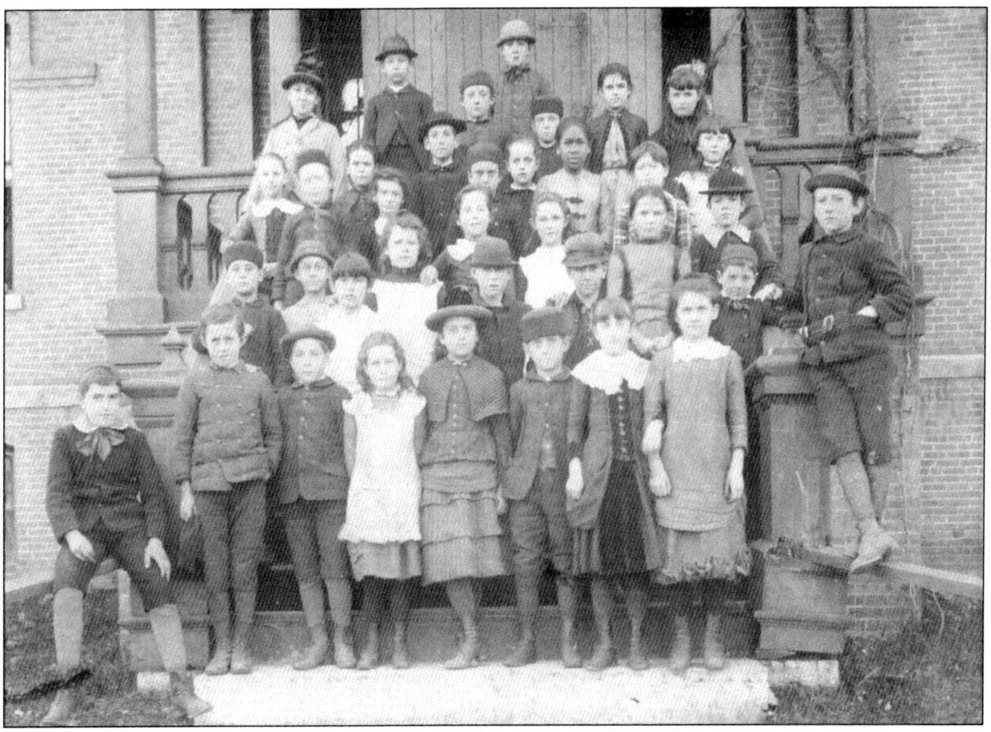

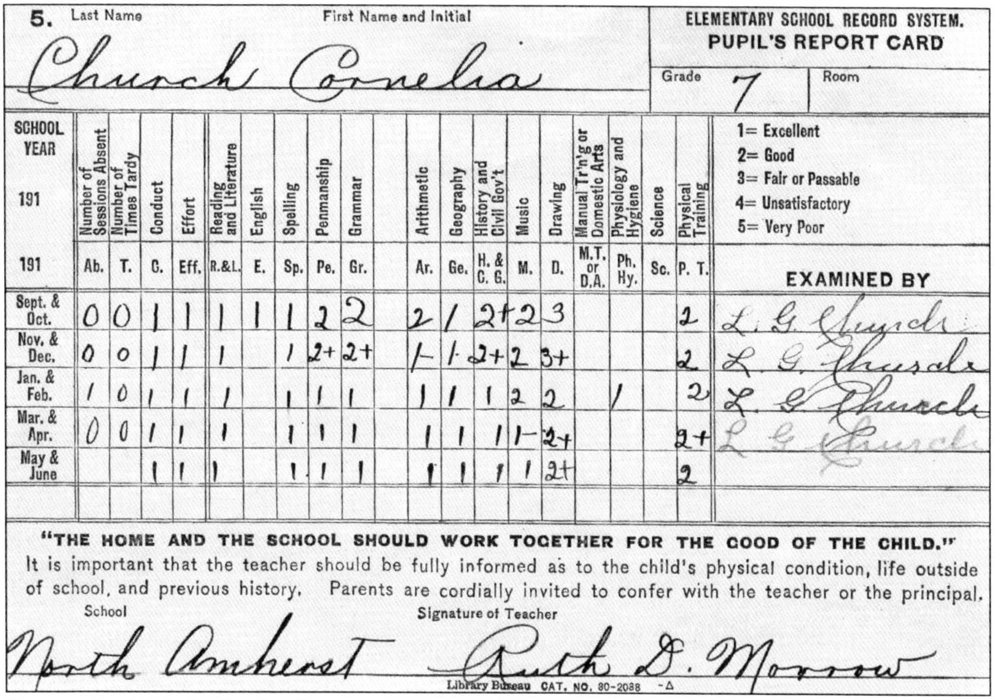

5. Last Name First Name and Initial

Church Cornelia

ELEMENTARY SCHOOL RECORD SYSTEM.
PUPIL'S REPORT CARD

Grade 7 Room

SCHOOL YEAR 191 / 191	Ab. (Number of Sessions Absent)	T. (Number of Times Tardy)	C. (Conduct)	Eff. (Effort)	R.&L. (Reading and Literature)	E. (English)	Sp. (Spelling)	Pe. (Penmanship)	Gr. (Grammar)		Ar. (Arithmetic)	Ge. (Geography)	H. & C. G. (History and Civil Gov't)	M. (Music)	D. (Drawing)	M.T. or D.A. (Manual Tr'n'g or Domestic Arts)	Ph. Hy. (Physiology and Hygiene)	Sc. (Science)	P. T. (Physical Training)	EXAMINED BY
Sept. & Oct.	0	0	1	1	1	1	1	2	2		2	1	2+	2	3				2	L. G. Church
Nov. & Dec.	0	0	1	1	1		1	2+	2+		1-	1-	2+	2	3+				2	L. G. Church
Jan. & Feb.	1	0	1	1	1		1	1	1		1	1	1	2	2		1		2	L. G. Church
Mar. & Apr.	0	0	1	1	1		1	1	1		1	1	1	1-	2+				2+	L. G. Church
May & June			1	1	1		1	1	1		1	1	1	1	2+				2	

1= Excellent
2= Good
3= Fair or Passable
4= Unsatisfactory
5= Very Poor

"THE HOME AND THE SCHOOL SHOULD WORK TOGETHER FOR THE GOOD OF THE CHILD."
It is important that the teacher should be fully informed as to the child's physical condition, life outside of school, and previous history. Parents are cordially invited to confer with the teacher or the principal.

School: North Amherst Signature of Teacher: Ruth D. Morrow

Library Bureau CAT. NO. 80-2088 -Δ

During the 1914–1915 school session, the school superintendent had a telephone in his office in Amherst's town hall numbered 4-M. Lucia G. Church signed the report card above for her daughter, seventh grader Cornelia Church, probably in 1919. In the 1917–1918 school year, Lillian Piper was teaching the fourth and fifth grades. Below, from left to right, are (first row) Joseph Kozloski, John Lannon, Clyde Spear, Walter C. Jones, G. Ross MacKimmie, H. Roy Holden, Joseph Jakimko, and Joseph Descavicz; (second row) Marion Leary, Marcia Esterbrook, Verebel Fulton, Hazel Burrington, Mary Barkowski, Annie Bukoski, Marcia Church, and Mildred Brown; (third row) Marcella Kuzminski, Katie Waskiewicz, Winifred Chenoweth, Ruth Larned, George Westcott, Barny Kolokoski, Raymond Bates, James Fitts, and Michael Waskiewicz. (Above, courtesy of the University of Massachusetts Amherst, Special Collections.)

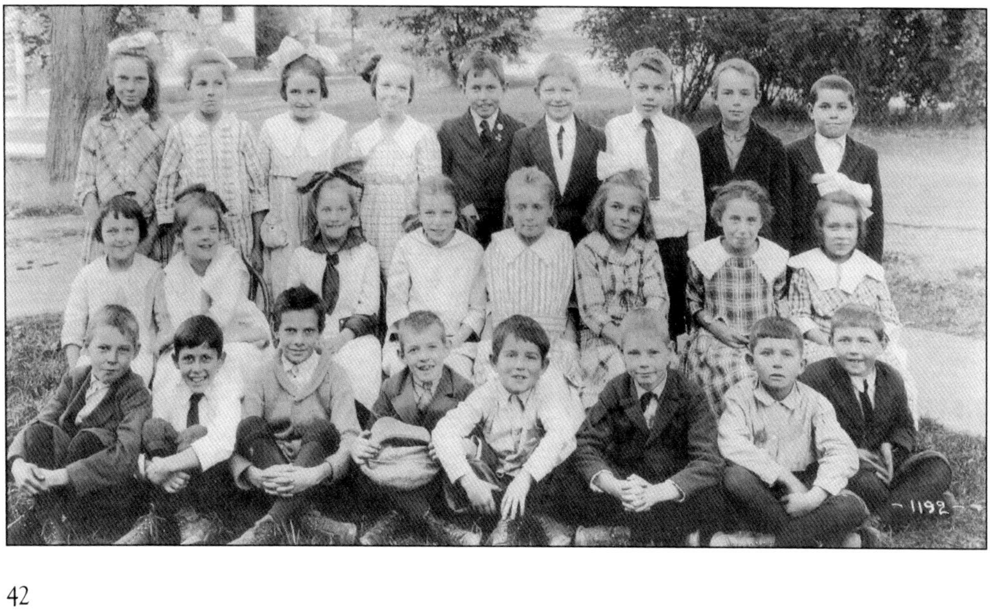

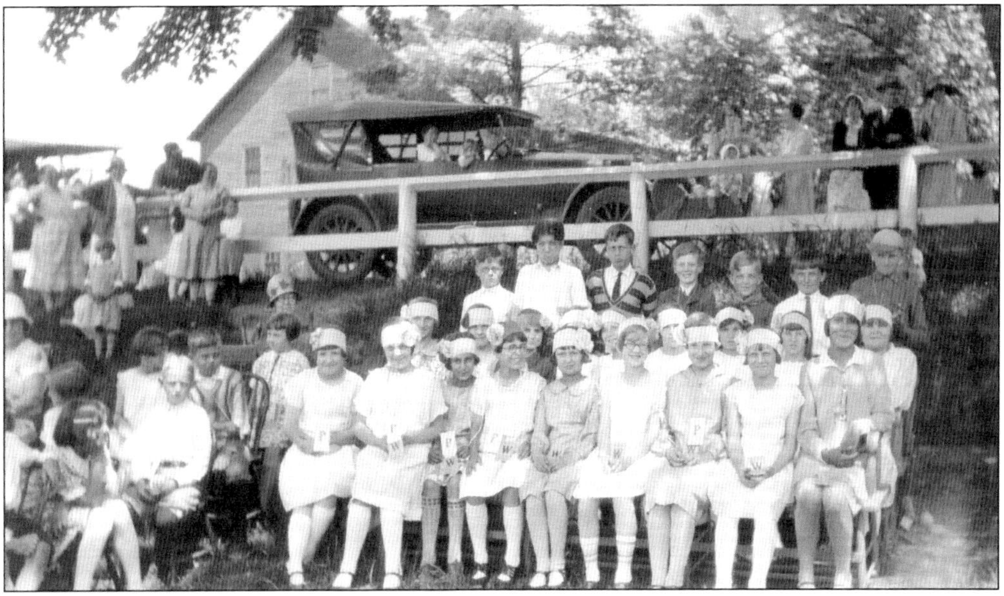

The school had three terms: fall, winter, and spring. Just north of the school was a large playing field, and in winter, people made a skating pond there. Here, students and families at the North Amherst School gathered on the edge of the school playing field to celebrate the annual School Health Day in 1928.

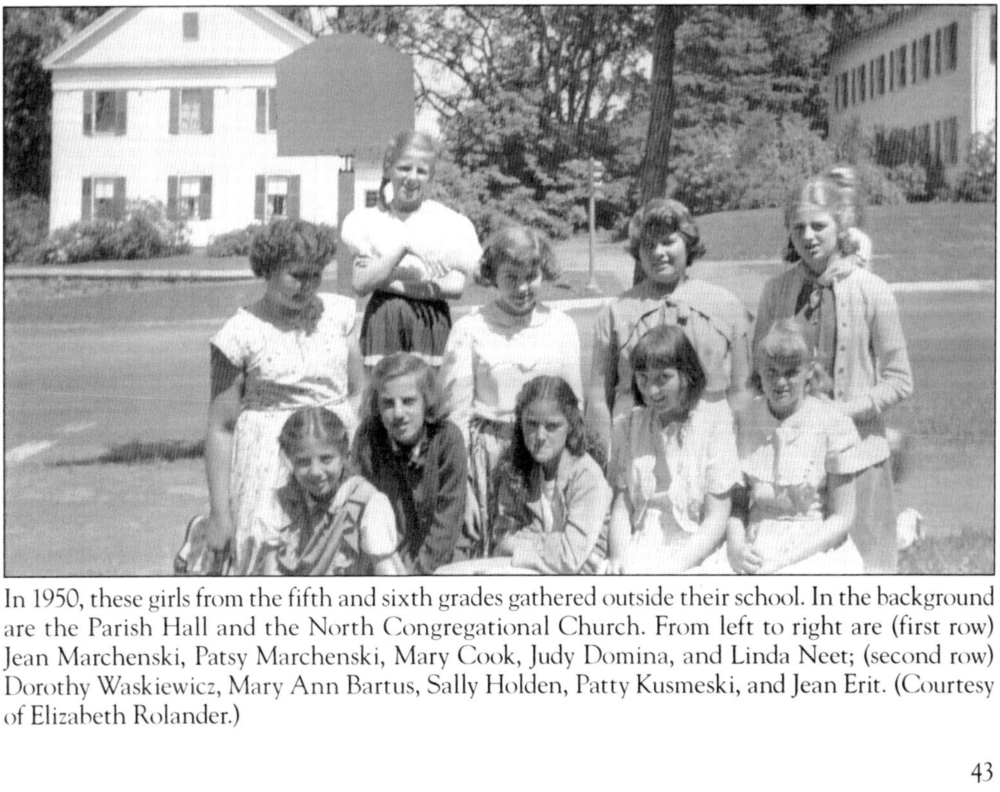

In 1950, these girls from the fifth and sixth grades gathered outside their school. In the background are the Parish Hall and the North Congregational Church. From left to right are (first row) Jean Marchenski, Patsy Marchenski, Mary Cook, Judy Domina, and Linda Neet; (second row) Dorothy Waskiewicz, Mary Ann Bartus, Sally Holden, Patty Kusmeski, and Jean Erit. (Courtesy of Elizabeth Rolander.)

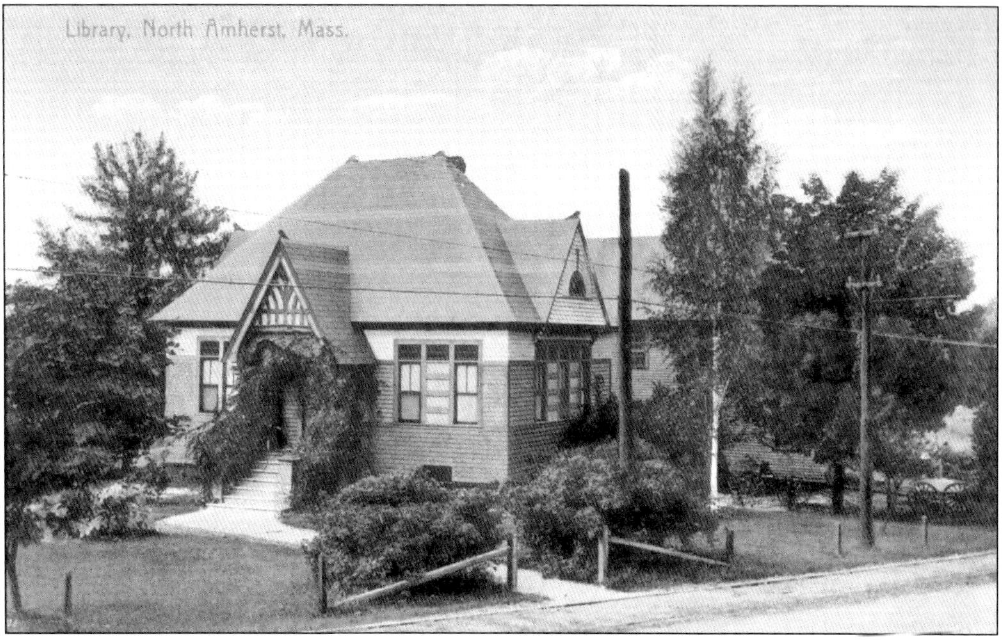

This early photograph shows the North Amherst Library across the street from the school. Before its construction in 1893, the library had been in the school. But then, in 1889, the two-story, wooden grammar school near the dam at Factory Hollow on State Street was destroyed by arson. The students had to be crowded into the North Amherst School, eliminating the room for the library. In the new library there was colored glass in the high windows and exquisite details on the woodwork. The exterior was painted in five different colors, but after the hard times of the 1930s, the town painted it all white instead, as seen in the 1993 photograph below. In 1996, the building was restored and painted in its original colors. The 1993 image shows a huge tree, a copper beech beloved by all; it had to come down in 2009. (Below, courtesy of Robert Winne.)

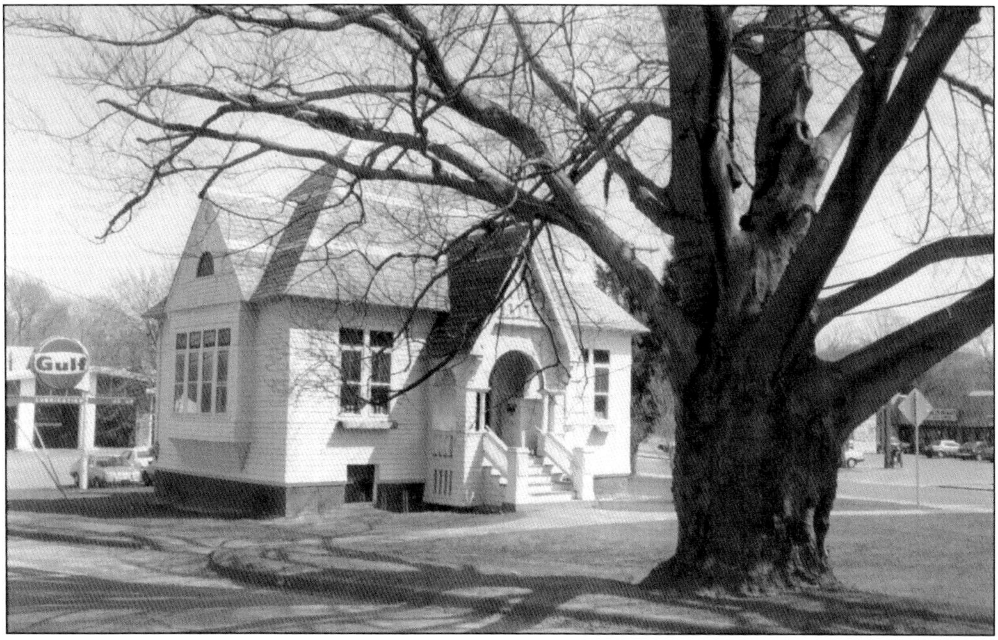

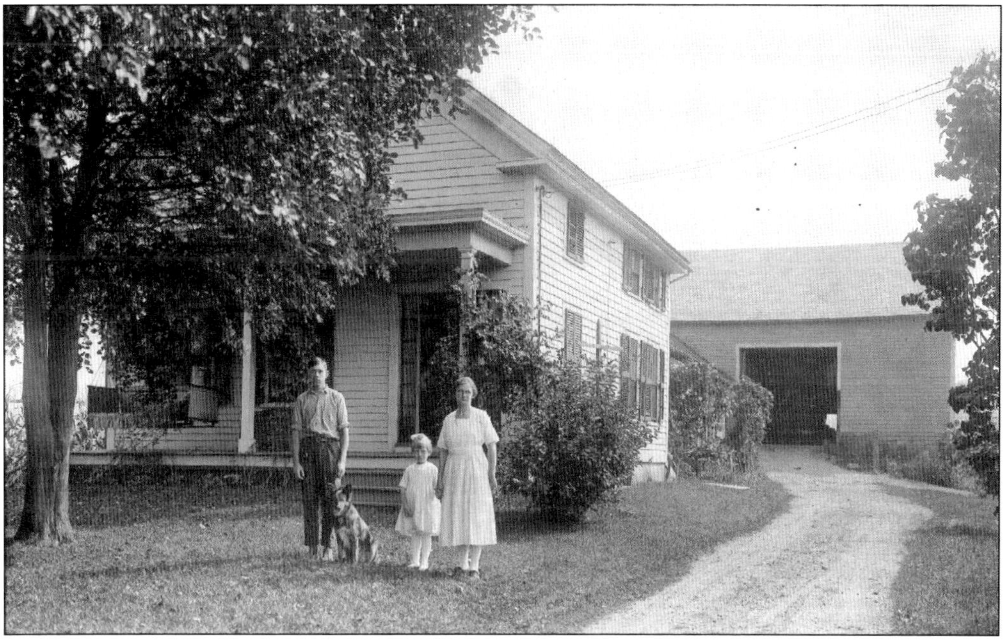

Sunderland Road, the road to Sunderland farther north, was a residential, tree-lined street in the first half of the 1900s. Judith (Westcott) Ingram remembers roller-skating there. People worked out of their homes. On the west side of the street, Ralph T. Staab had his fuel oil business. The photograph above shows the house of the Westcott family at 127 Sunderland Road with young George, his sister Marion, and their stepmother, Florence Westcott. George was born in 1907. The house was located where a modern business, Cowls Building Supply, has stood since the 1970s. The Westcott house was moved farther north to the opposite side of the road. John S. Westcott, shown below in the 1950s, had founded a trucking business 30 years earlier that his son George developed into an interstate concern. (Both courtesy of Houghton and Judith Ingram.)

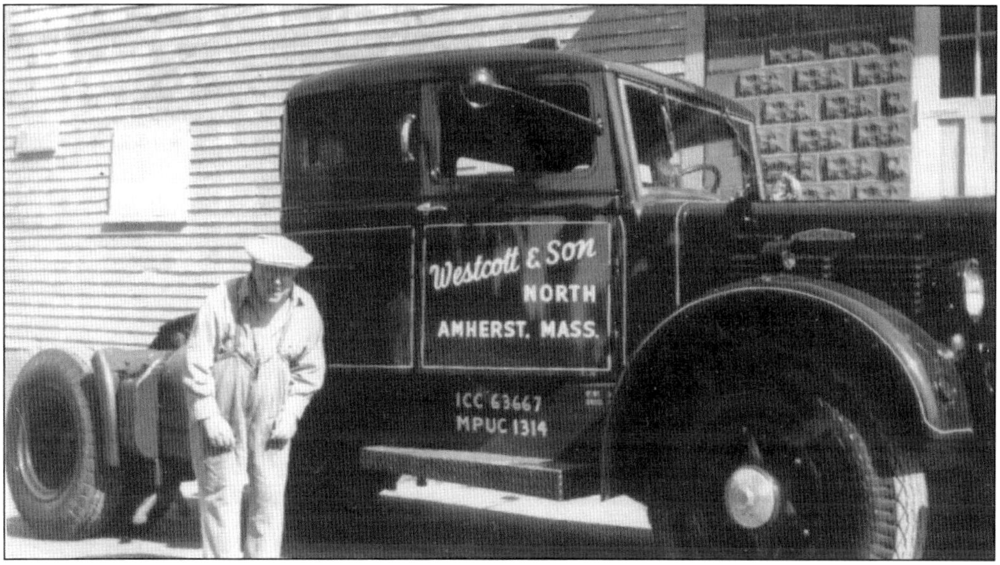

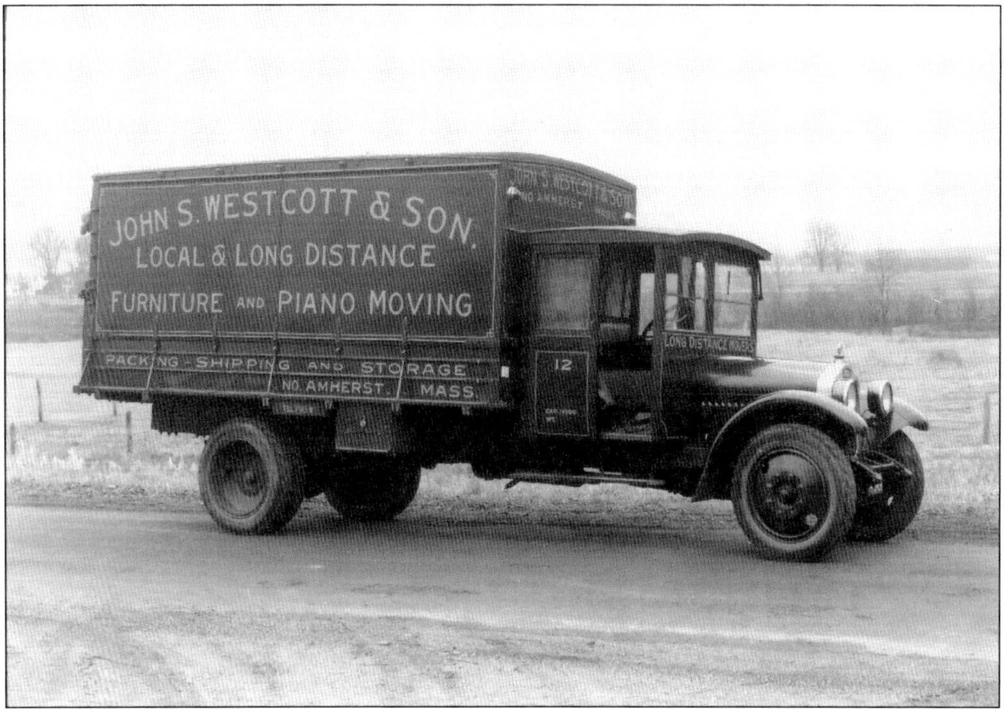

Above is a truck from the early days of the business. In the mid-1940s, the director of the Pratt Museum at Amherst College hired Westcott Movers to bring a plaster cast of a dinosaur from New York City to be installed in its museum. The college was well-known for its collection of dinosaur bones, many of which had been found in the area. There are several spots in the valley where the footprints can be seen in the rock. In the photograph below, the loaded truck drives past a dormitory at the college. (Both courtesy of Houghton and Judith Ingram.)

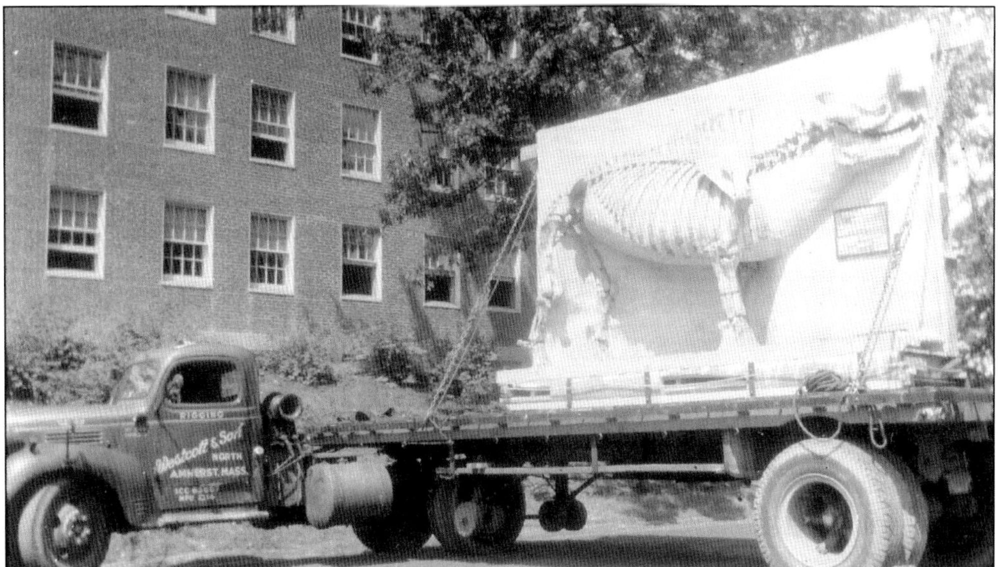

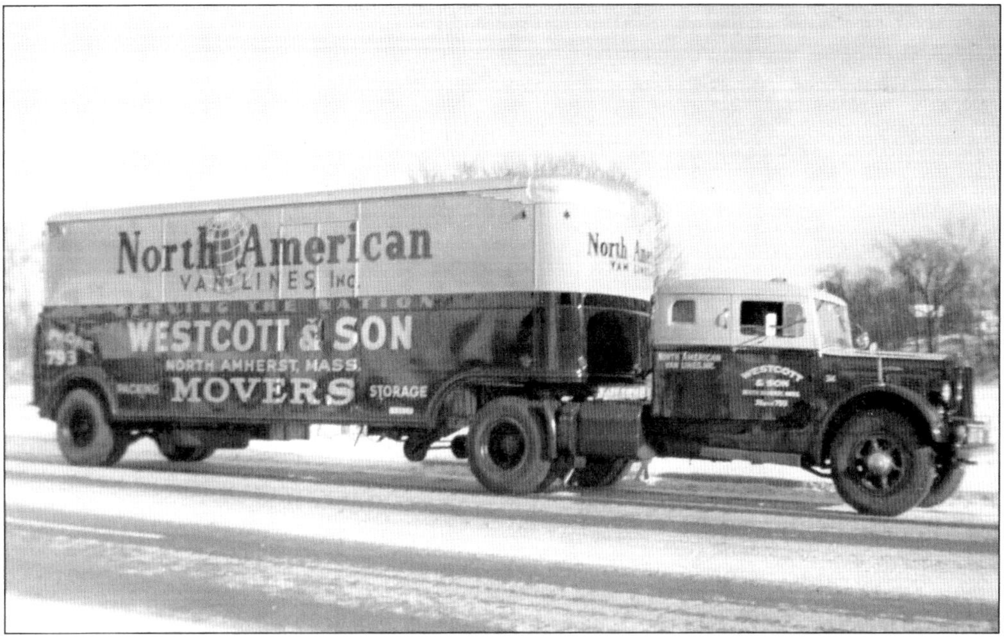

Here is their truck in 1950, affiliated with North American Van Lines. After George Westcott retired from trucking, he went on to make specialized crates for unusual objects. Once he crafted a box for a valuable crystal chandelier to be shipped to Los Angeles. (Courtesy of Houghton and Judith Ingram.)

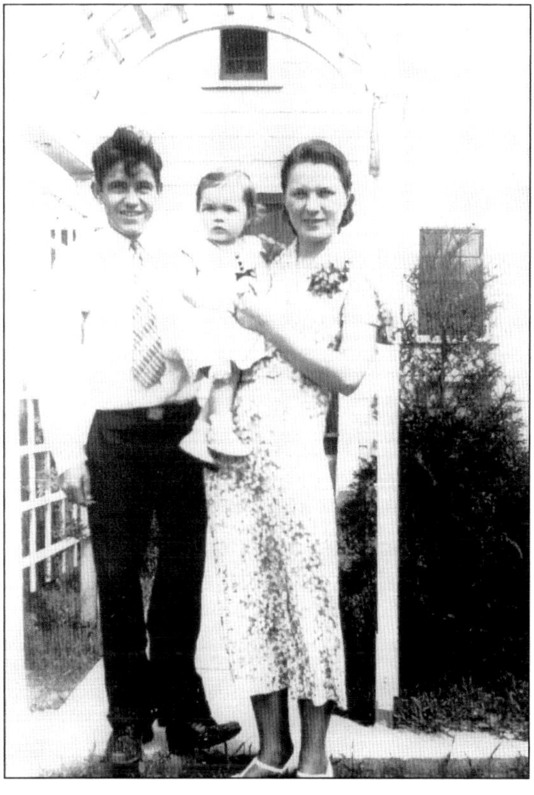

Michael Waskiewicz was a neighbor of the Westcotts on Sunderland Road. He is shown here in the 1930s with his wife and baby. Part of a farming family, he had a twisted leg that ruled out farm work, so he started the Westview Cafe. (Courtesy of Mark Power.)

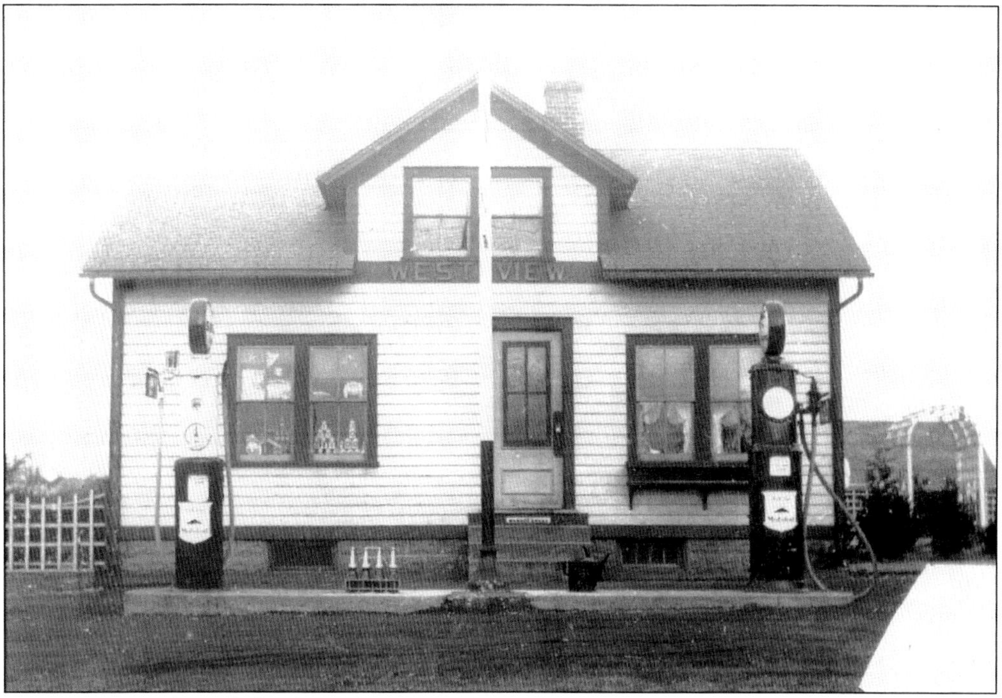

At the corner of Sunderland Road and Cowls Road was the Westview Cafe, shown above as it was in the 1920s, with the house on the right, and below in the 1940s. The school bus used to stop in front of the store, and the children waiting there delighted in finding dropped change. The store evolved into a bar, and in recent years, has become a bar with an Irish theme called The Harp. (Both courtesy of Mark Power.)

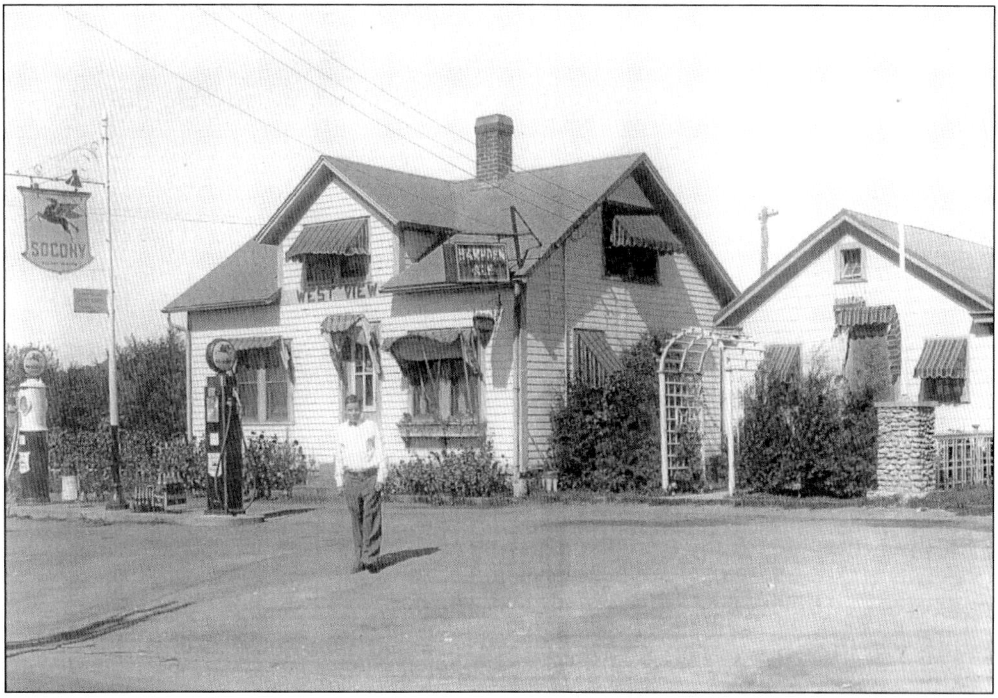

Three

Summer Street, Puffer's Pond, and the Mills

From Cowls Road, up Summer Street, there is Puffer's Pond. The pond and the land around it have been a bucolic conservation area since 1977. The Mill River runs through it, the fishing is good, and it is a wonderful place to cool off in the summer and ice fish in the winter. But back in the 1700s, and especially in the 1800s, the river powered mills. In 1739, the town of Hadley gave Nathaniel Kellogg permission to build a gristmill "at the great falls," but instead he erected a water-powered sawmill, then a very modern invention. By 1744, he also had a gristmill. The whole area was called Factory Hollow. Summer Street used to be Factory Street, laid in the 1830s to reach the factory. In 1860, there was a wood-planing mill, powered by a canal off the Mill River. In the 1890s, A.W. Hall manufactured wagons, carriages, and Concord buggies where 111 Summer Street is now. The second section of Summer Street was called Slab City for the wood mill at the far end. It was also called "Little Lithuania" for all the Lithuanians who lived there. Workers lived in the small houses and duplexes that are still there. After the trolley service ended in 1928, many Catholics found it hard to get to center Amherst for church. During the 1930s, a fellow Catholic, Edward Dowd on State Street, just across the river, arranged for them all to have services in his barn. As the big mills upstream stopped functioning in the early 1900s, more people were out of work. Still, people recall good times. The site of Ebenezer Kellogg's corn mill in 1725 became a swimming hole in the Mill River. Before the dam on the river up in Cushman was removed, people used to skate on the millpond and dance in the empty factory buildings. Factories depended on a drywall dam which held back the Mill River and formed a millpond northeast of the present bridge; that was for a long time a favorite place to go swimming. The river still flows, but the millpond has turned into forest.

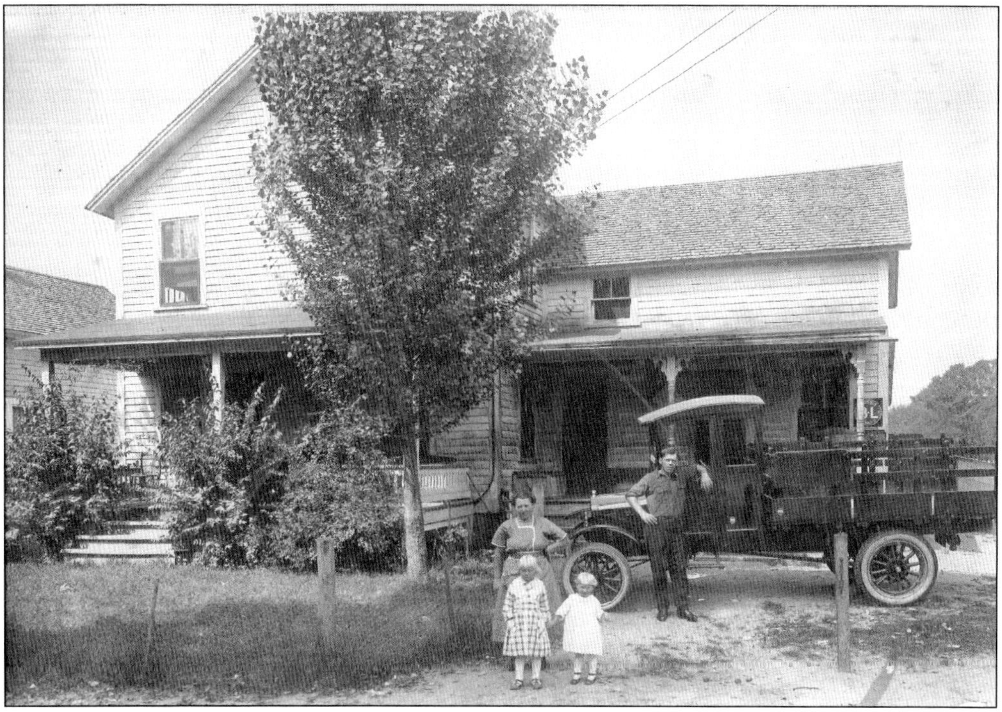

At 134 Summer Street, Victor Lozoski had a store with gas pumps. He sold kerosene, and in 1932, got a liquor license. He is pictured above with his Model T truck. Across the street was Frederick Crafts's blacksmith shop, shown below in 1937. The 1938 hurricane tore off the front. The shop remained until 1945. The school bus stopped there, and the place became a hangout for the children. Crafts would fix wagons for the children and make basketball rings. Sometimes, they would have parties there. His son Fred Jr. also fixed cars there. (Above, courtesy of Peter Kaslauskas.)

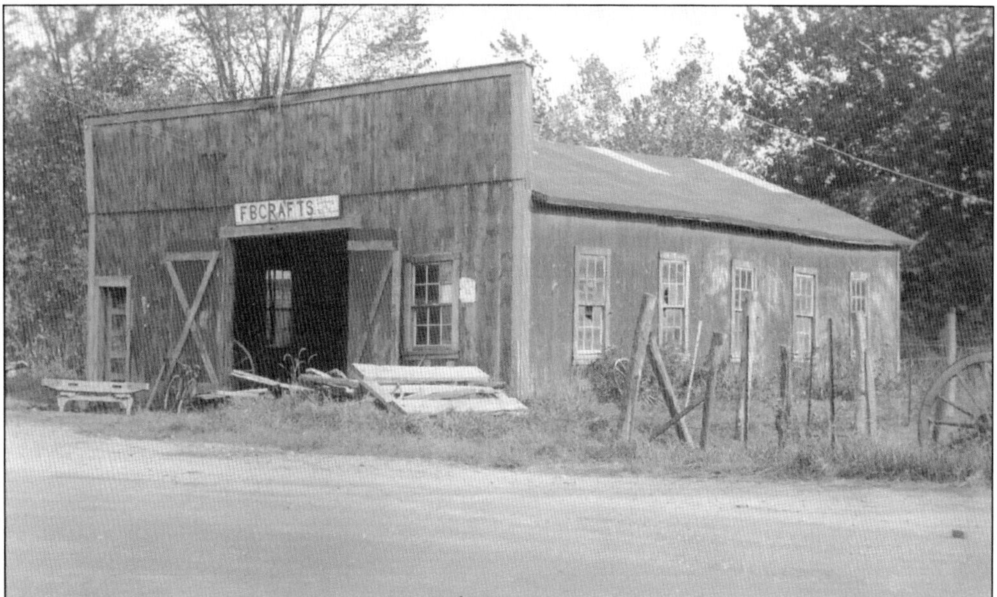

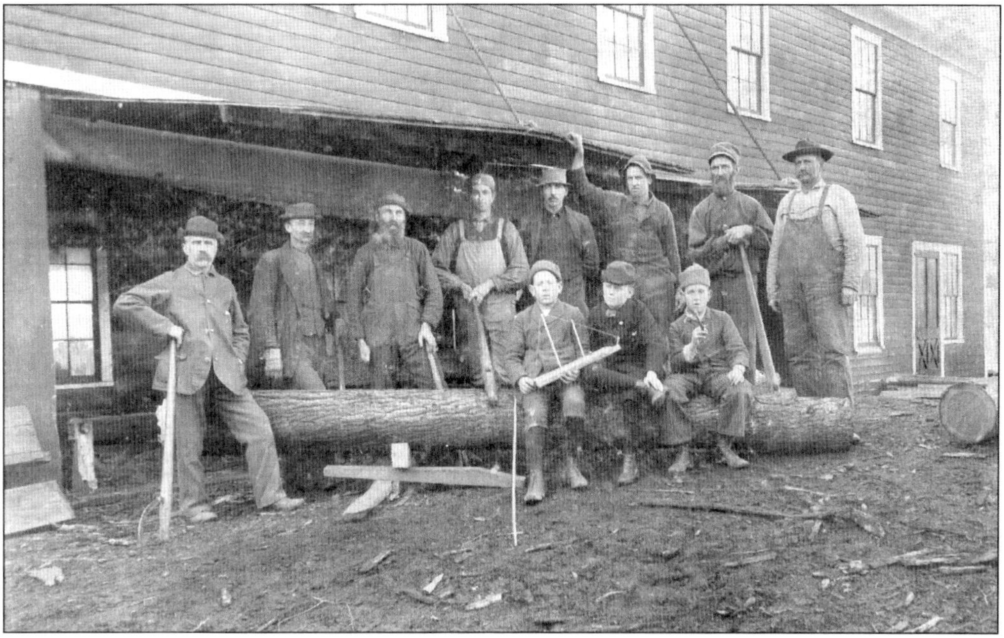

At the end of the road was the mill, powered by water from the dammed-up Mill River. In 1809, Ebenezer Dickinson built a three-story cotton mill there. In the 1840s, Thomas Jones owned three mills there. He manufactured Kentucky jean, a fabric woven with cotton warp and woolen weft for making blue jeans. The brothers Ephraim and John Cushman built this dam in 1850 on the site of a smaller one. The Cushmans then built paper mills. In the last half of the 1800s, Dwight Graves made doors, sashes, and boxes. Pictured above is the Amherst Woodworking Mill; the men and boys are unidentified. It was started in 1880 and burned down in 1940. The Mill Hollow apartment complex now occupies the site. The photograph below shows the dam and sluiceway in 1888. (Above, courtesy of Houghton and Judith Ingram.)

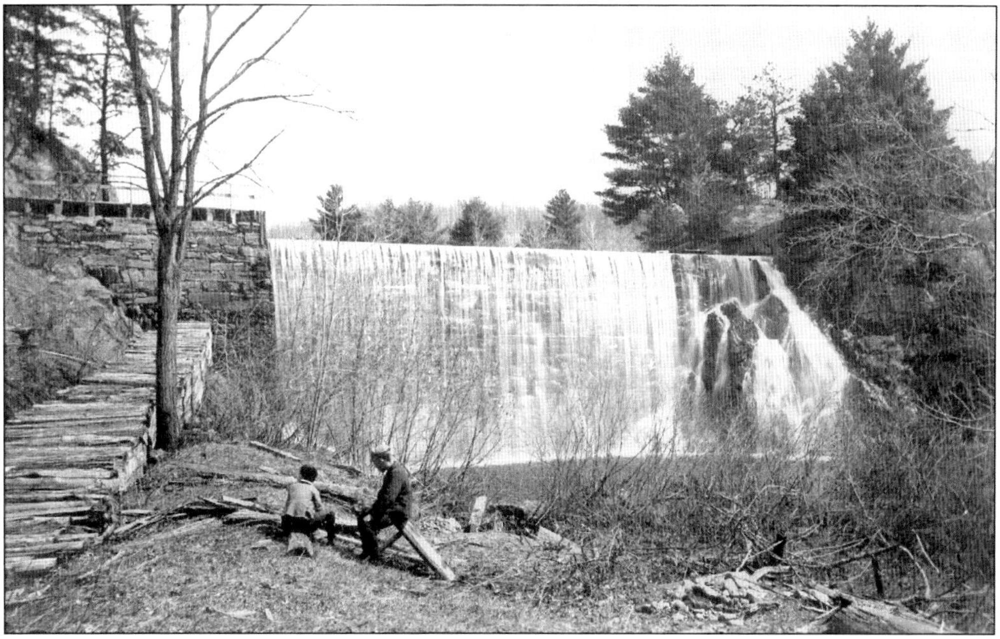

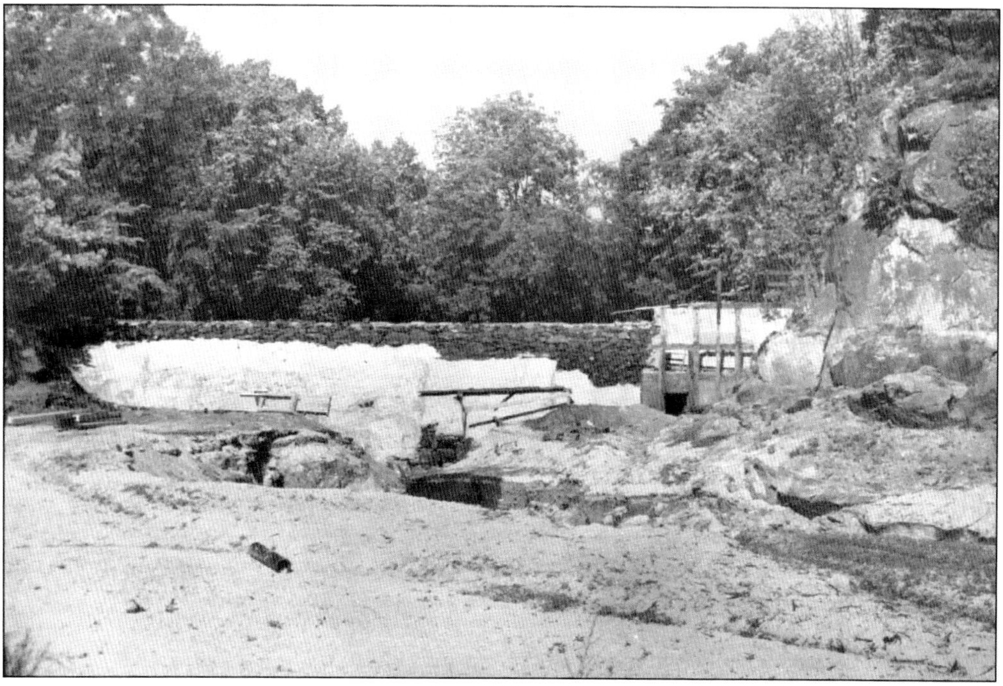

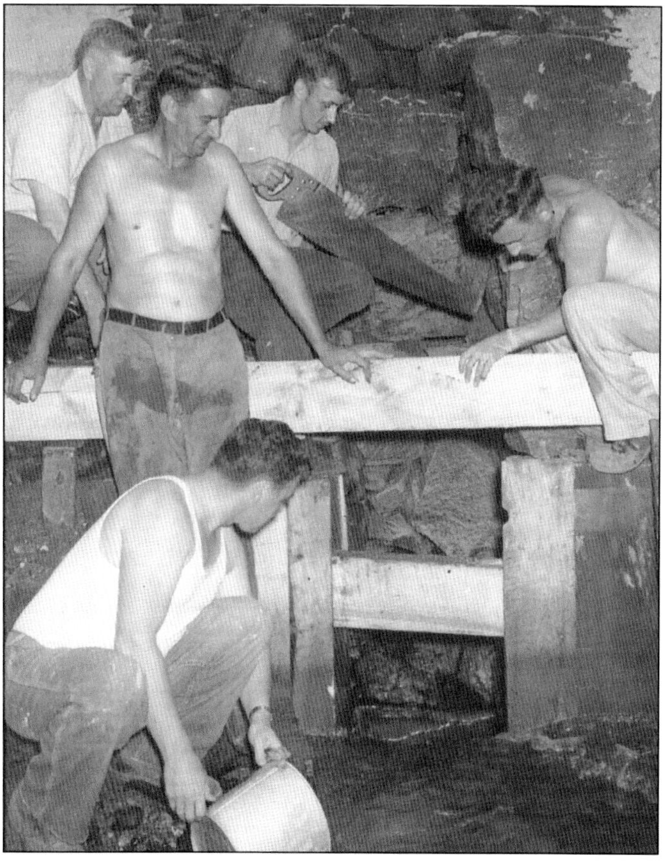

On August 11, 1863, a tragedy occurred. The bridge crossing the river below the dam gave out during a flood. Three women were killed as they stood on the bridge: Mary Wheelock, age 42; her daughter Welthy, age 14; and Rachael Barrett, age 27. The Wheelocks lived in the house just right of the dam. Every so often the dam still has to have repairs. It is shown above from the upstream pond side in the mid-1900s. At left, the workers are, from left to right, (first row) probably Victor Giard; (second row) Leon Shumway, George Mellen, Art Ely, and Gordon Hobart. In the summer of 2012, the state declared the bridge below the dam unsafe. It is now open only to bicyclists and pedestrians.

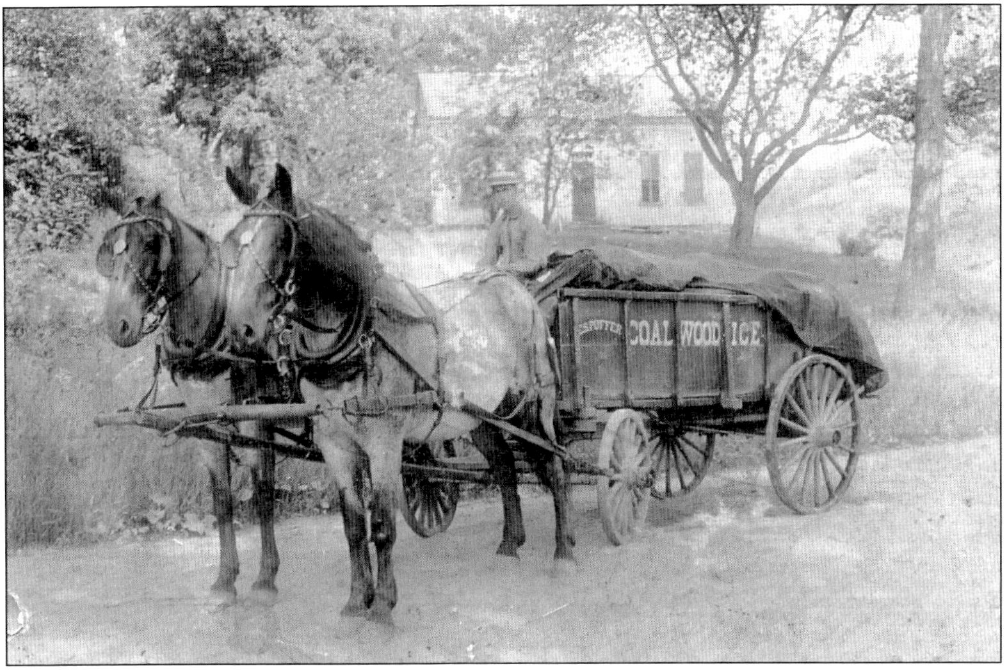

In 1912, Edward S. Puffer built an ice elevator on the southern shore of the pond above the dam and in 1916, added an icehouse. The ice was cut on Puffer's Pond and stored in sawdust in the huge icehouse. The blocks were 23 inches square, about 16 inches thick. A machine could cut through the ice about six inches, and the rest had to be sawed by hand. Workers said that if the pond froze before Christmas you had a good Christmas. Shown above is Winfred Page driving the Puffer wagon. The house behind him was on a knoll above the dam. Customers would set out a square card with numbers in the corner telling how many pounds of ice they needed. At right is a company receipt. (Above, courtesy of Edna Ball.)

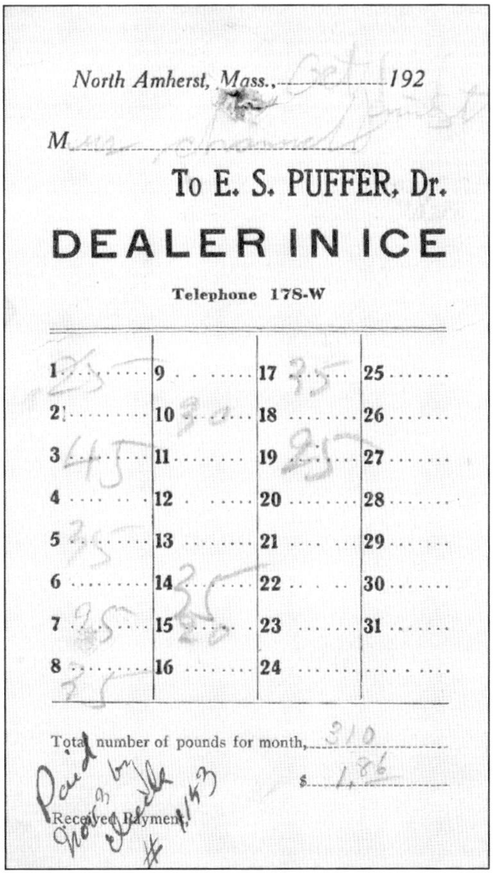
North Amherst, Mass., ... 192

M..........

To E. S. PUFFER, Dr.

DEALER IN ICE

Telephone 178-W

1	9	17	25
2	10	18	26
3	11	19	27
4	12	20	28
5	13	21	29
6	14	22	30
7	15	23	31
8	16	24	

Total number of pounds for month, 310

$ 1.86

Received Payment,

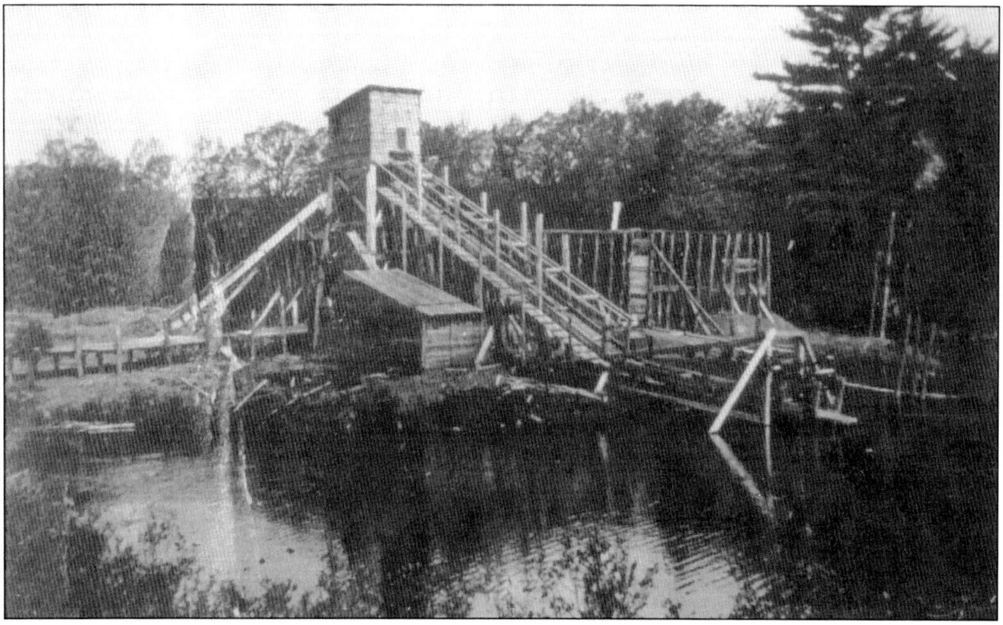

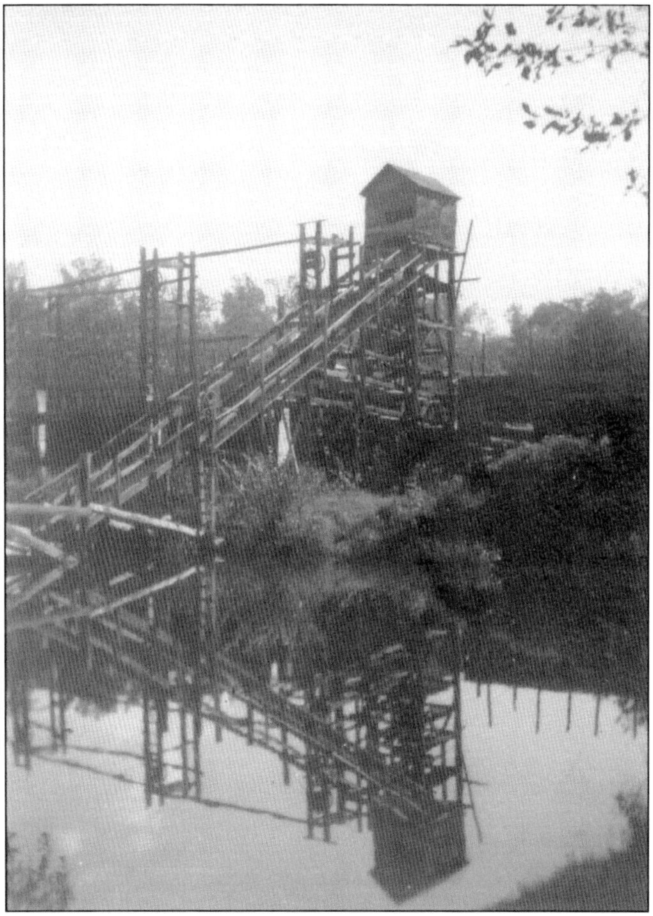

Pictured above, the elevator and icehouse are under construction. At left is a photograph by Robert L. Coffin, taken in 1942 with a Kodak Brownie camera. The works burned down later that year. The site with its old foundations became a popular swimming place. The town was aware of the ecological value of this river site and in 1961, began acquiring conservation lands below Factory Hollow Dam including the flood plain of the lower Mill River that stretched from Puffer's Pond to Montague Road. There used to be an apple orchard on the hill near the pond where Puffers Circle is now. Over the years, the ice works site had been shaped into a family-friendly spot, and local neighbors hold a pancake breakfast in June to raise money for a summer caretaker. (Left, courtesy of Stewart Coffin.)

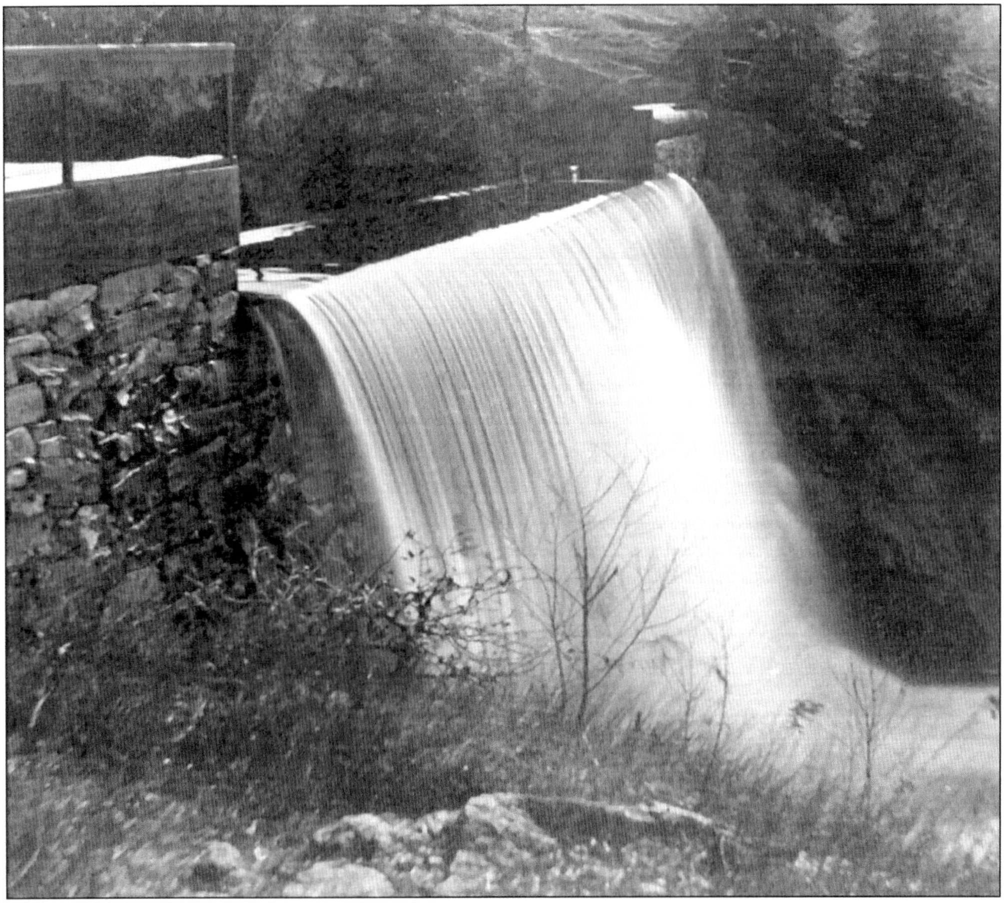

John L. Lovell, a photographer in Amherst who died in 1903, took this photograph of the waterfall from the pond. He titled it "Golden Gate Falls" and the pond "Golden Gate" pond. The photograph below, taken by Edgar Scott on June 2, 1934, shows an island that no longer exists. Changes in the river flow from storms and beavers mean that islands appear every now and then and later disappear. The Mill River had excellent fishing after all the mills were gone.

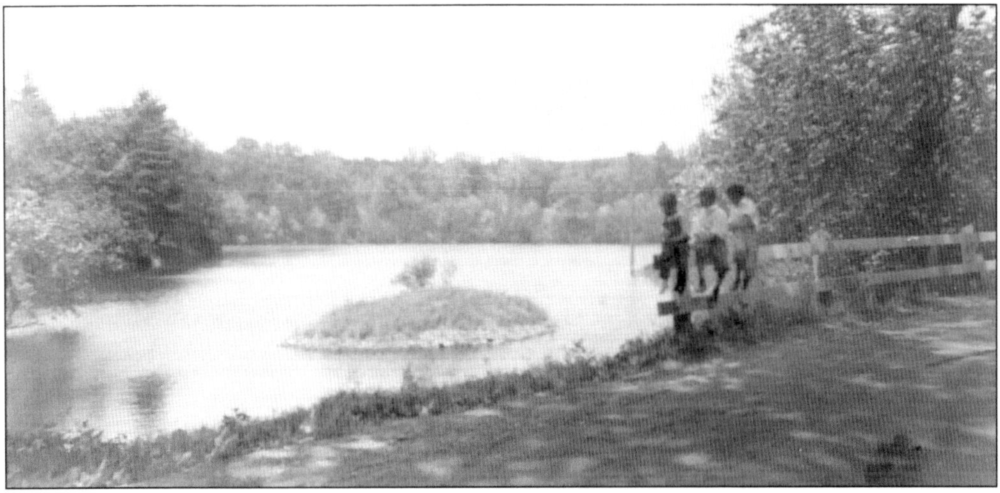

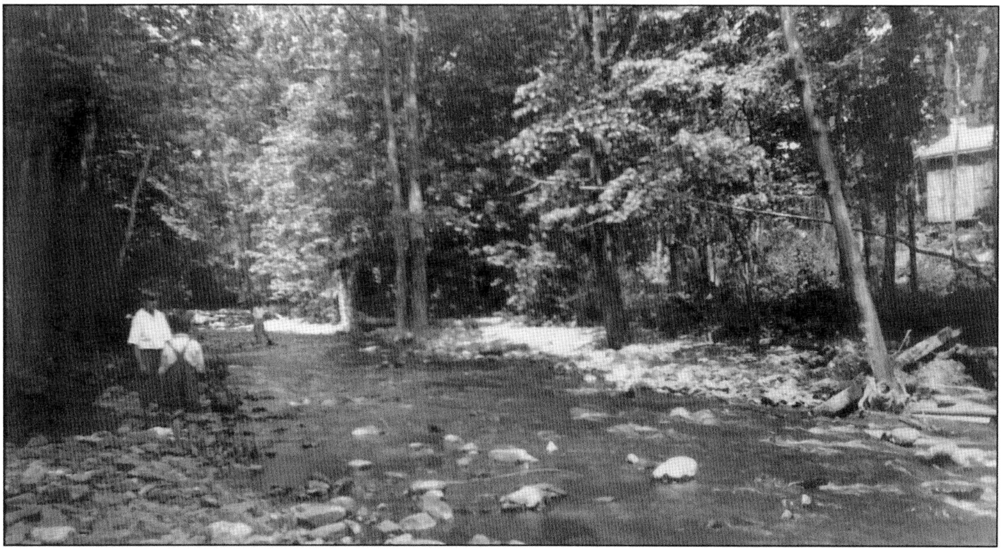

Upstream from Puffer's Pond by the Mill River there used to be the Cushman Clam Club, a place for local parties. In the photograph above, the club is above the stream on the right. After nearly all the mills closed in the 1920s, the blacksmith Clifton Ashley hauled lumber from the Red Mill to build the cabin and fashioned the boiler and steamer pots plus the wire baskets. The menu was clams, crackers, cheese, coffee, and a keg of beer. The members of the club were men only, and sometimes things got rowdy. Sometimes, a wedding party took place there. The place stayed active for at least 15 years and left behind a lot of clamshells. You can still find the foundations of mills. Below is a photograph of an old dam; the railroad bridge is above.

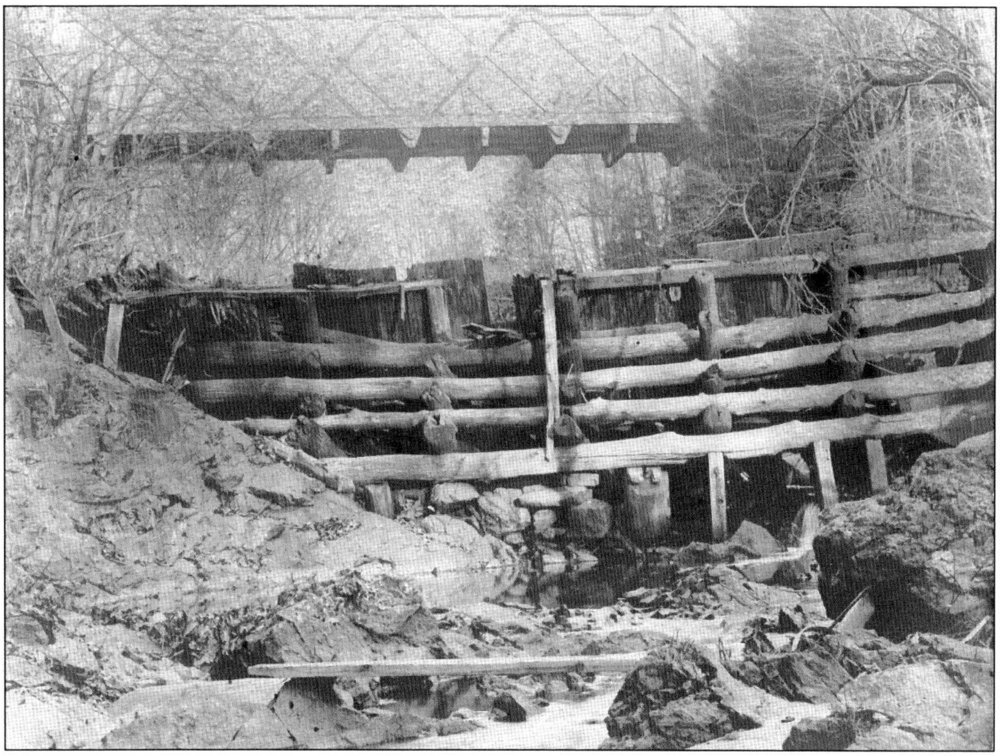

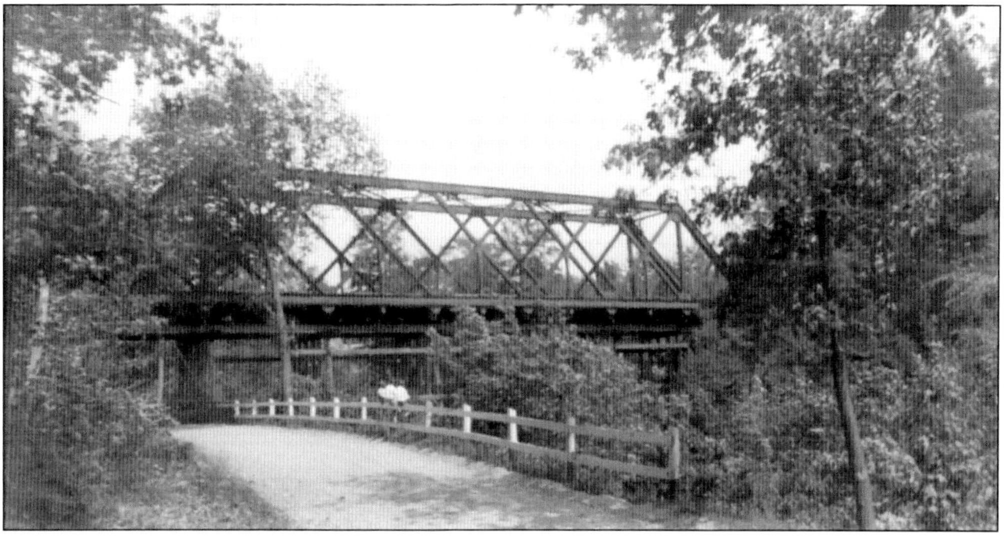

Railroad service came to Cushman in 1866 with the New London Northern Railroad. Above are three boys in the early 1930s looking from State Street into the Mill River; the railroad bridge is above them. One of the boys may be Peter Kaslauskas. Having access to quick transportation for their goods meant even more prosperity for the mill owners. Below are the remains of one of the factory dams, possibly one of the paper mills. In 1771, John Adams had a mill near the Cushman bridge; the Kellogg family had another. Passing under the railroad bridge, factory housing, consisting of a few small houses and duplexes, can be seen. That area was called "The Patch." (Above, courtesy of Peter Kaslauskas.)

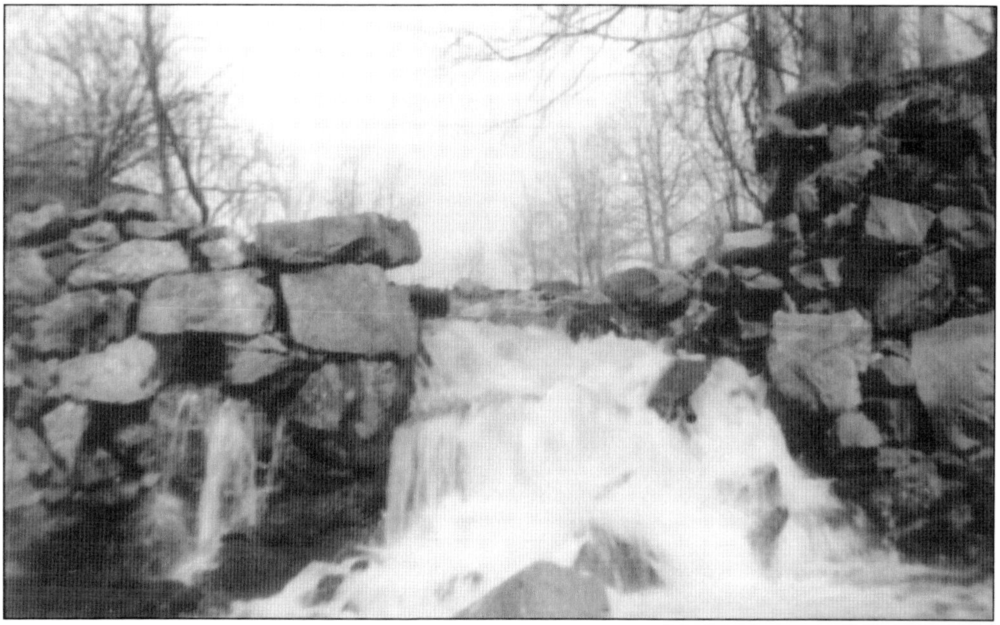

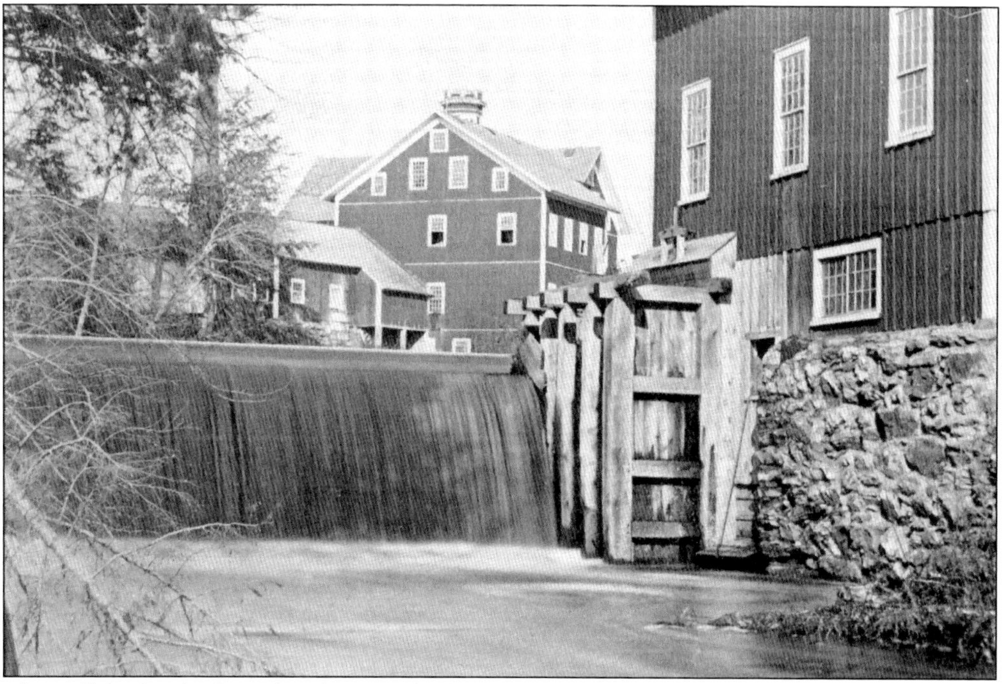

The mill farther back in the photograph above is the Cushman Paper Mill, known as the Red Mill. Peter Ingram built a woolen mill there in 1830 and sold the water privilege to the brothers Ephraim and John Cushman in 1835. They began making paper on the Mill River and erected the Red Mill in 1859. It stayed in the family until 1909. They made straw board, a coarse, yellow paperboard made of straw pulp, used in packing and for making boxes, and leather board, an imitation of sole leather, made of leather scraps, rags, and paper. The bunghole in the right foreground housed several industries. One was a shop that forged railroad frogs, which are the crossing points of two rails, parts of railroad switches. The term "frog" is taken from the part of a horse's hoof it closely resembles.

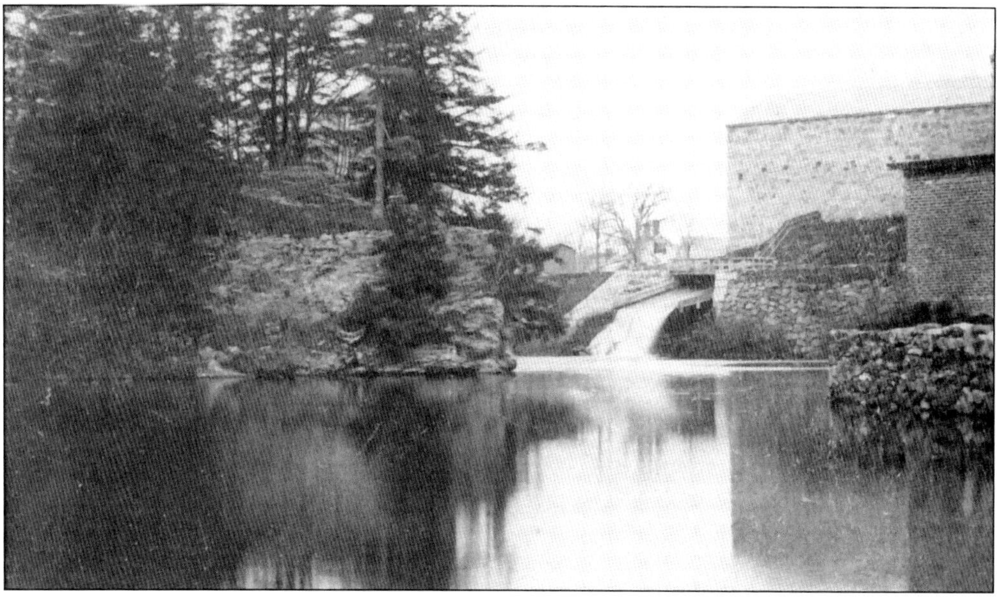

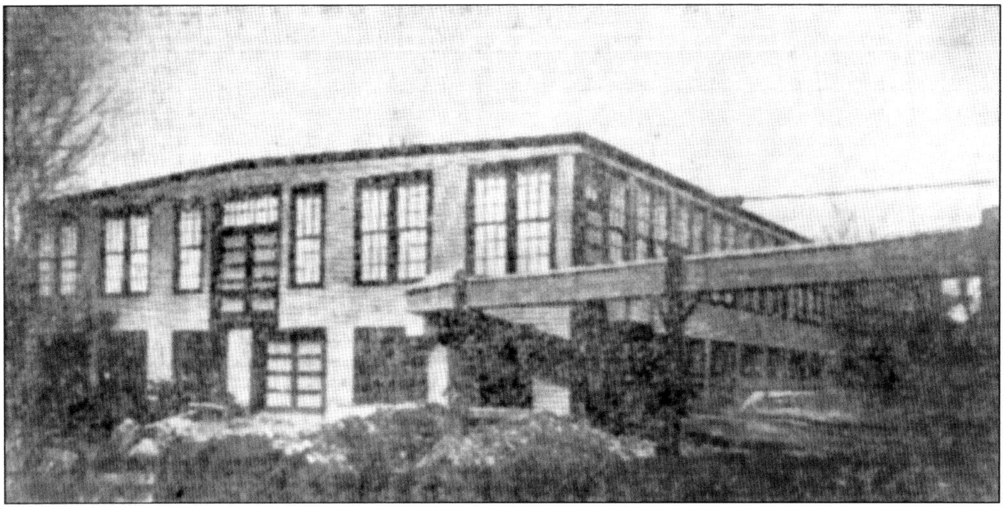

When the Red Mill was torn down, the water privilege was bought by J.L. Perkins, who owned the American Tissue Mills of Holyoke, Massachusetts, and a new mill was erected in 1912, shown above in a poor-quality image from a newspaper clipping. In 1917, Perkins sold the factory to the Japanese Tissue Mills of Holyoke. (Japanese tissue was a type of paper used for paper towels.) In 1912, the state passed a law requiring paper towels rather than cloth in public places. The Cushman shop made waxed paper and novelties, and the products were shipped all over the United States. An example of the product is shown at right. When it opened, 20 hands were employed, and the owners expected to hire 30 more. In 1927, the mill moved to Holyoke, where the company had its headquarters. By then, it was employing between 35 to 40 people, about half men, half women. After the mill closed in Cushman, according to Peter Kaslauskas, the local people used it for dances.

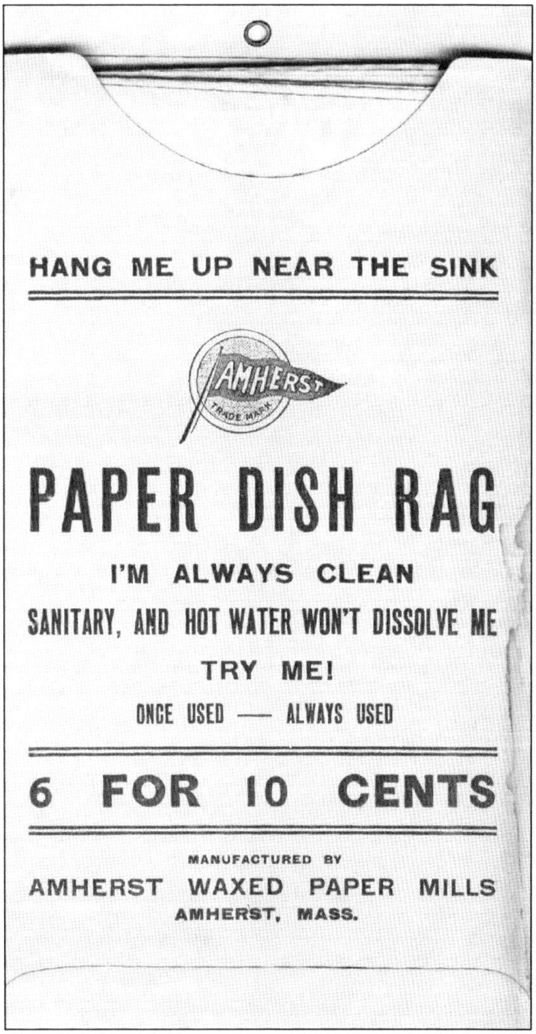

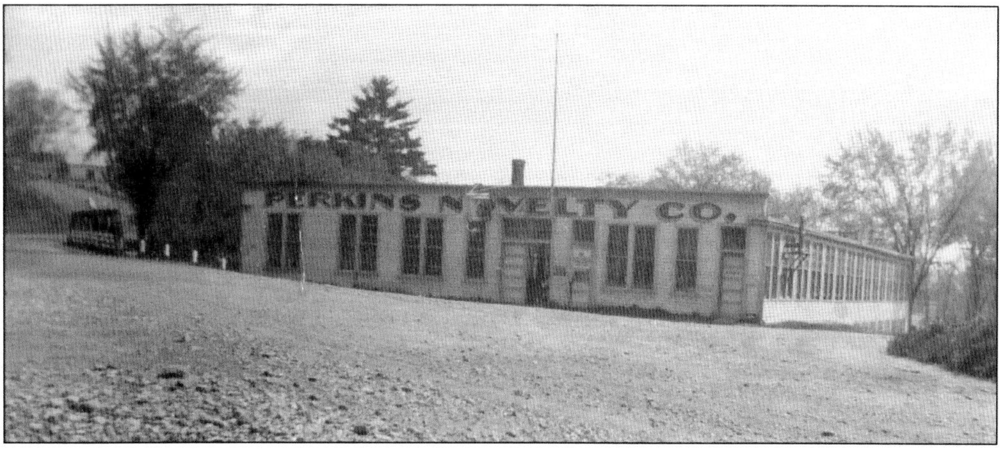

The photograph above shows what was left of the mill, a place where Victoria Pratt remembers buying paper dolls in her childhood in 1936. Isabelle Callahan remembers products such as old-fashioned silhouettes of women to go in round frames. Below is a photograph taken in 1976, when the old bridge over the Mill River in Cushman was being replaced. The photograph shows the house of Peter Ingram, whose father, Ebenezer Ingram, ran a gristmill and later, wool-carding and fulling mills, and a clothier's shop. In the center is the dam that created a large millpond. Mills were built along the northern edge of that pond. By 1830, the area was beginning to be known as North Amherst City. (Above, courtesy of Victoria Pratt.)

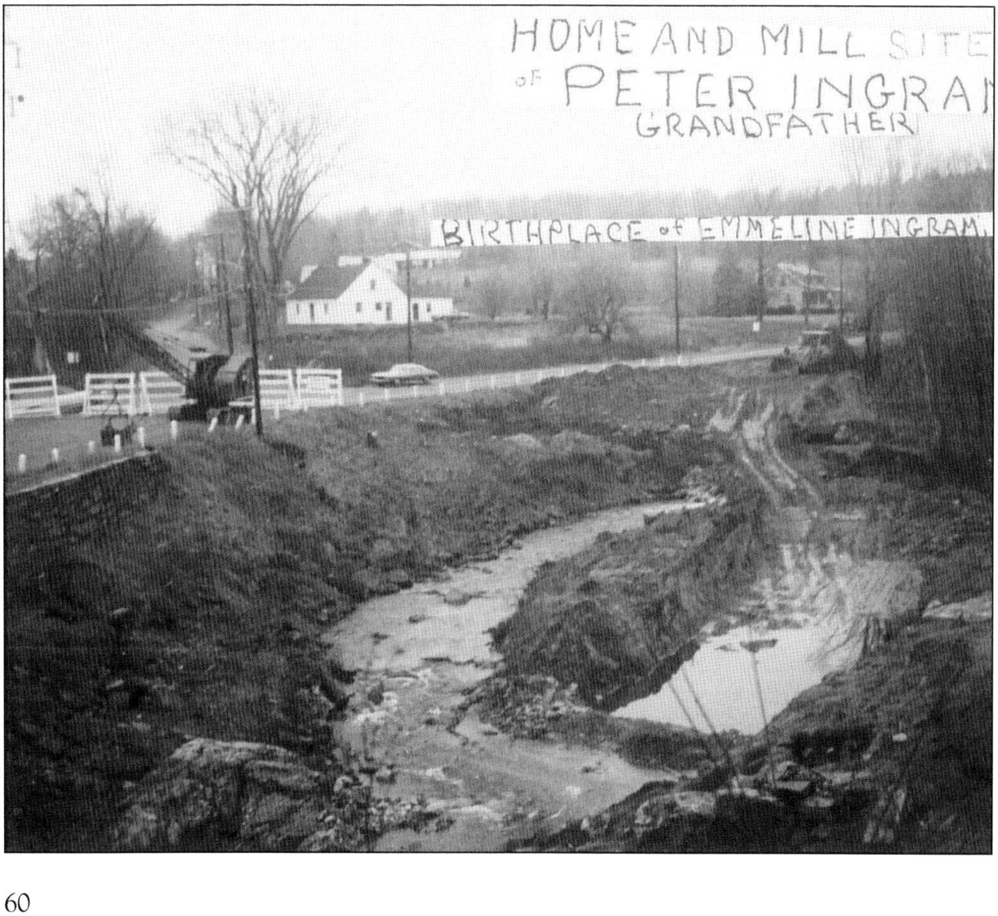

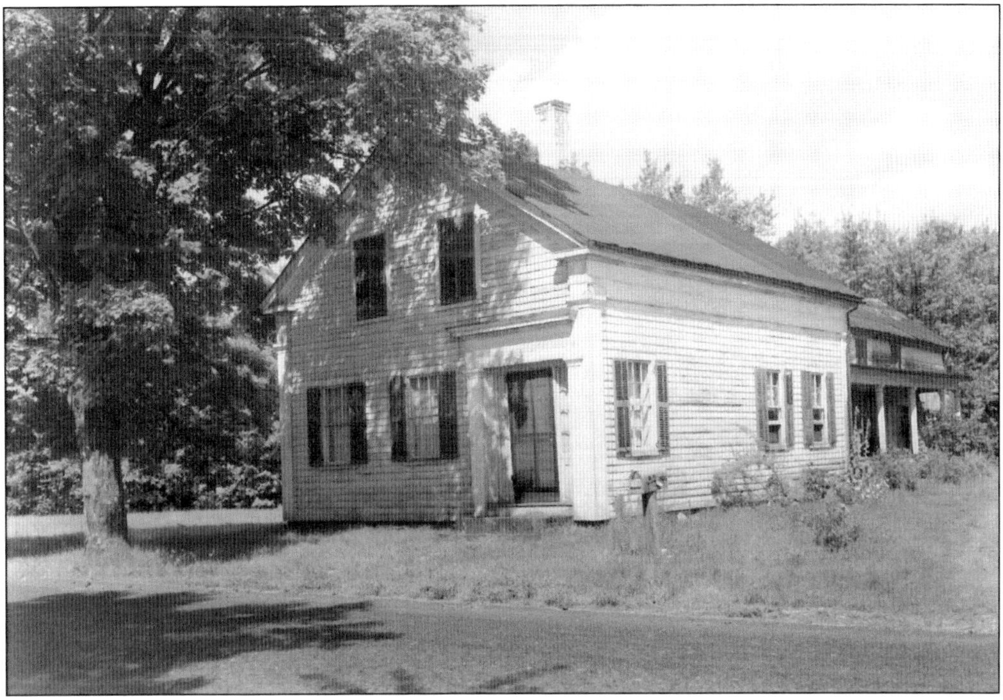

The Peter Ingram house, above, at 51 East Leverett Road, is situated on a rise with the Mill River flowing in the rear. Peter Ingram finally sold his properties to the Cushman family in 1849 and joined relatives in Fond du Lac, Wisconsin. Frank and Emma Bowen lived in part of the house in 1934. The kitchen had a woodstove.

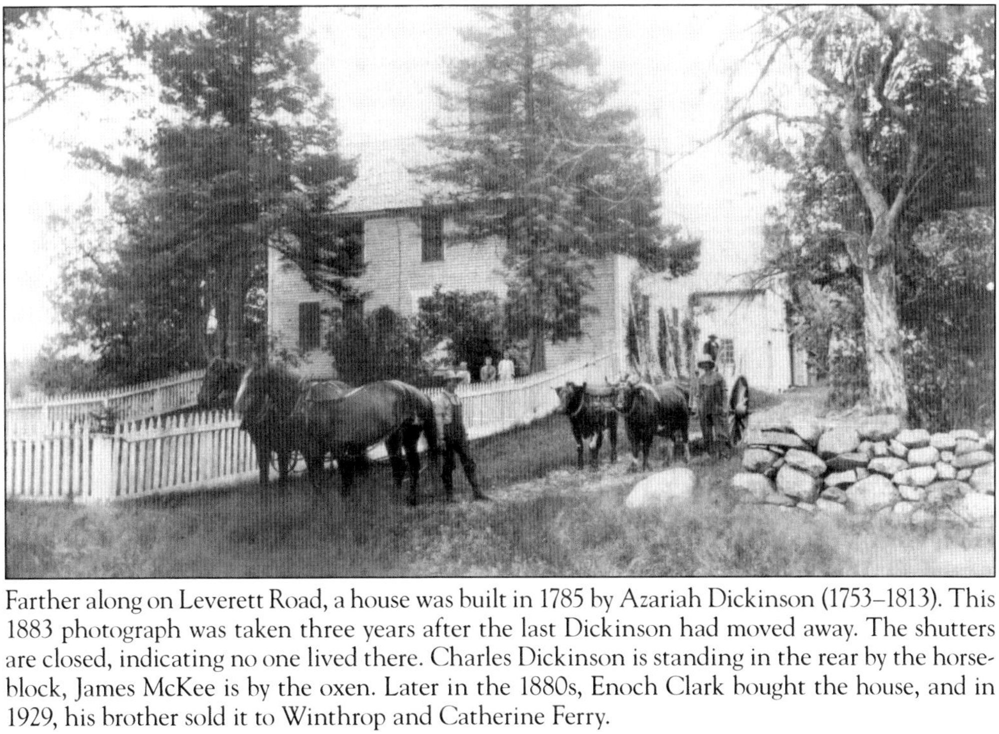

Farther along on Leverett Road, a house was built in 1785 by Azariah Dickinson (1753–1813). This 1883 photograph was taken three years after the last Dickinson had moved away. The shutters are closed, indicating no one lived there. Charles Dickinson is standing in the rear by the horse-block, James McKee is by the oxen. Later in the 1880s, Enoch Clark bought the house, and in 1929, his brother sold it to Winthrop and Catherine Ferry.

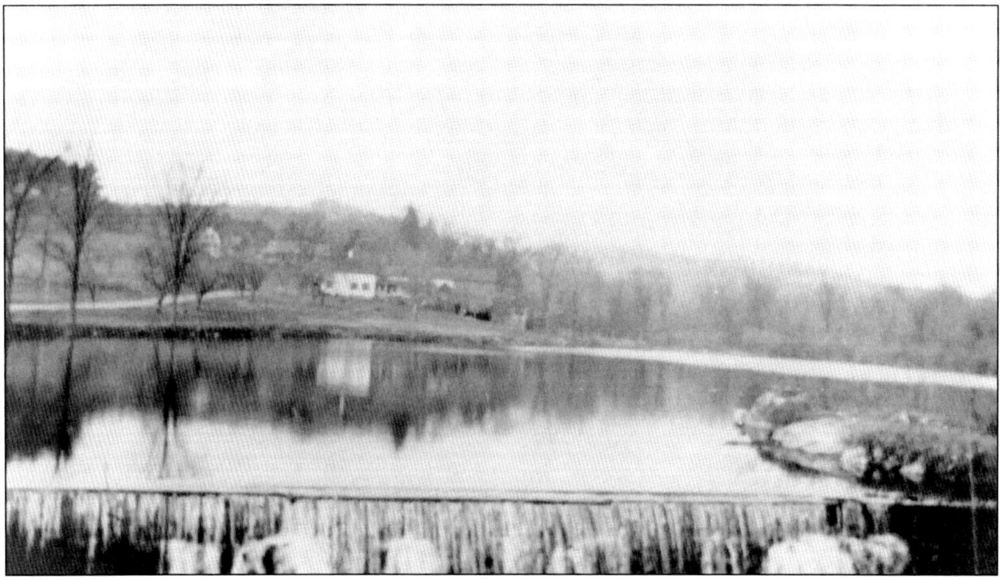

In 1744, Ephraim Kellogg had established a corn mill and a sawmill using power from a pond on the upstream side of the bridge; later, many small mills were built on that west side of the pond. This photograph shows the millpond behind the dam that powered the factories. Since the dam was removed and the pond drained, this area is now completely forested, though the houses remain.

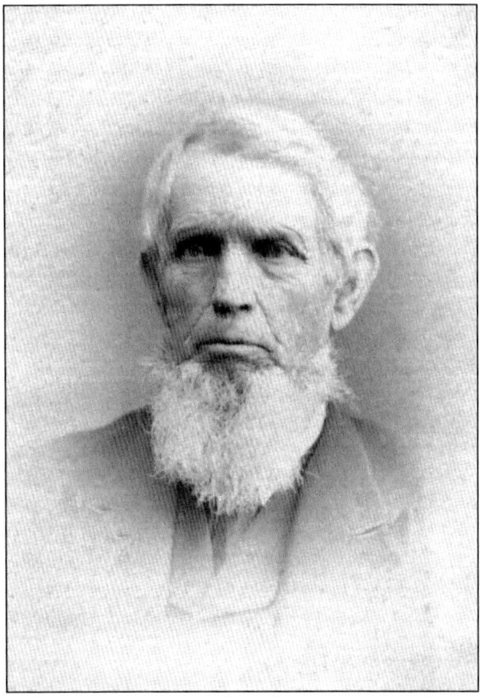

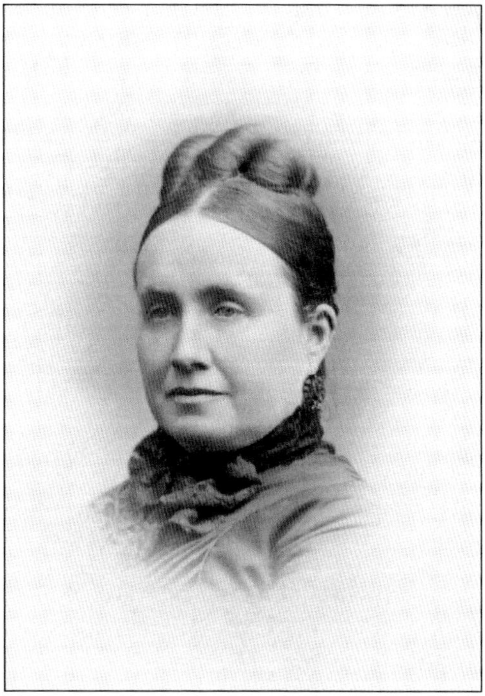

Moses Cushman married Martha Souther on June 24, 1857. In 1898, North Amherst City was renamed Cushman in honor of the family that for generations ran successful paper factories from 1835 up until the early 1900s. It is said the renaming was eased by a large donation to the Town of Amherst.

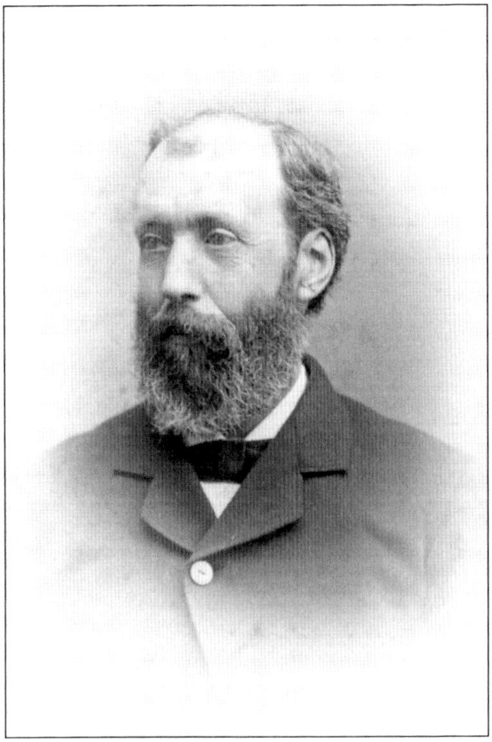

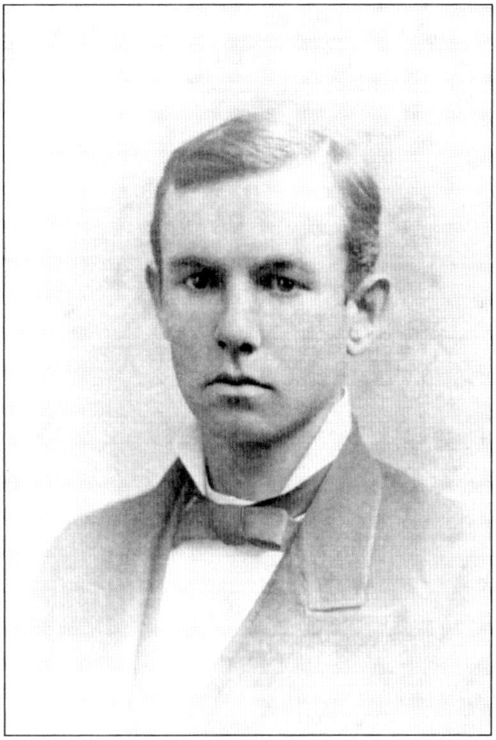

Above are Moses Cushman Jr. (left) and Fayette Cushman, Amherst High School class of 1878 (right). At right is Carrie (Cushman) Hall. At the start of 1927, when Franklin S. Clark of North Amherst wrote a paper on the mills, only three remained: the gristmill in North Amherst, the woodworking shop at Factory Hollow, and the plant for finishing waxed paper at Cushman. By 1940, all were closed.

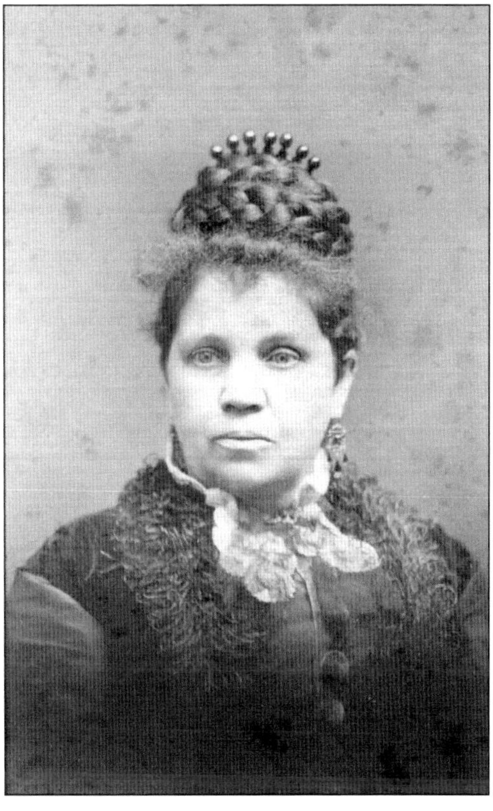

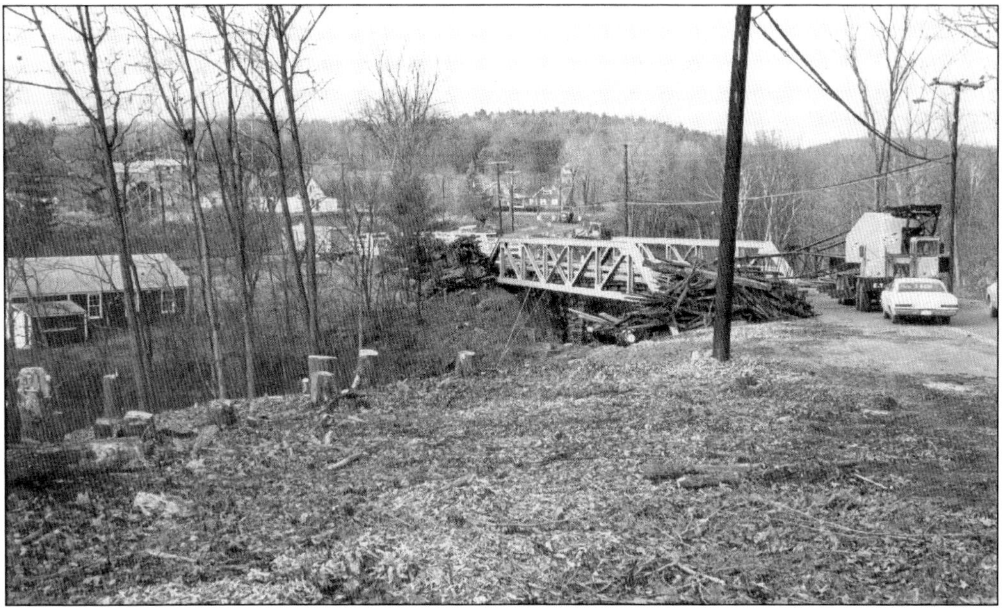

In 1972, the old bridge was removed and the street straightened out, widened, and a new bridge put in. Residents loved the old bridge, but the highway department said it was unsafe. The old bridge, formerly a railroad bridge that Stephen Puffer installed in 1935, had used the remains of the old factories for its supports. Isabelle Callahan remembers when the 1936 flood tore away two bridges over the Connecticut River at Hadley and Sunderland, and traffic to Greenfield and Deerfield had to go by their house on Leverett Road to get to the Montague Bridge over the river.

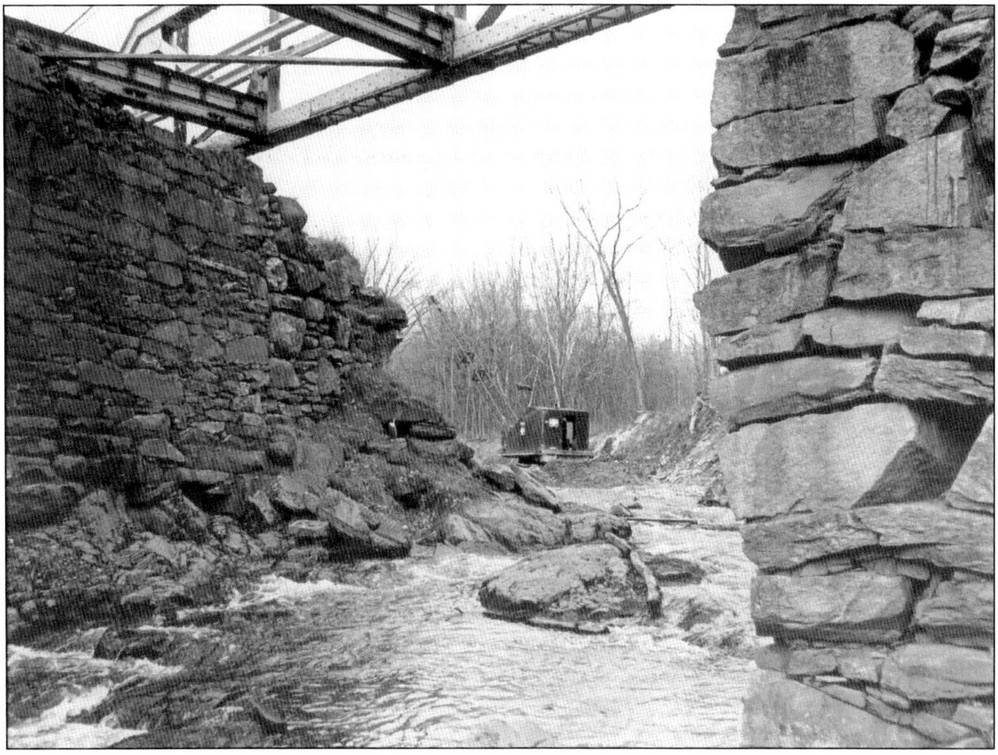

Four

CUSHMAN

Traveling over the new bridge in Cushman today, one comes to a triangular green in the center. A railroad track crosses the green and small houses on Bridge Street face it. Cushman is listed in the National Register of Historic Places as a small, largely 19th-century workers' village. In the 1600s, the way through this village was an old Native American trail called the Nashaway Path, as it connected with a northern route that went to Nashua, New Hampshire. This path, later used by colonial settlers and recognized as one of the early east-west routes, connected residents of Hadley with communities in eastern Massachusetts. In the early 1700s, the road brought people from the east part of the state through Amherst and Hadley to the west. Inns and taverns served the travelers. In the mid-1700s, Ezra Rood opened a store, and Moses Cook and Jacob Samson did the blacksmithing. When the mills expanded in the 1800s and more workers were needed, modest houses were built. Because the houses were so close together, the place came to be called North Amherst City. In 1889, Cushman residents created a Village Improvement Society to make sidewalks and install and maintain gas lamps. In 1897, North Amherst City was renamed Cushman. In 1911, electric lights replaced gas lamps. According to a 1916 Sanborn map, there was a passenger station for the Central Vermont Railroad on the common across from the store, and north of that was a freight house with a siding. On that same map, Bridge Street was called State Street. In 1920, the dam at the river was partially removed, greatly decreasing the size of the millpond. Isabelle Callahan, who grew up in Cushman, remembers all the peddlers. There was a man who walked all the way from Greenfield to fix sewing machines. And there was Mary, the Pack Peddler, who wore a floor-length skirt with about 50 pockets in it, and "if one needed something, she had it." People remember that in the 1920s and 1930s, there were as many as five general stores there. At present, there is one.

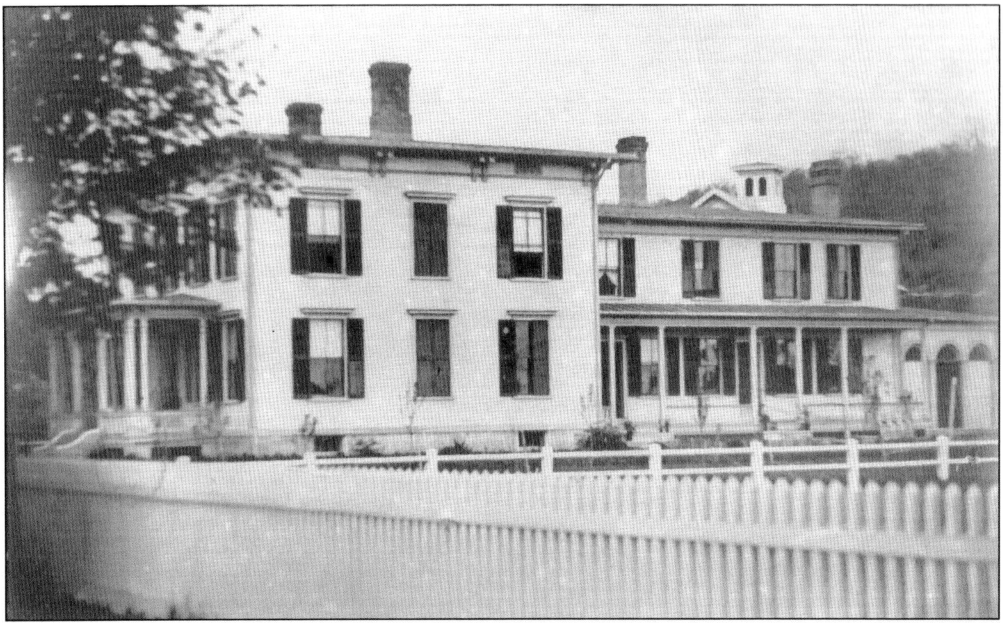

The Cushman Inn, shown above, used to house travelers and factory workers. The house was believed to have been built around 1790 by Nathaniel Peck, who also had a water-powered corn mill on the nearby Mill River. Peck opened a tavern there; the road was once a well-traveled route between Boston and New Hampshire. It was torn down in 1930.

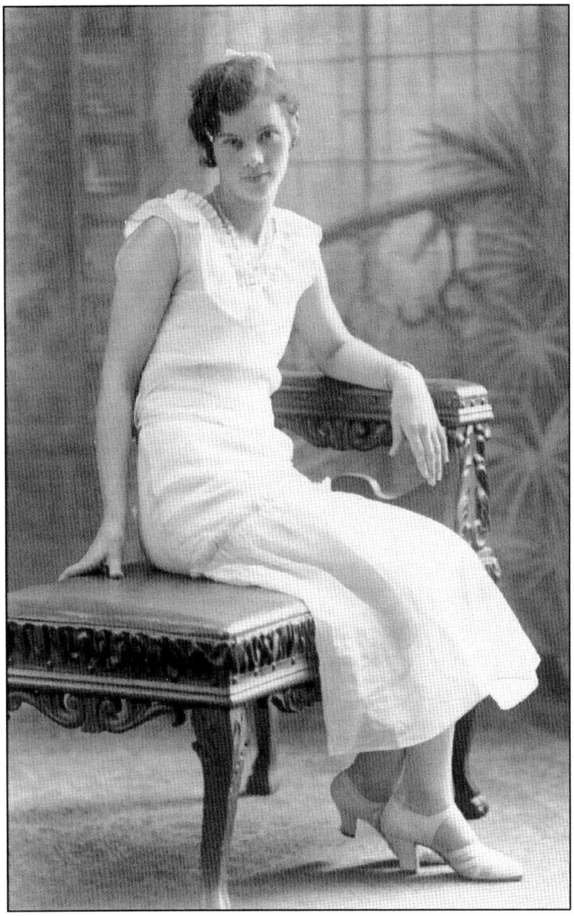

In September 1922, William and Julia Keet moved into the old Cushman house, where they raised their three sons and one daughter. Keet was a foreman at the paper mill, and one of his sons worked there too. Their daughter Florence, shown here, was born August 1, 1911. (Courtesy of Charlie Clark.)

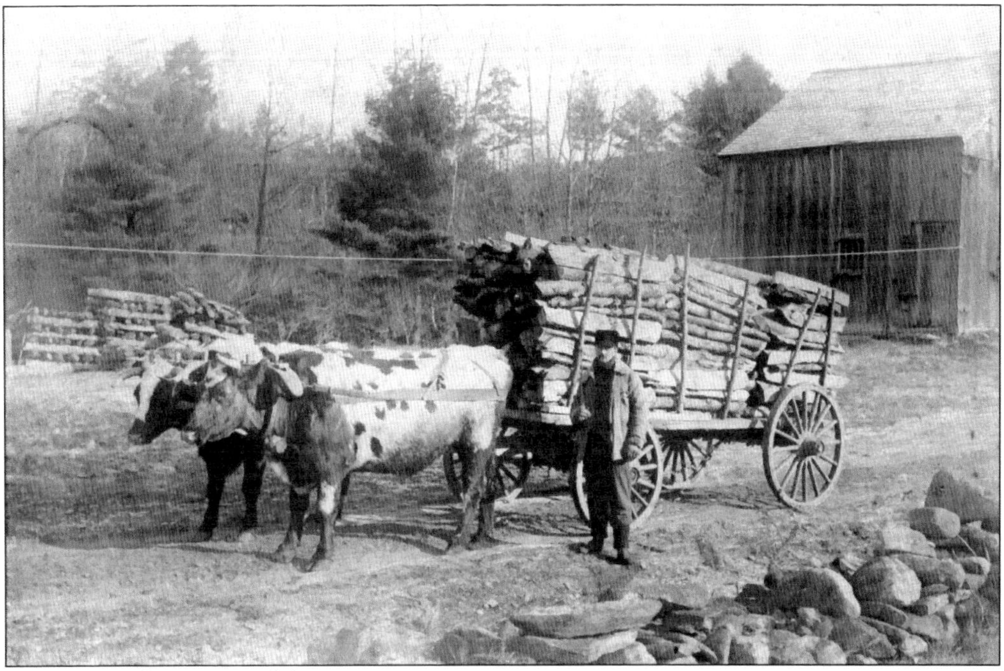

Bill Keet used oxen to pull his logs. He farmed and worked at the local paper mill. Mildred Britt, a cousin of the family, remembered visiting the house with its big porch and spacious kitchen. "There was a player piano," she said, "and we'd all sit around and sing songs." Florence, their beautiful daughter (right), lived all her life with her parents and never married. She died in Amherst on August 12, 1988. (Both courtesy of Charlie Clark.)

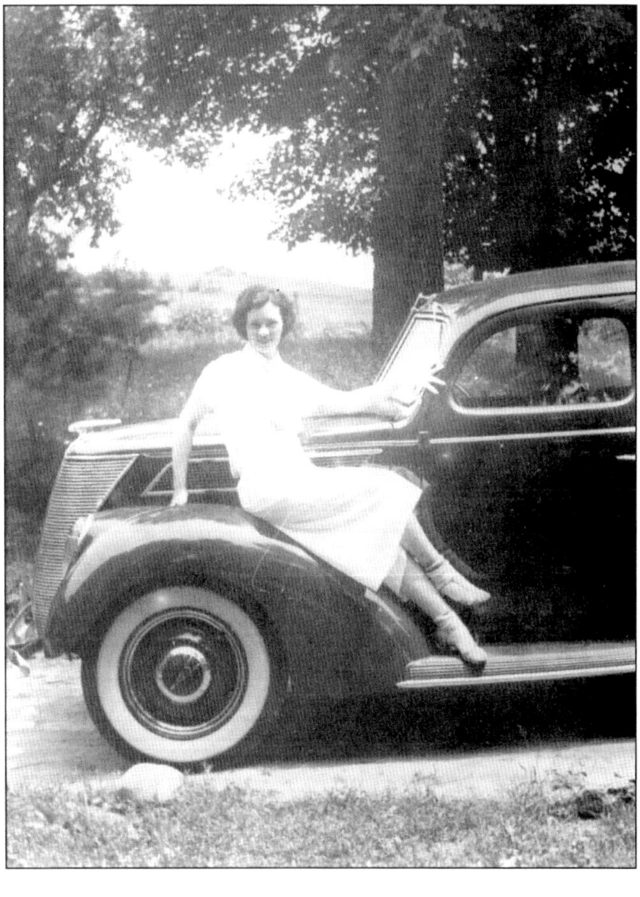

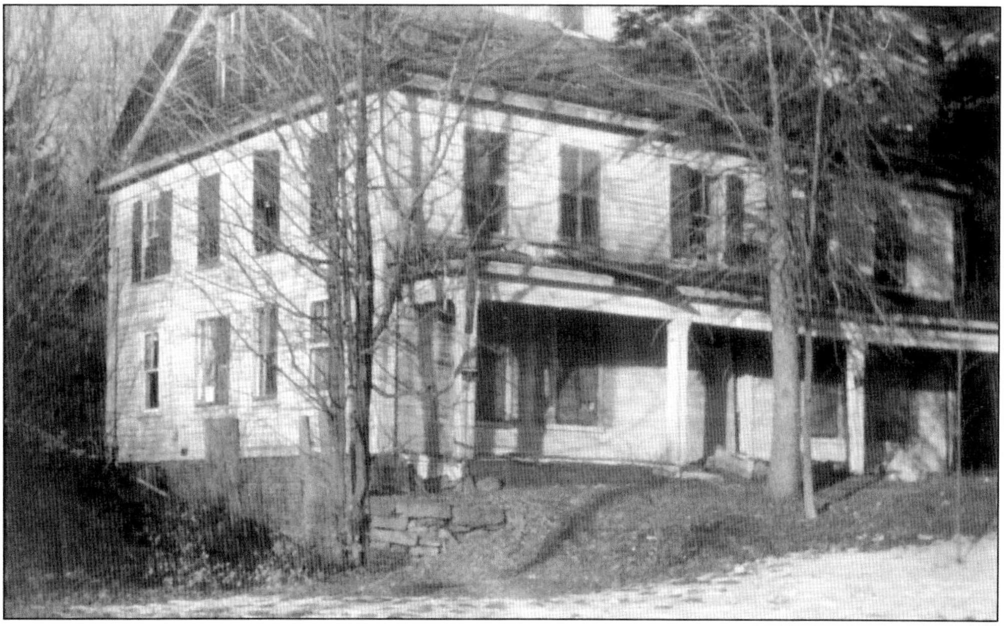

As shown above, the Cushman house became completely dilapidated. The town had acquired the house in 1986, and Cushman residents learned it would be torn down. Sidney Poritz, a local developer with a concern for history, proposed that instead of demolishing the house he would renovate it for low- and moderate-income housing. In 1988, arson destroyed the Keet house, but despite this destruction, Poritz promised to rebuild the house, keeping the outside as it was. And so he did, as shown below, and added another housing unit of similar design. Where the driveway is now used to be the beginning of Market Hill Road, which was moved to the south.

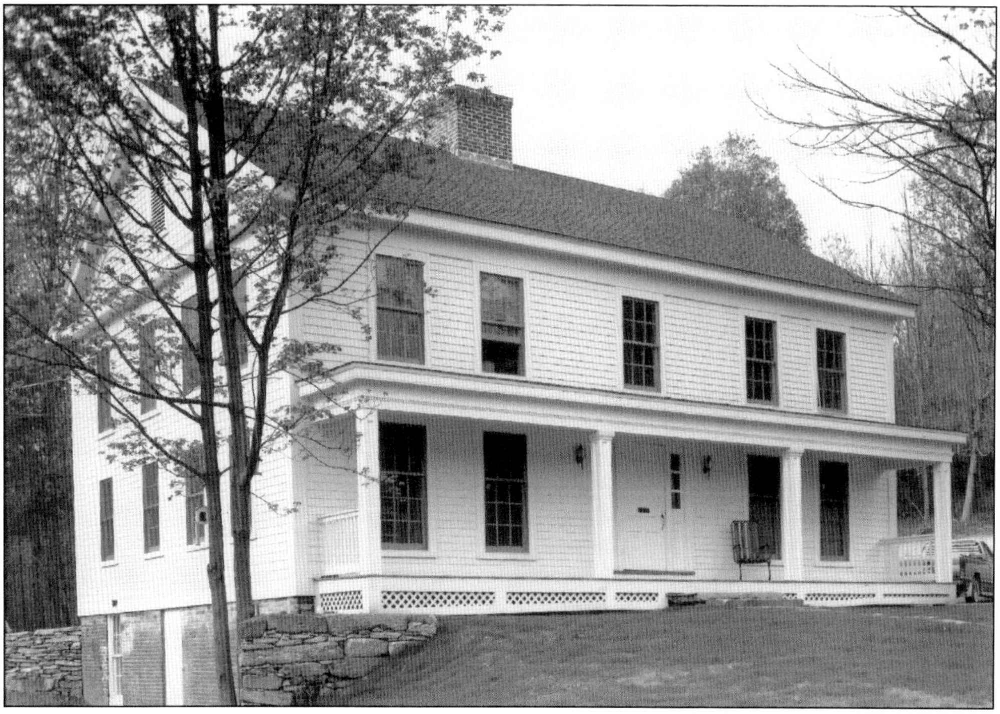

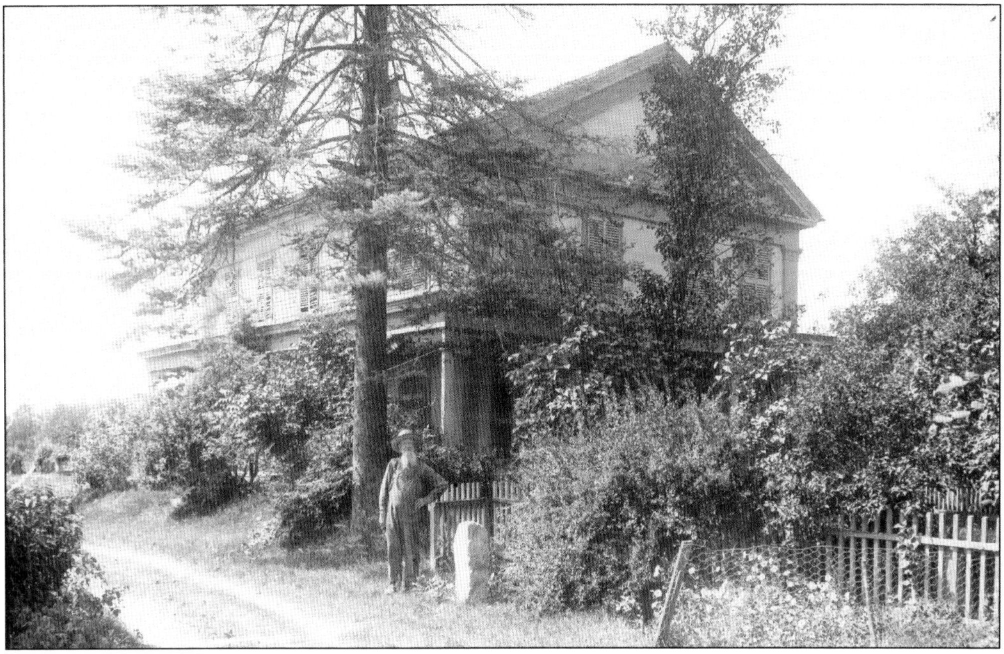

Across Bridge Street had been Lewis Draper's Tavern in the 1800s. In 1885, Reuben Roberts sold it to Leonard Pierce. The man in the photograph may be either Draper or Pierce. In 1944, the Leonard family bought the place. They had a successful egg business for many years and later ran a breakfast and lunch restaurant in North Amherst called Roosters.

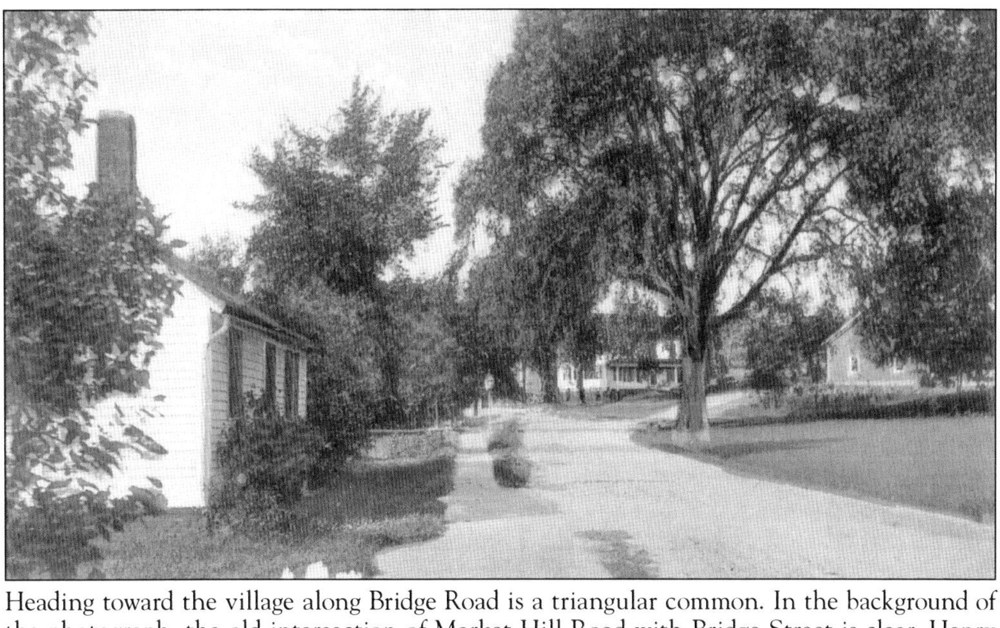

Heading toward the village along Bridge Road is a triangular common. In the background of the photograph, the old intersection of Market Hill Road with Bridge Street is clear. Henry Street also intersected there. The barn of the old Keet House was across that road. (Courtesy of Reed Kaynor.)

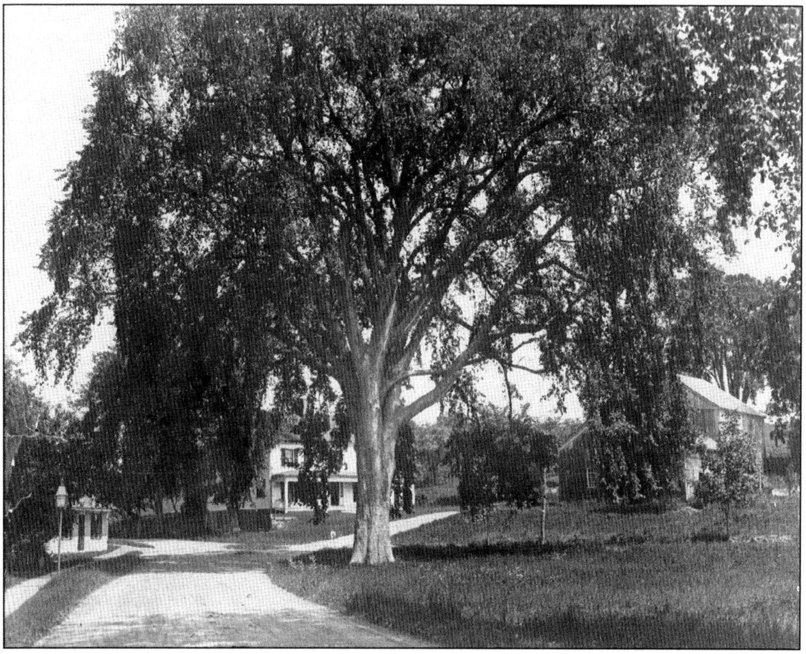

In 1789, Luther Henry planted an elm tree on the common, and it stood for over 145 years. The Village Improvement Society also installed a plaque on the tree. In 1901, when the tree was 115 years old, it stood 106 feet high and 6.5 feet through at the base. The plaque was often stolen and replaced and is now in private hands. The tree stood at the junction of Market Hill Road and Henry Street. It succumbed to elm disease and was taken down in 1964 by Amherst's tree warden. The tree is shown below in the winter. (Above, courtesy of Victoria Pratt.)

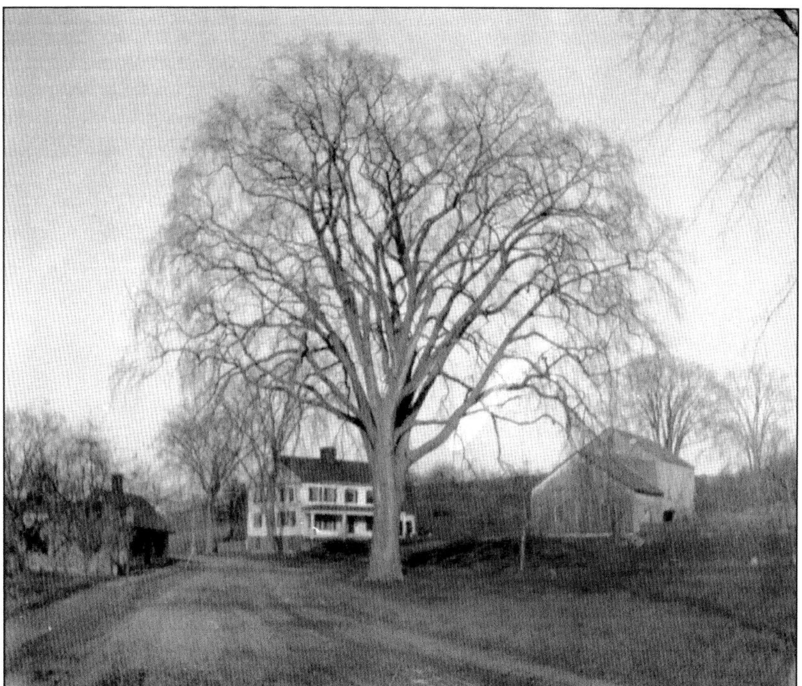

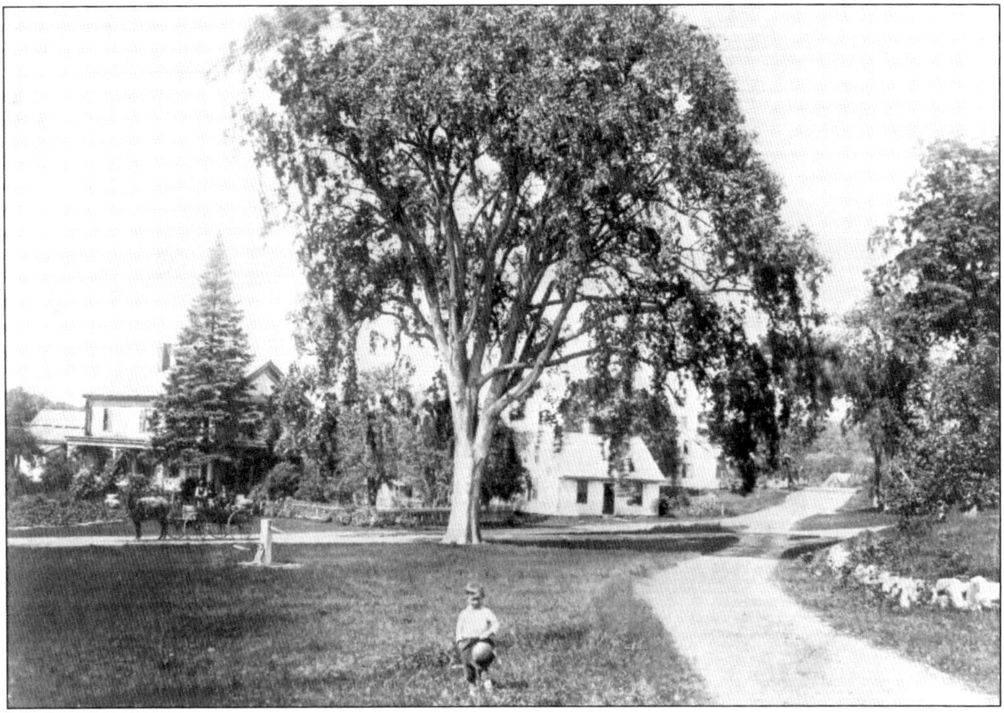

The above view of the common looking north shows Henry Street in the foreground, Market Hill Road coming in on the right, and Bridge Street coming across from the left. Near the Luther Henry elm tree is the village well where people drew their water. Below is the house at 74 Bridge Street. In 1957, Charles Ryznic lived there with his family. (Above, courtesy of Reed Kaynor.)

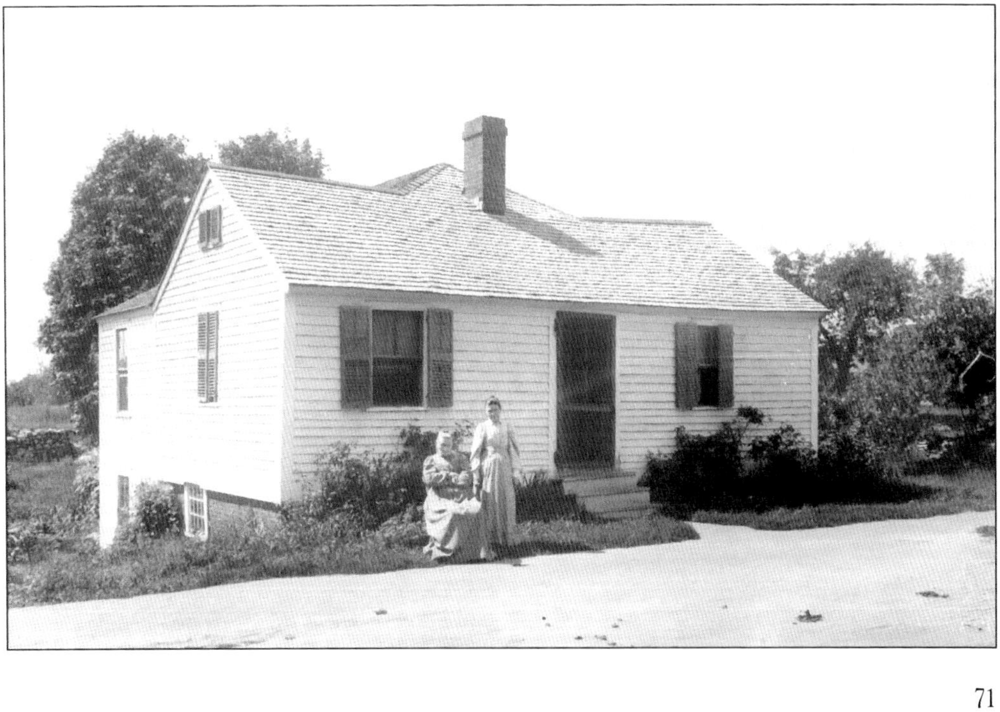

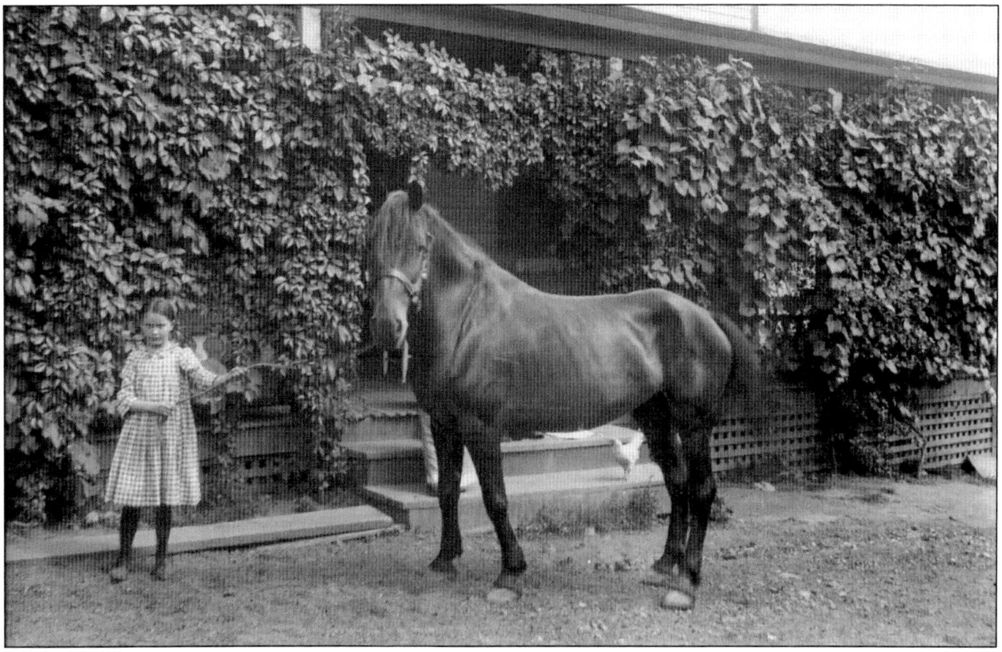

This c. 1890 photograph shows a house in Cushman; its location is undetermined. The young girl seems very proud to show off her horse despite his bony backside. Notice the variety of vines on the porch and the chicken on the step.

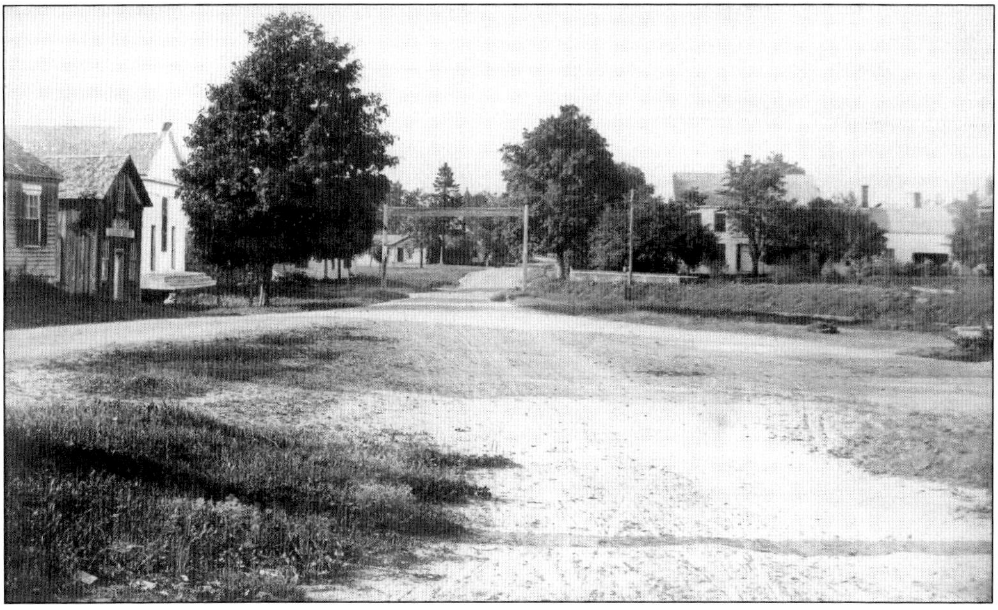

Looking north toward the railroad crossing in the late 1800s are the closely set houses along Bridge Street, including the Methodist Church with a tree in front. Later, the Village Improvement Society would build a sidewalk along the road, as seen on the opposite page.

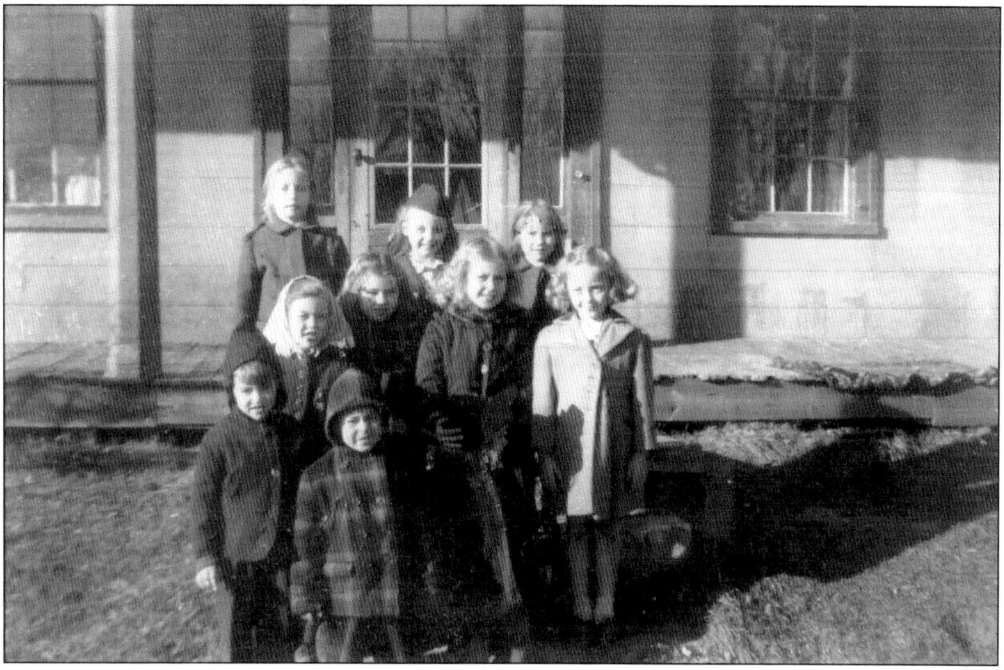

Sunday School was sometimes conducted in local homes. Here is a class standing outside what is probably the Leonard family house on Bridge Street in 1946. From left to right are (first row) Charles "Tommy" Stockwell and Freddie "Boo-Boo" Felton Jr; (second row) Evelyn Stockwell, probably Loretta Page, unidentified, and Cliffie Felton; (third row) Leona Stockwell, Marjorie Rockwell, and Judith Stockwell. The mother of the Felton children was the Cushman postmistress. (Courtesy of Judith Schaefer.)

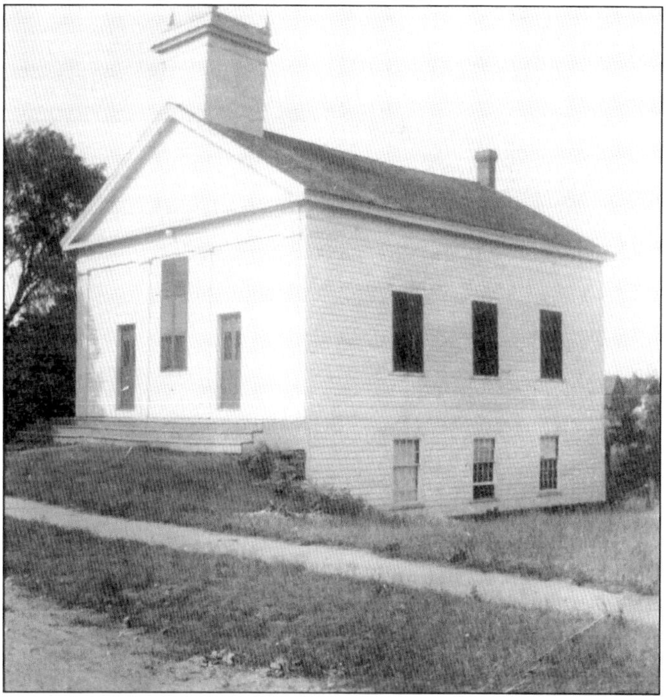

In 1842, a congregation of the Methodist Episcopal Church began meeting in the village. Rev. William White preached first in the local schoolhouse. The Methodists were known for their outdoor camp singing, and at first local Congregationalists harassed them. In 1844, they decided to build a church of their own on Bridge Street. In the 1950s, the congregation merged with the Wesley Methodist Church in the center of Amherst. The building was taken down in 1960 when someone misread the language of the original deed and thought it said the building could only be used for a church. (Courtesy of Paul and Leona Searle.)

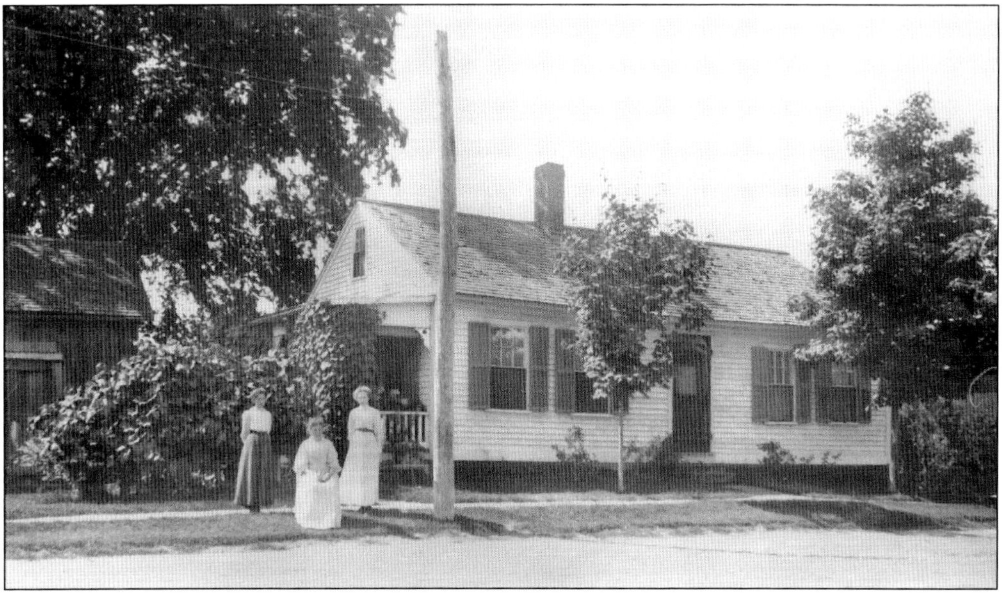

This 1890s photograph shows the house at 16 Bridge Street. It appears to have both electricity and phone service. The women are not identified. In 1957, John J. Romancier lived there with his family. He was a chef.

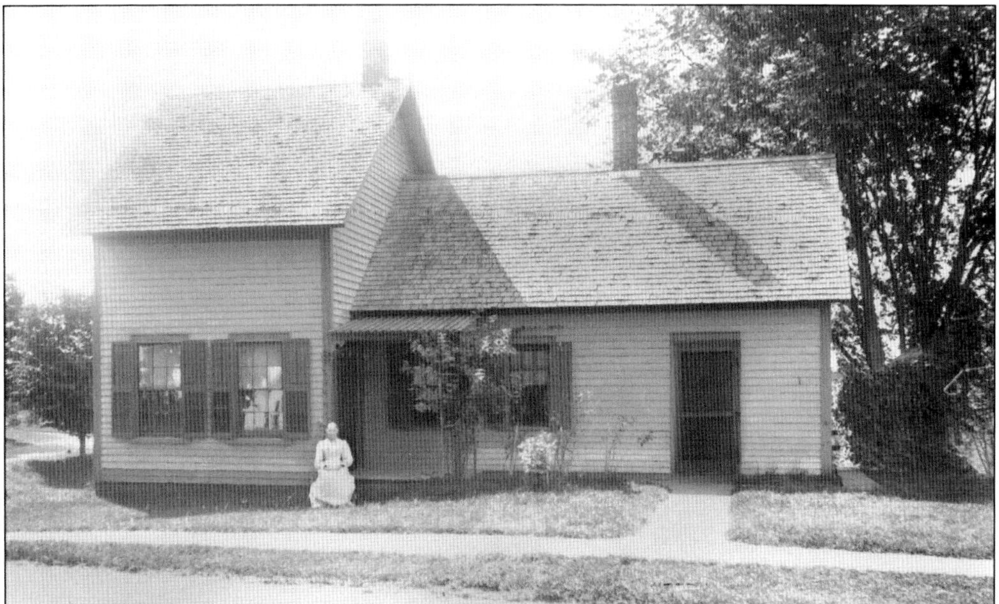

The house at 2 Bridge Street was, and still is, on the corner of Pine Street. In 1937, the family of Frank and Emma Bowen moved to the corner of Pine and Bridge Streets. The railroad went through nearby, leaving cars of grain and coal on side tracks by the Cushman Store. On July 7, 1944, Harry F. Sherman, whose parents were living here, was killed in action in World War II while flying over Holland.

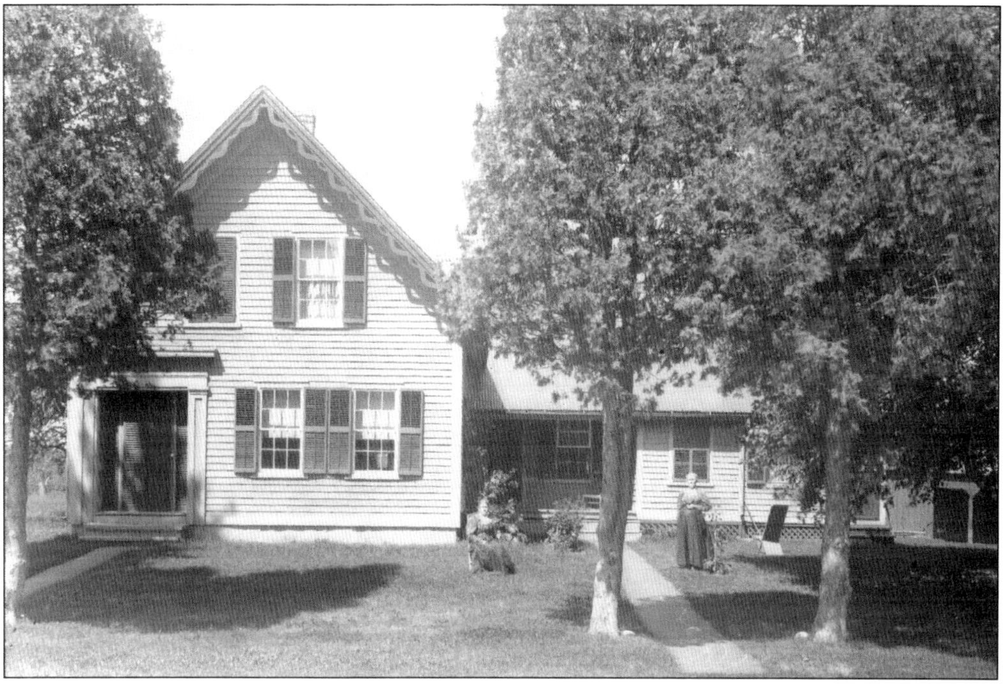

The house at 436 Pine Street, probably built about 1840, is around the corner from Bridge Street, heading west. In 1882, when John H. Stetson sold it to Marshall B. Cushman, it was known as the Thompson house. Mary Cushman owned the house in 1900; she is perhaps one of the women in the photograph above. Farther on, 428 Pine Street, below, was probably built in the 1880s. In 1957, John R. Lee lived at 436 Pine Street, and Robert A. Drake and his family lived at 428 Pine Street. Both houses are still standing. In 2009, two professors, Amber Douglas and Joshua Rosenthal, lived at 436 Pine Street, and William and Elizabeth O'Neil lived at 428 Pine Street.

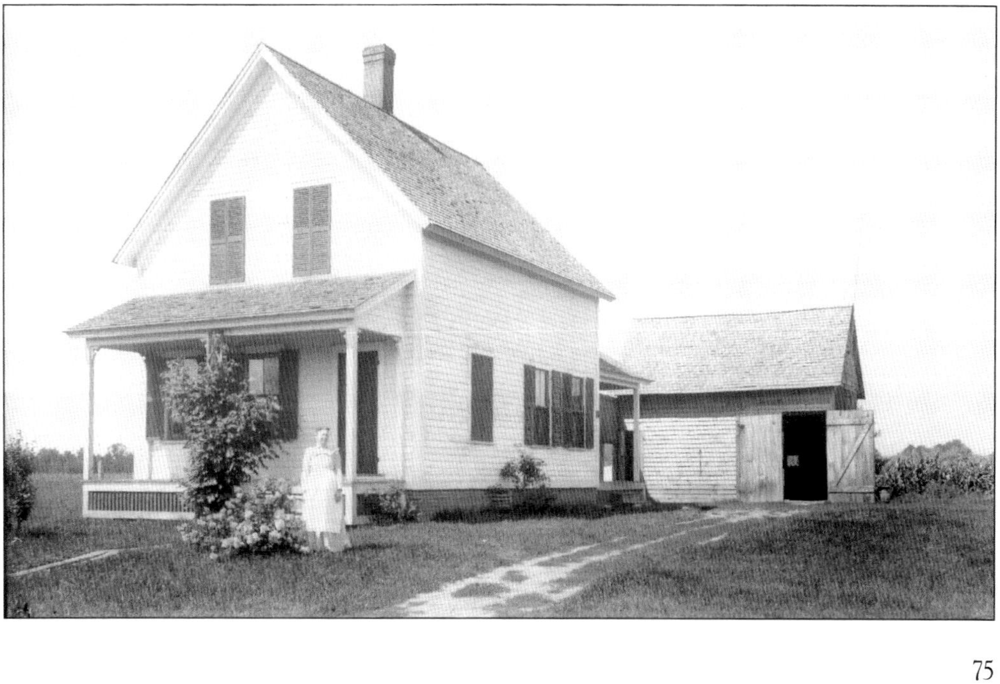

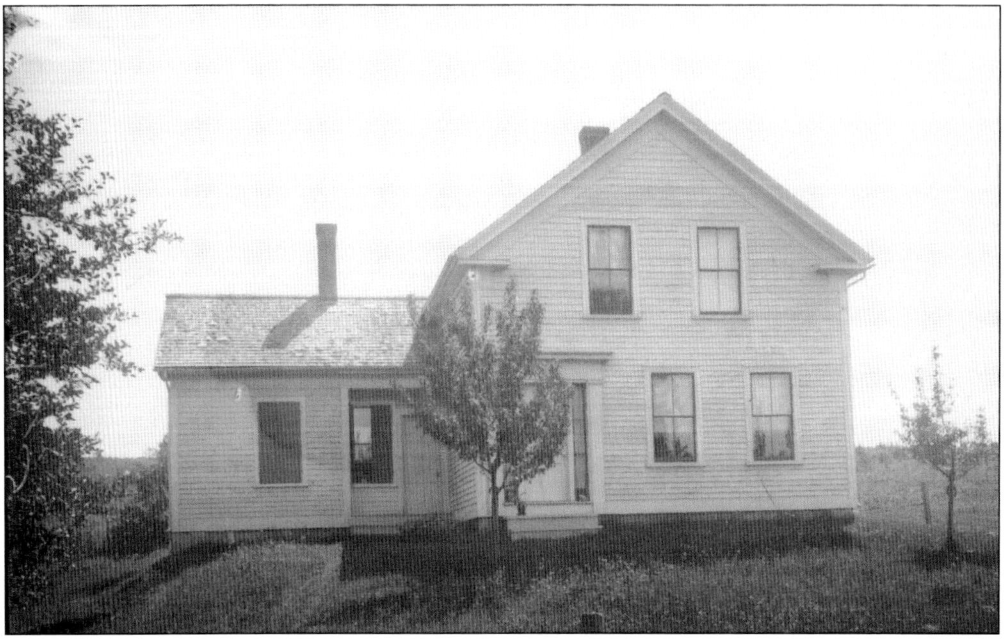

Pictured above is the house at 435 Pine Street. J. Parsons lived here in 1873, Edward A. Parsons in 1957, and Erika Schluntz and Shivonne St. George, both in the education field, in 2009. Pictured below in the 1890s are George and Tabitha Burak, next door at 449 Pine Street. In 1957, James L. Hunter lived here with his family; James and Patricia Coopee lived here in 2009.

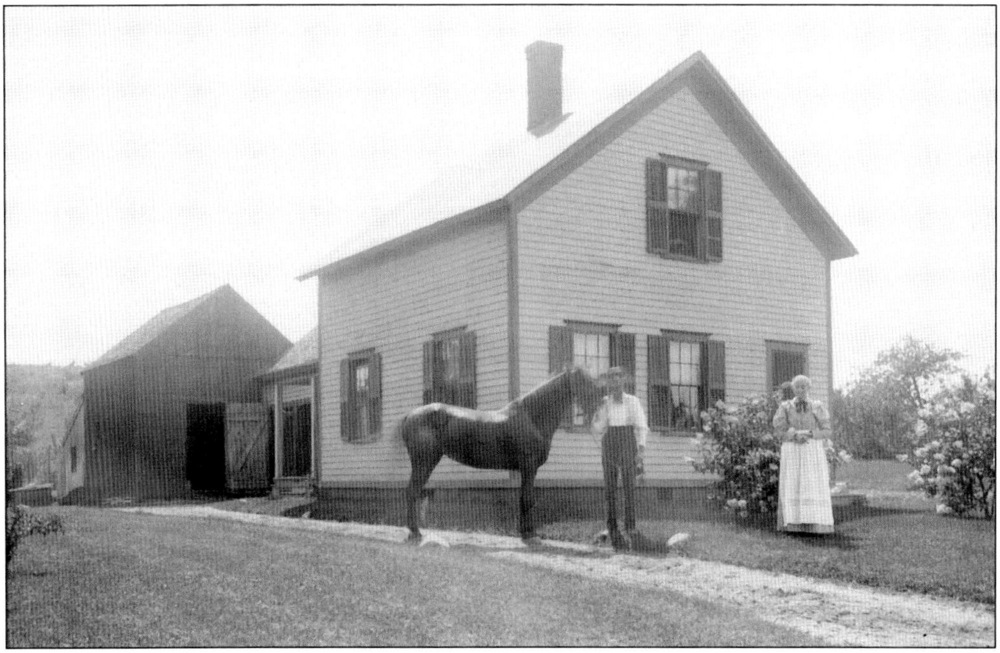

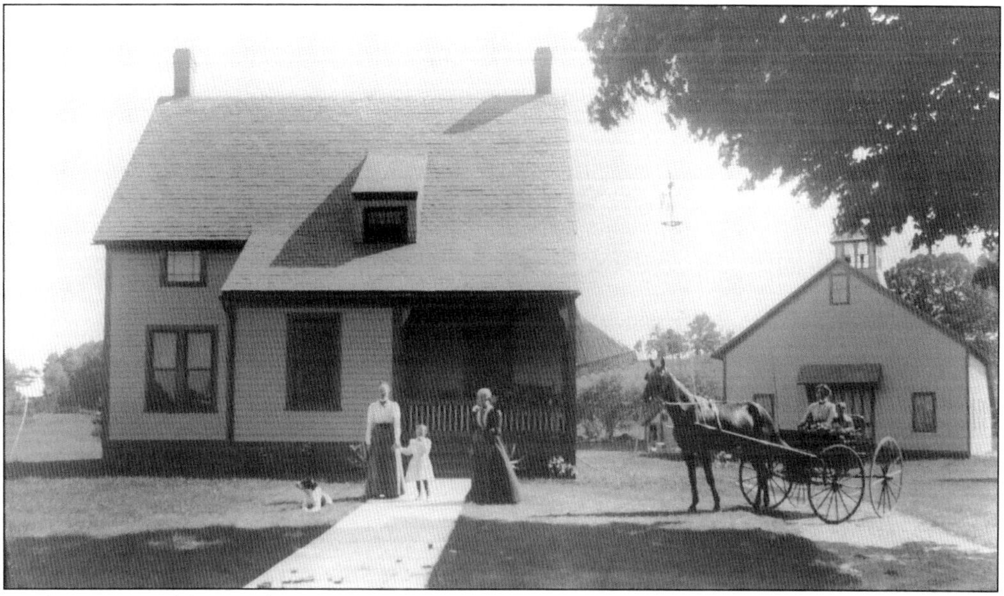

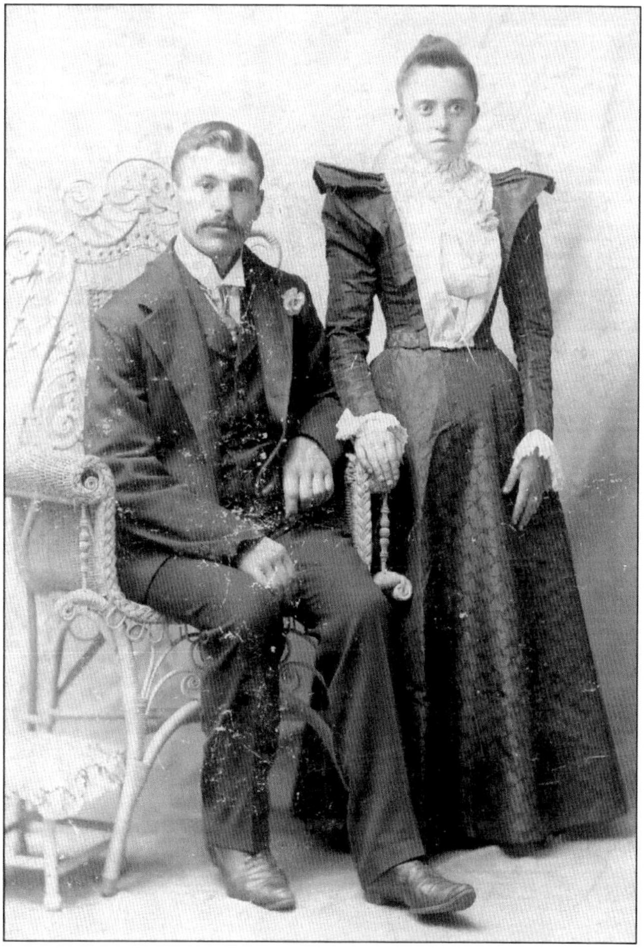

Farther east, and facing the green, is 473 Pine Street, pictured above in the 1890s. On the left is now Hitching Post Road leading to the housing development of University Heights, built on land once owned by the Japanese Tissue Mills. In 1941, the house became the home of Etore and Marcella Battistoni. Etore Battistoni's father, Eugenio, was born in Italy in 1875, came to America at the age of 20, lived in Leverett, Massachusetts, and worked making railroad ties out of chestnut trees, known as the "northeastern redwood" for their durability. He is shown at right with his wife, Angelina, in their wedding portrait. She was born in 1879 and came from the beautiful Lake Garda district of northern Italy at the age of 17, ending up in Springfield, Massachusetts. In 1930, the couple were living on Market Hill Road with their five sons and four daughters. (Right, courtesy of Eugene M. Battistoni Jr.)

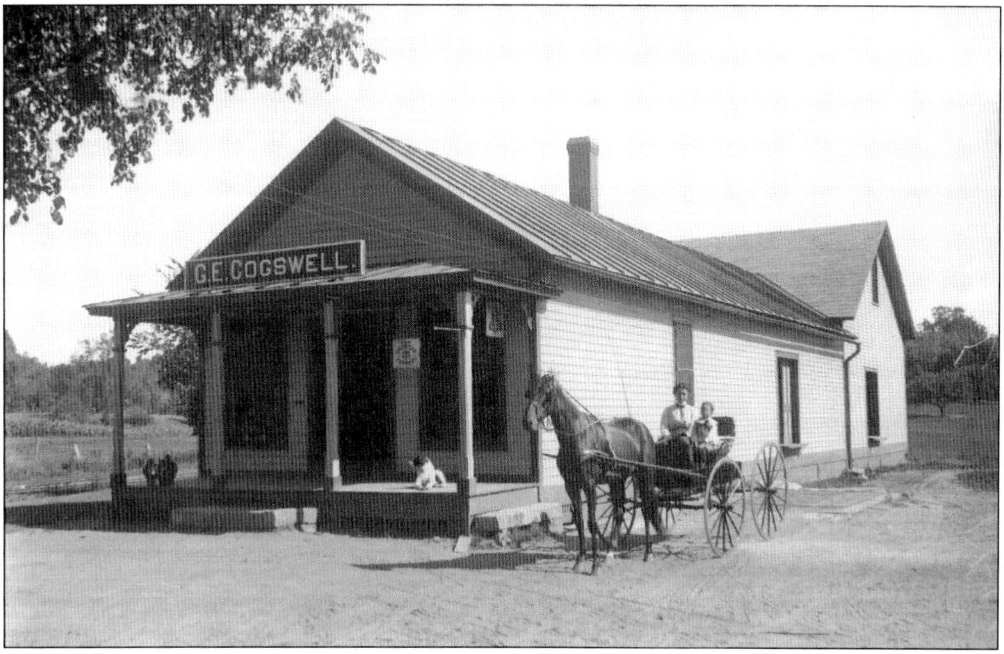

George E. Cogswell started the Cushman Store in 1893. Perhaps it is his wife, child, horse, and dog pictured here; the same carriage and people are in the top photograph on page 77. The railroad tracks are just to the left. In 1912, Cogswell sold the store to Peter F. Hawthornwaite. Attached behind the store was the Peter Hawthorne Feed Mill, which made corn crackers. Right next to the tracks there was a coal shed. The store had an outdoor scale on the west side. John and Martha Germain owned the store from 1919 to 1930 and are likely pictured below.

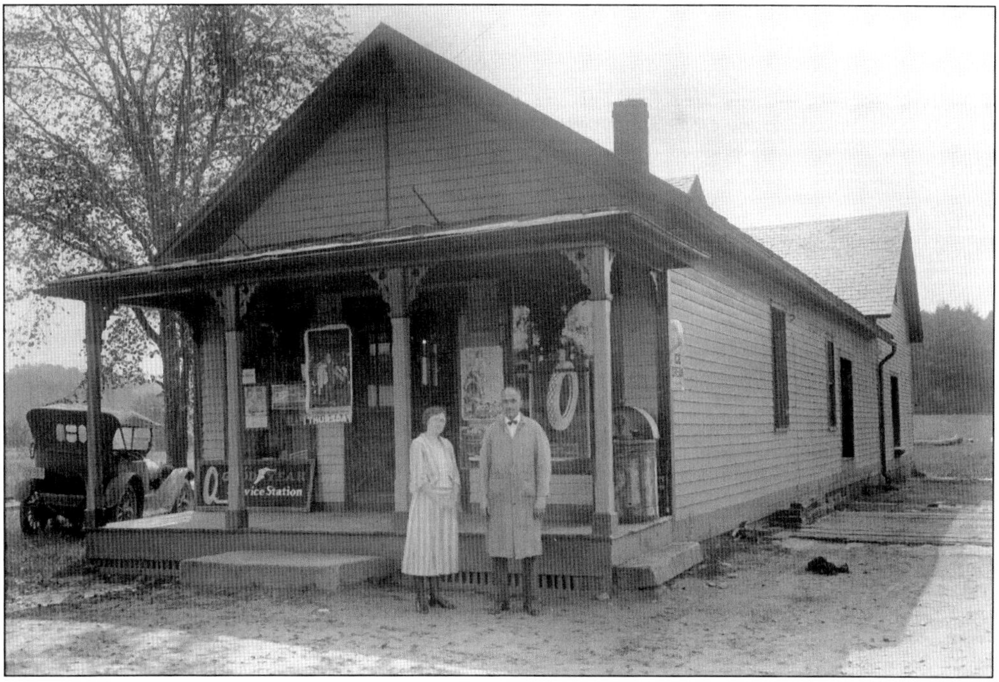

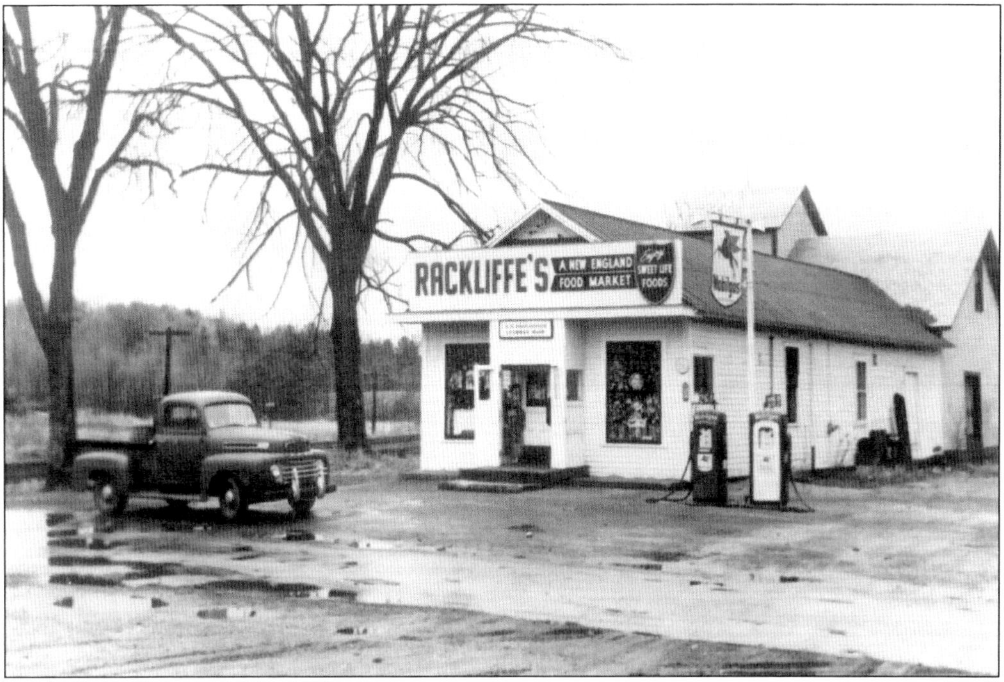

William Rackliffe later owned the store and in 1937, established a post office there. William and Evelyn Rackliffe had no children and were always generous to local families. They were kind about giving a customer more time to pay if needed. The car shown here was a Ford F-100, a 1950 half-ton pickup. From 1965 to 1983, William and Shirley Whittemore ran the store. The current owners of the Cushman Market & Café are Pete Sylvan and Rebecca Schwartz.

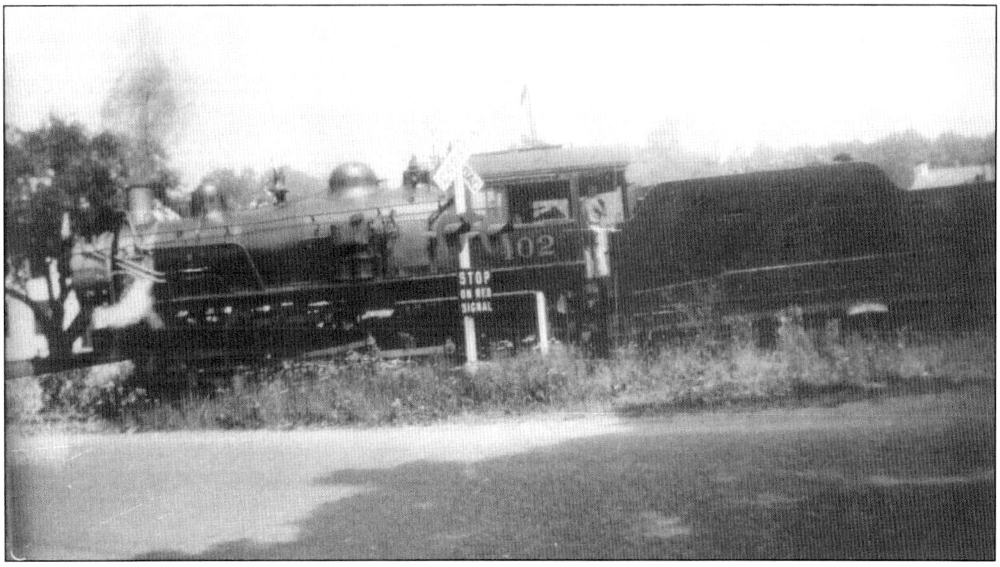

The railroad station used to be across Pine Street from the Cushman Store. There was passenger service and mail was delivered every day. The postmaster from North Amherst would come up to Cushman each day to collect it. This photograph shows the last run of the steam engine in 1957. The railroad still carries freight and passenger traffic, but there is no longer a stop. There have been a few instances of people committing suicide by throwing themselves in front of a train.

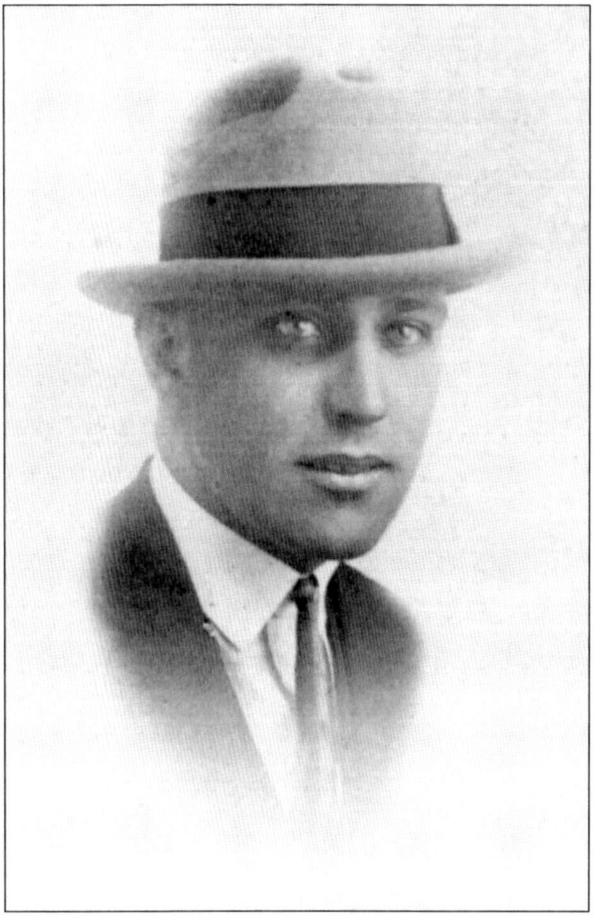

This is a portrait of Lester "Jack" Cunningham, a native of Cedar Rapids, Iowa. He married Doris Harlow of Amherst in 1926, and they lived in California and Colorado before moving to Cushman. Their son lives at 509 Pine Street.

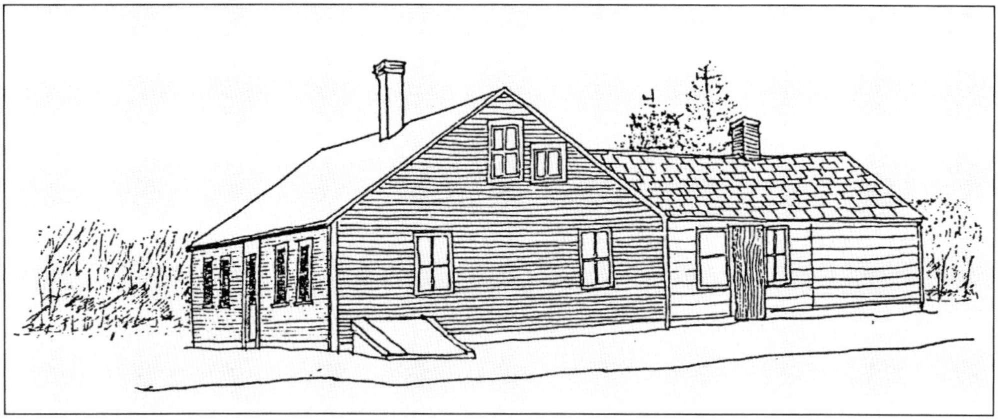

The house at 107 Henry Street on the southwest corner of Pine and Henry Streets is listed in the National Register of Historic Places as the Samuel Henry House. It was built around 1770, with the rear ell and other additions dating from the 1800s. In 1900, Jeremiah Stockwell, a veteran of the Civil War, owned the house. South on Henry Street is a salamander crossing. In 1987, the town and local nature groups built two tunnels under the road so spotted salamanders could safely migrate to vernal pools to mate and lay eggs. (Drawing courtesy of David John Miller.)

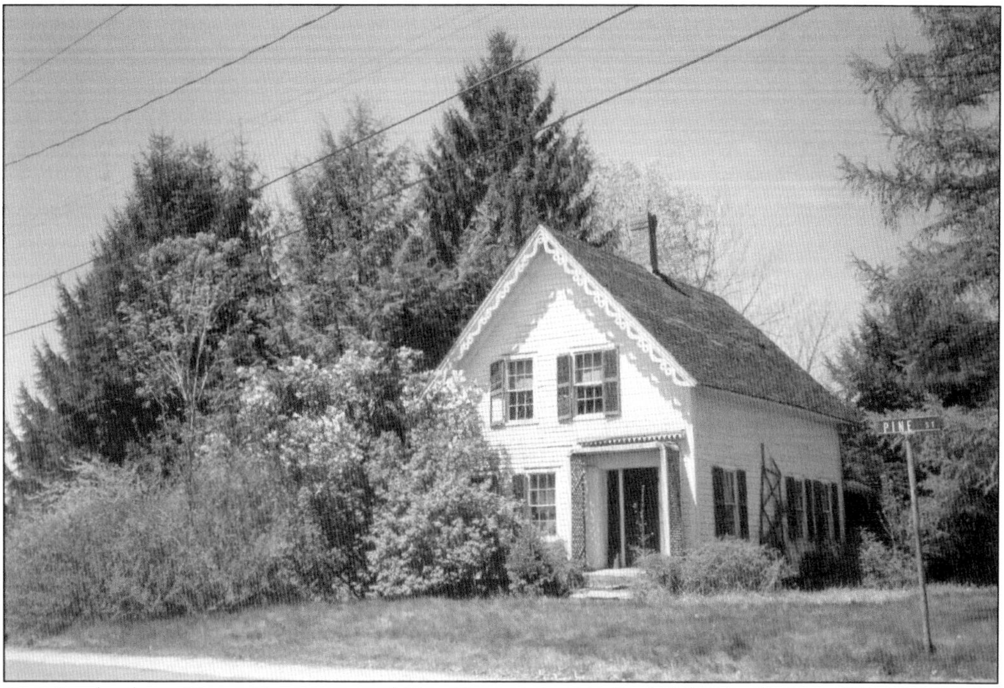

Coming back on Henry Street toward Pine Street, the original Ephraim Roberts House is at the northwest corner. When the railroad came through in 1866, the house was right in the way and so it was moved farther up Henry Street. It is a Greek Revival house with Victorian Gothic details added in the 1880s. In the 1950s, it belonged to Archie Goldthwaite.

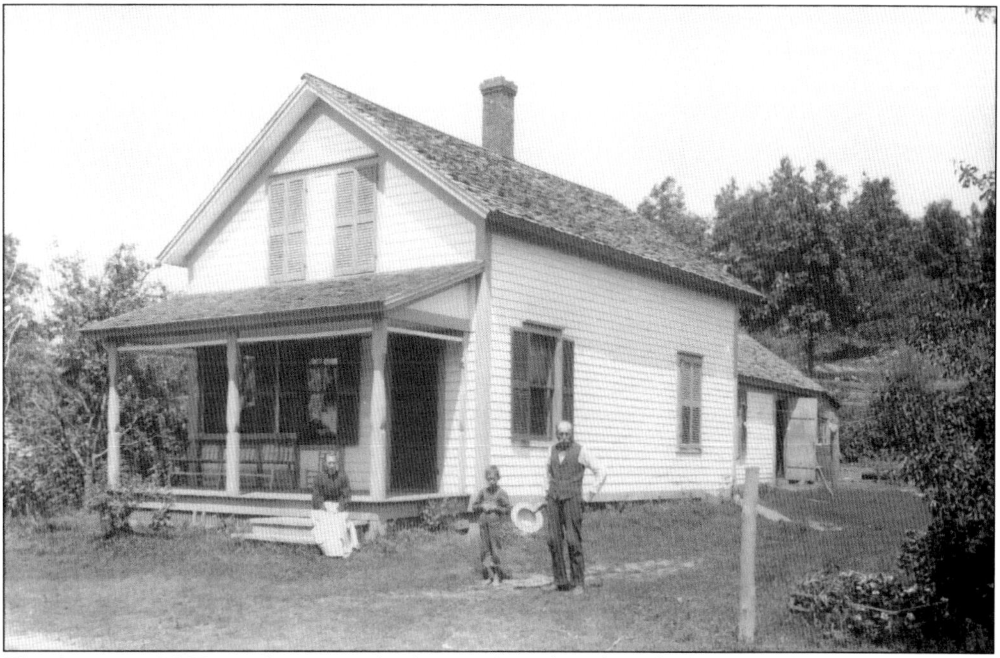

This house at 86 Henry Street was built in 1850. It has three bedrooms. The Stockwell family used to own the place, and in 1957, it belonged to Alfred J. Therrien. Amherst Community Acupuncture has operated out of the house.

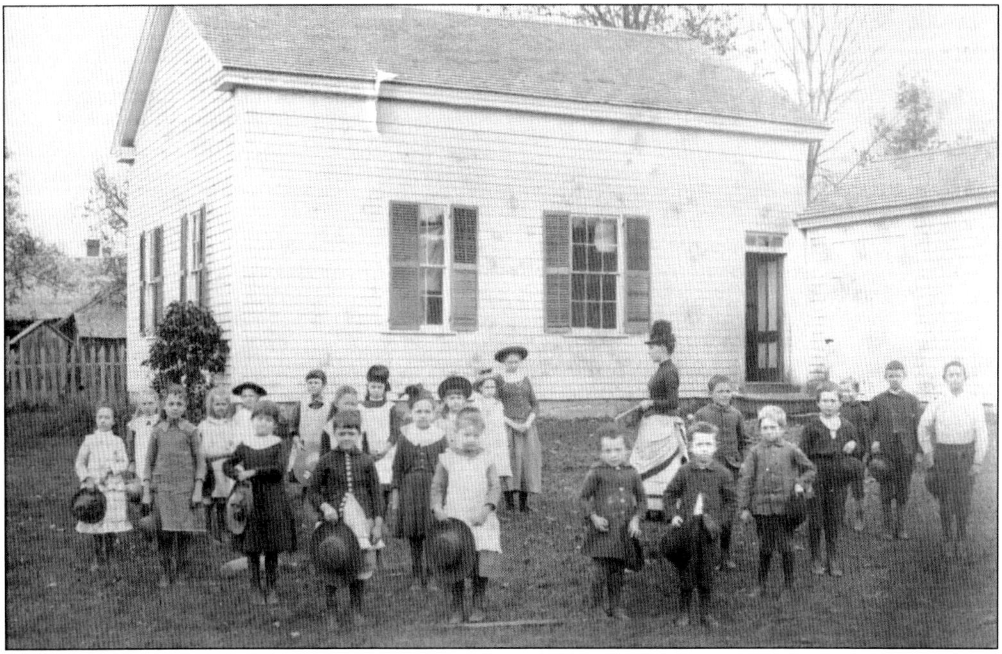

There have been three schools in Cushman. The photograph above shows the second-built school to the east or uphill side of Henry Street. The photograph below shows the Cushman school that used to be on the west side of Henry Street. That building was demolished, and a new school was built, shown here. In the 1880s, the teacher at the North Amherst City Primary School was Ella Roberts. Though their locations in the photograph are not known, the children include Sadie Spear, Sadie Hardaker, Edith Heald, Emma Tracy, Edmund S. Wilbur, Susan F. Wilson, and George Spear.

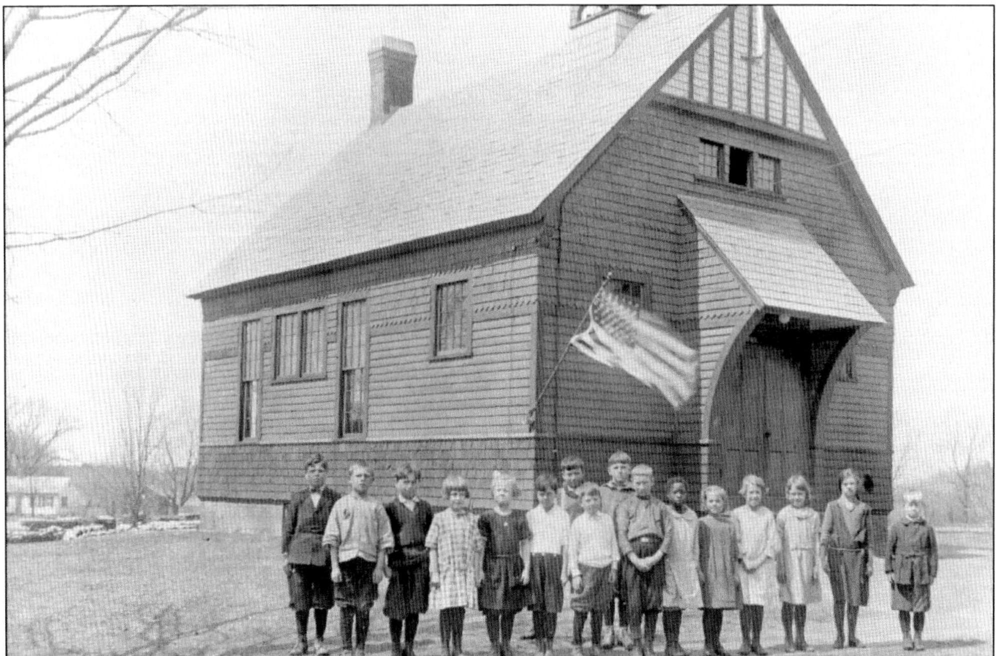

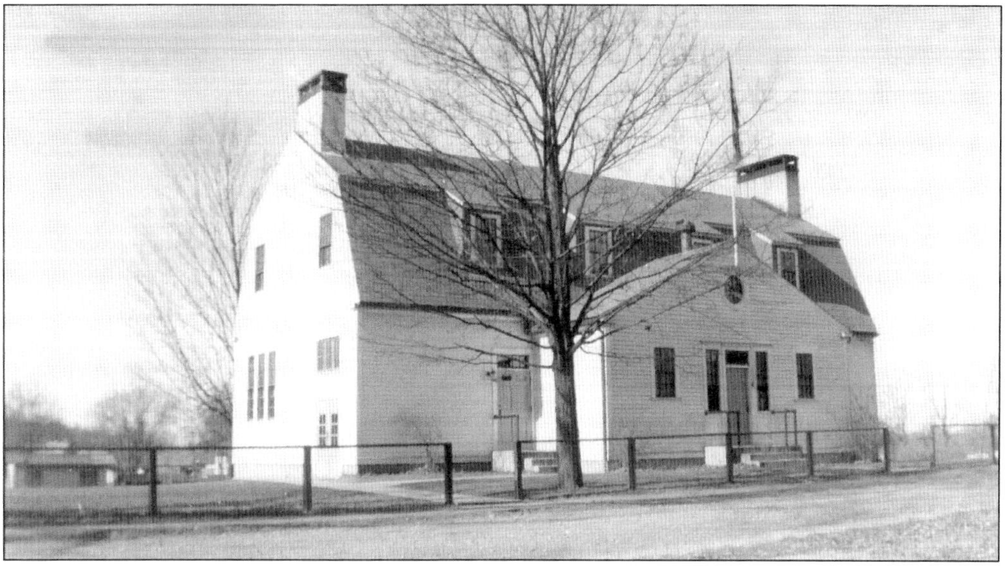

A new school, pictured above on November 11, 1936, was built in 1927. Health Day is being celebrated below, about 1928. Isabelle Callahan remembers that when she went there in the early 1940s, her teacher Mrs. Walsh let them sit in her car in front of the school to listen to the radio and follow the election of Franklin D. Roosevelt. The Cushman Scott Children's Center, serving children ages 15 months to 6 years old, occupies the building now. The school's educational philosophy is based on the Reggio Emilia approach.

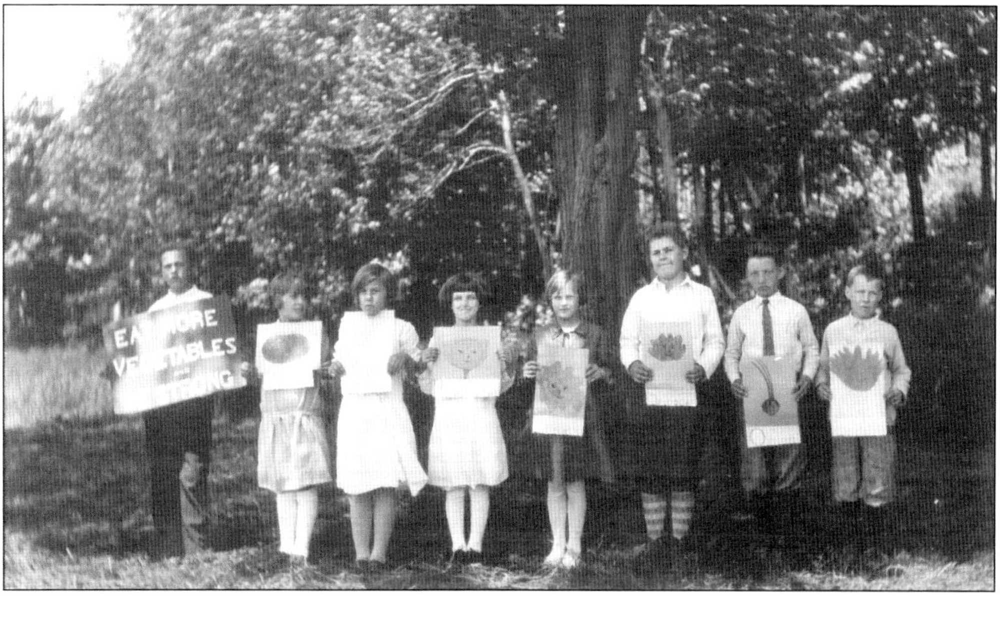

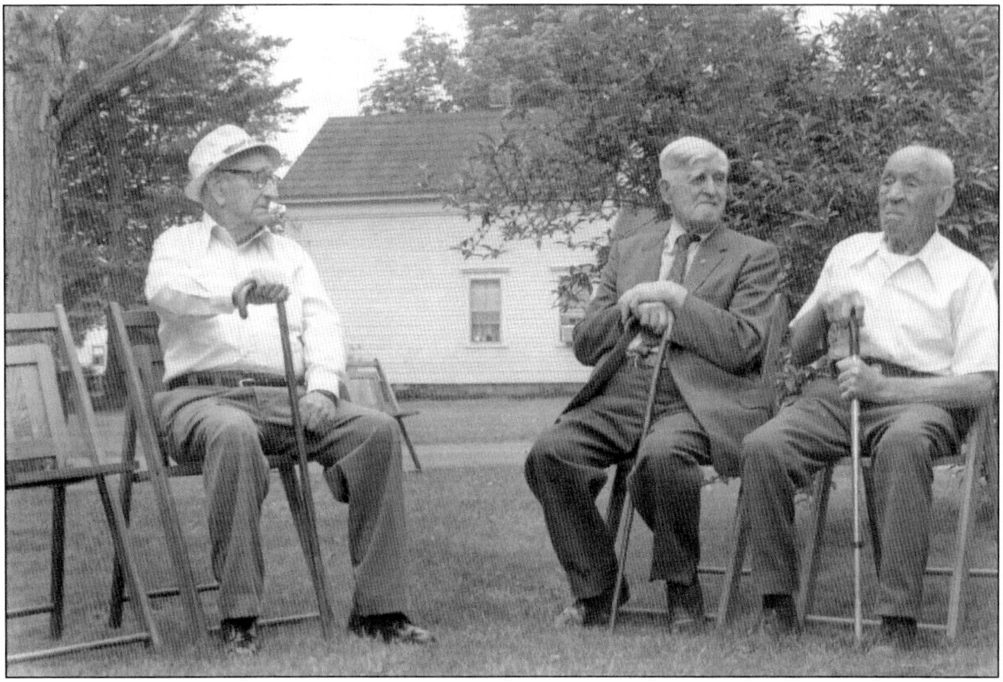

In October 1924, Cushman celebrated Old Home Day for the first time, and the custom continued for many years. The photograph above shows, from left to right, Ray Spear, Archie Goldthwaite, and Guiseppi Sacco, all long-time residents of Cushman, at the 1978 School Bell ceremony. Guiseppi and Giovannina Sacco lived at the farmhouse shown below, south of the village on Henry Street. They bought it from Frank Brighenti in 1930. The house was separated from the road by the railroad tracks, and over the years, Sacco built several bridges so he could cross over the tracks safely. In the 1990s, the farm became an upscale housing development, and the house was burned down by the fire department.

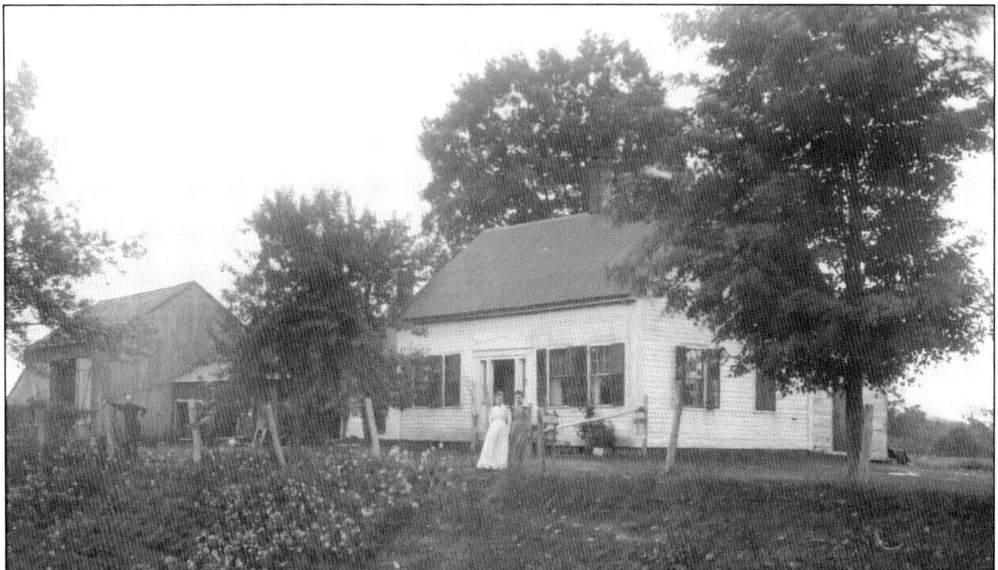

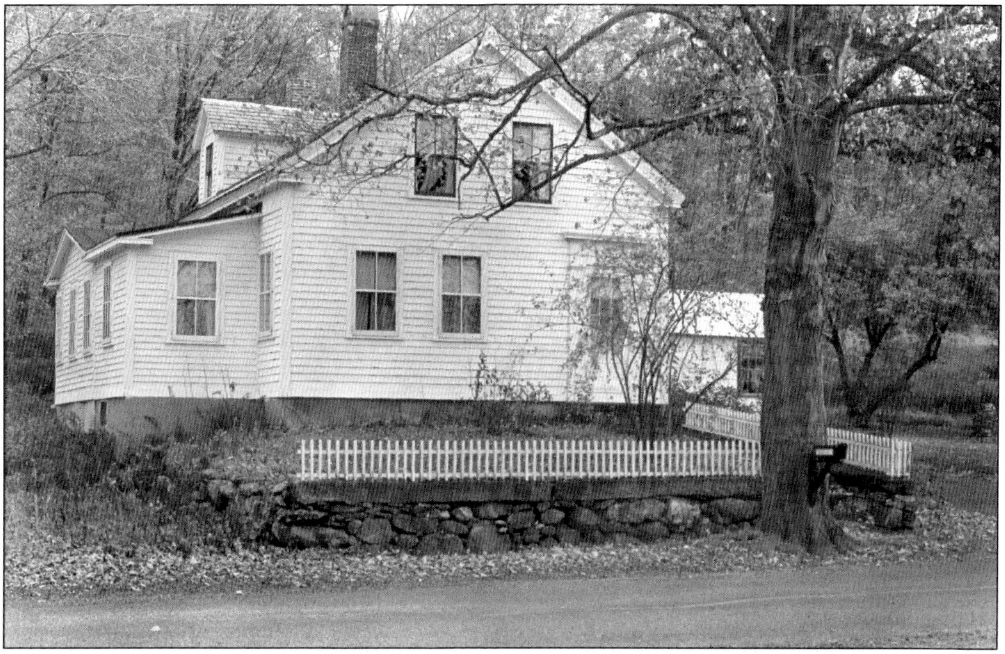

The National Historic Register lists this house at 58 Henry Street as the Barnard House, built in 1856. It is another one-and-a-half-story Greek Revival structure, sited gable end to the street and set close to the road. The stone retaining wall may be part of the original construction. In the 1950s, it was the home of J. Clifton Ashley. His blacksmith shop, which he inherited from his father, Frank Ashley, was across the street, shown below. In 1972, the shop was still functioning. (Both courtesy of Almon Acker.)

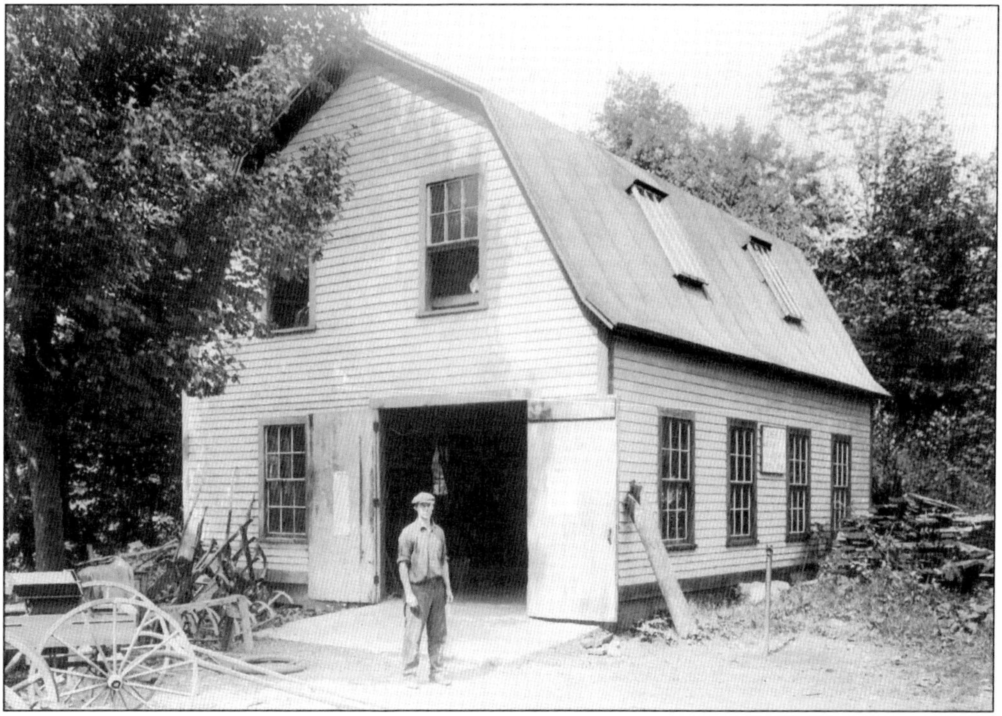

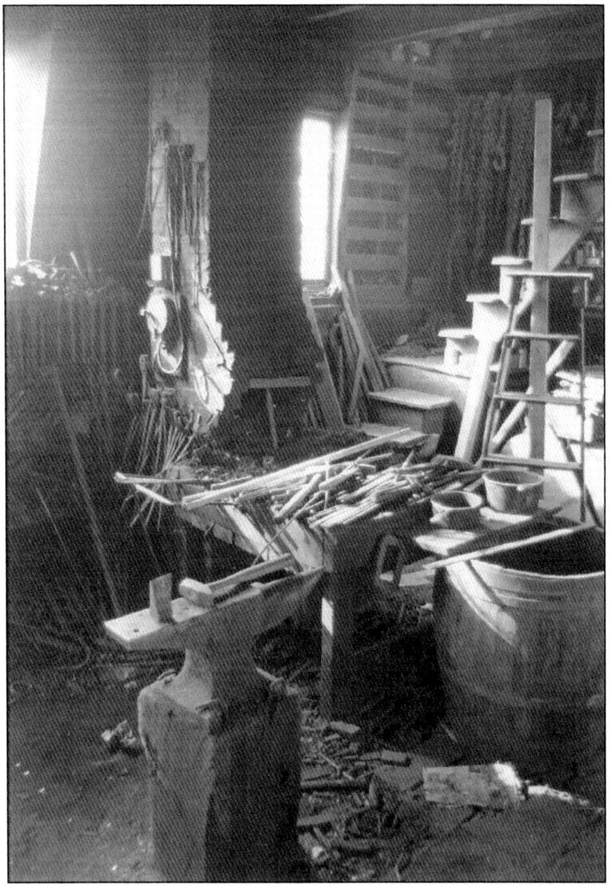

At left is the interior of the blacksmith's shop, with its old anvil and forge. Below, this house at 50 Henry Street, shown in the 1890s, was later owned by Percy Spence. He used to be a machine operator at Worthington Pump in Holyoke, Massachusetts. He was known for his great strength and was also a ham radio operator. In 1947, Spence struck a southbound Central Vermont train in a Willys sedan. There were no signals at the crossing, and the weather was sleeting and raining. Lester Cunningham and Dr. Peter Merzbach helped him. Spence survived his severe cuts; he died in 1958. The house was eventually torn down by Clate Pratt. (Left, courtesy of Alvin Acker.)

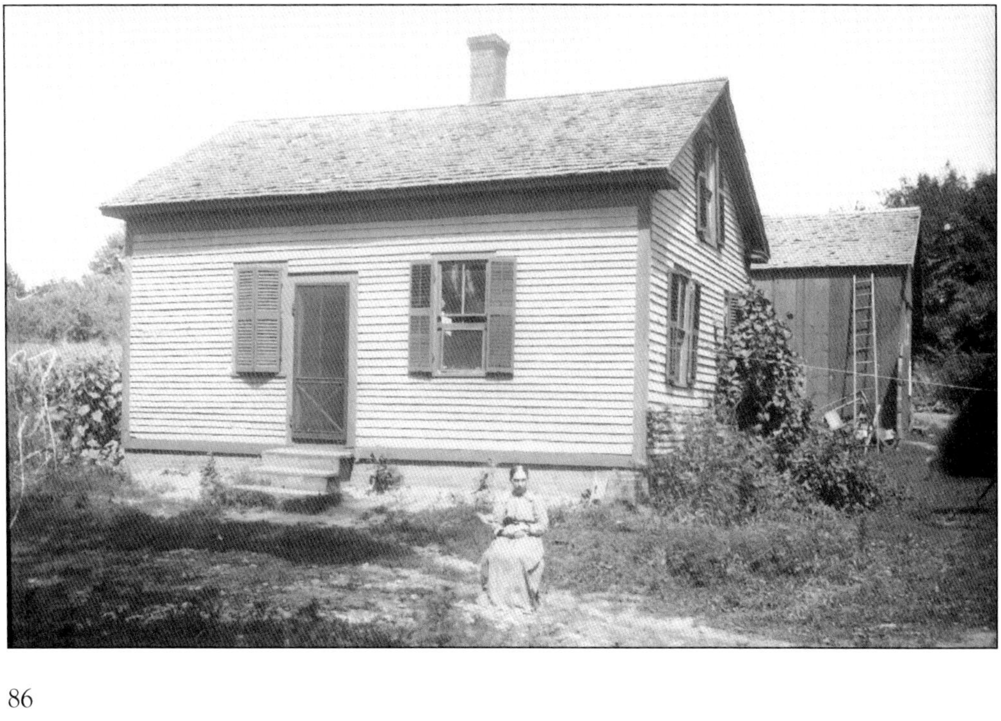

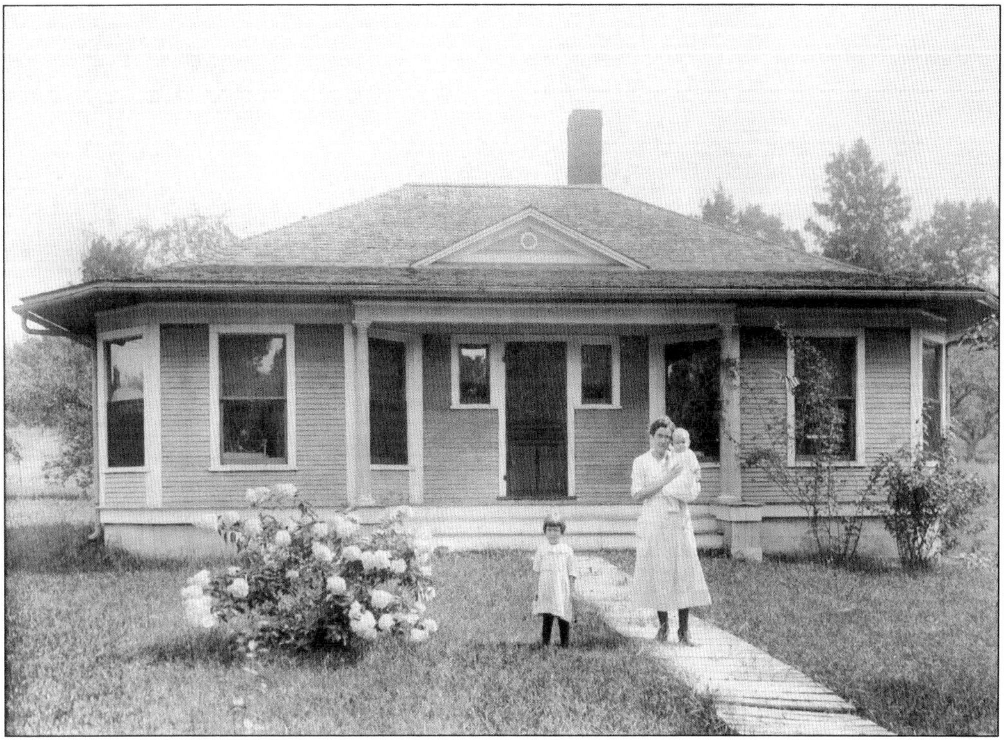

The Benjamin and Hannah Holden house used to stand beyond the Spence house. In 1890, they experienced a tragedy. At 4:00 a.m. on September 20, after a dance party on Flat Hills, a young man named John Davis, from Ware, shot and killed Eva May Holden, pictured at right. She and her escort were riding home on Pine Street; she was 16. Her escort, James Hardaker, was shot in the groin but survived. Davis reportedly told people he would shoot Eva if she went with anyone else but him. He was convicted of murder in the second degree. Eva was the youngest of five sisters. (Both courtesy of Deborah Carroll.)

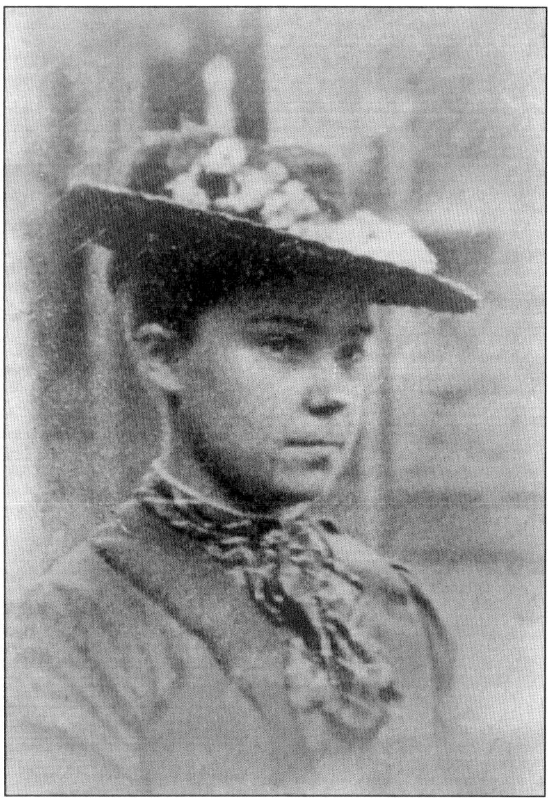

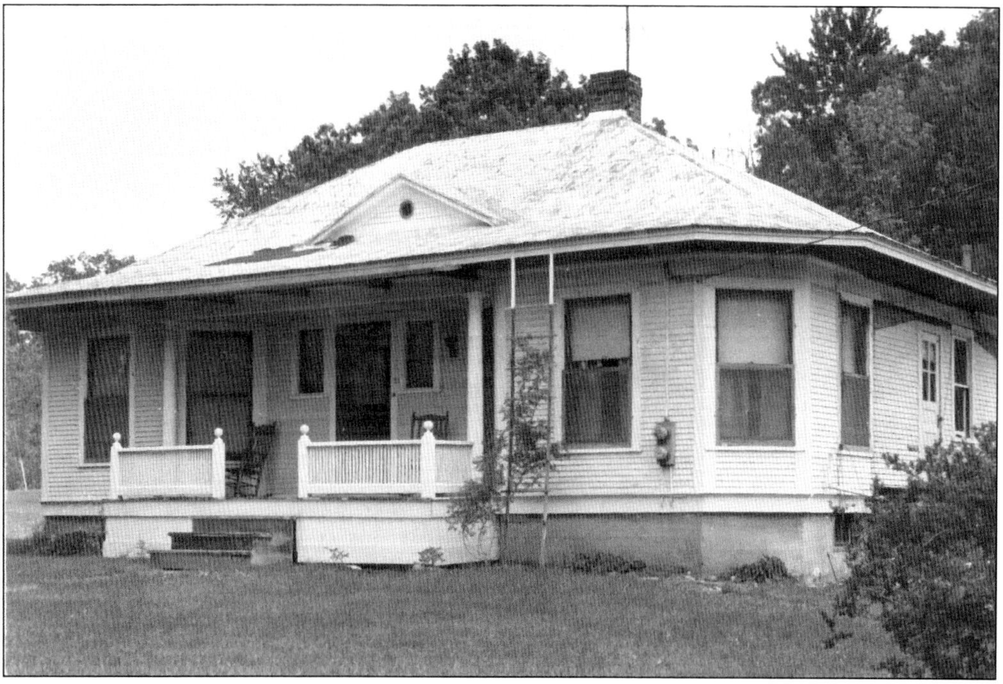

The Holden house at 28 Henry Street was locally famous because it was ordered from a Sears Roebuck catalogue. In the 1950s, it was owned by Herbert Holden. Below, Eva Holden's four older sisters are, from left to right, Grace (Hatt), Hallie (Blair), Effie (Stockwell), and Eddie (Lemon), with their arms linked. The photograph may have been taken shortly after the murder. There were also two brothers, Henry and Herbert Holden. (Both courtesy of Deborah Carroll.)

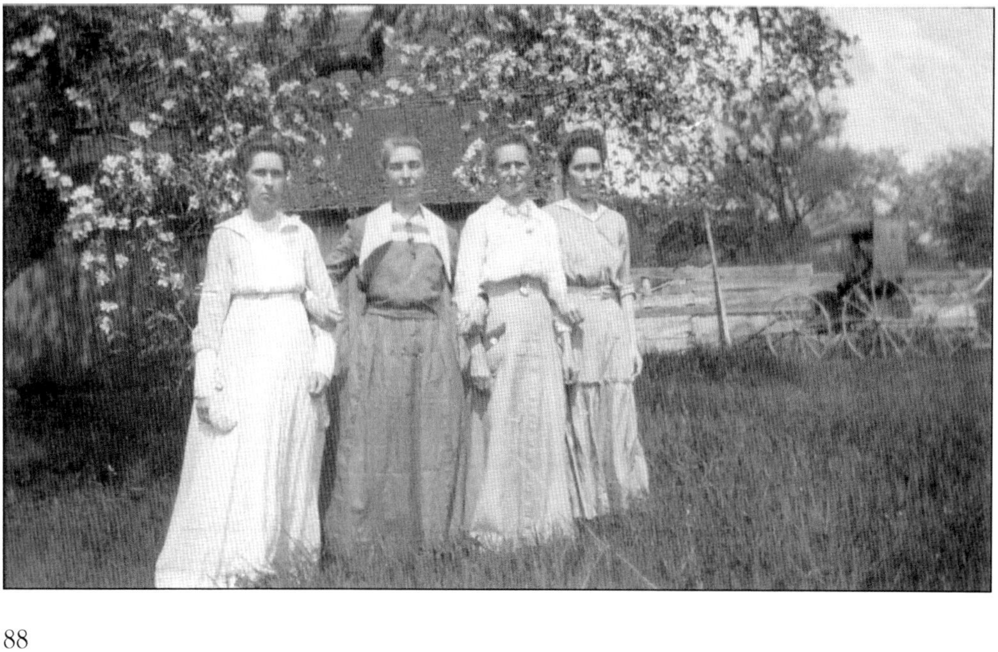

Five

Market Hill Road, Flat Hills Road, and North East Street

The poet and essayist Robert Francis came to Amherst in 1926, three years after he graduated from Harvard. He was a bachelor and in 1937 moved to 51 Leverett Road. In 1940, he built a small cottage on Market Hill Road he named Fort Juniper. He wanted to live quietly with "plain" people. Children thought he might be a hermit. He wrote there and entertained his visitors, including his friend, Robert Frost. He died in 1987, and his cottage is still reserved for local poets. Near the top of Market Hill Road there used to be a fortune teller, Wilda Chicoigne, who kept fierce dogs and read palms. At the top of Market Hill Road and just over the Amherst town line in Shutesbury is the Atkins Reservoir. Pratt's Pond was the basis for the reservoir, which was fed by springs and streams; work began on the reservoir in 1929. The water has been supplying the northern half of Amherst including Cushman, North Amherst, and the University of Massachusetts; a treatment plant is near the bottom of Market Hill Road. In 1909, a local writer, W.R. Brown, described the narrow, shady road through the Flat Hills area in the northeast corner of Amherst as the most picturesque in town, with only four houses on it. An early settler was Peter King, a soldier during the Revolutionary War, who went there with his family from nearby Pelham in 1820. He planted a grove of maple trees and several generations of his family remained there as farmers.

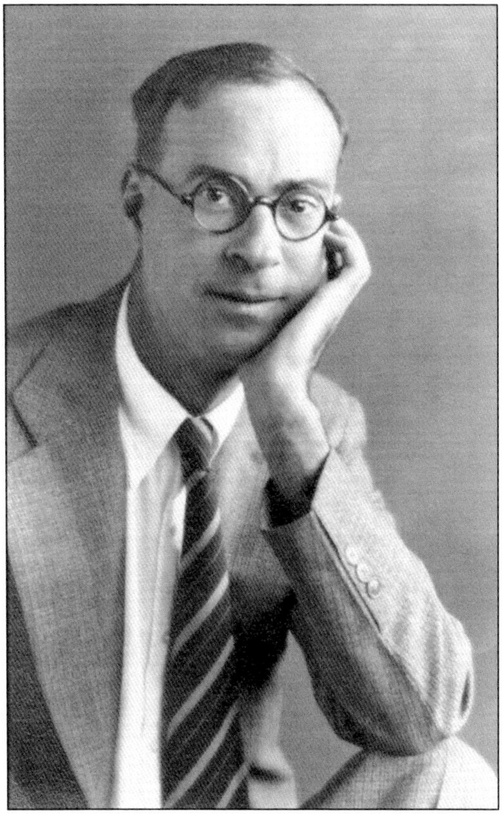

Robert Francis, shown at left, was the son of a Baptist minister who had a church in West Medford, Massachusetts. After finishing college, he came to Amherst to teach school, and after several years doing that, he decided he wanted to write full-time. He published articles in magazines and two books of poems, and had to learn to live extremely cheaply. He would give violin lessons. When his father died in 1940, there was a $1,000 legacy, and Robert Francis decided to have a cabin built on a half acre of land that overlooked the old Cushman mill pond. Below is a photograph of that cabin, built by Chester Woodard. It had one small bedroom, and another room for cooking and everything else including his upright piano. (Courtesy of the University of Massachusetts Amherst, Special Collections.)

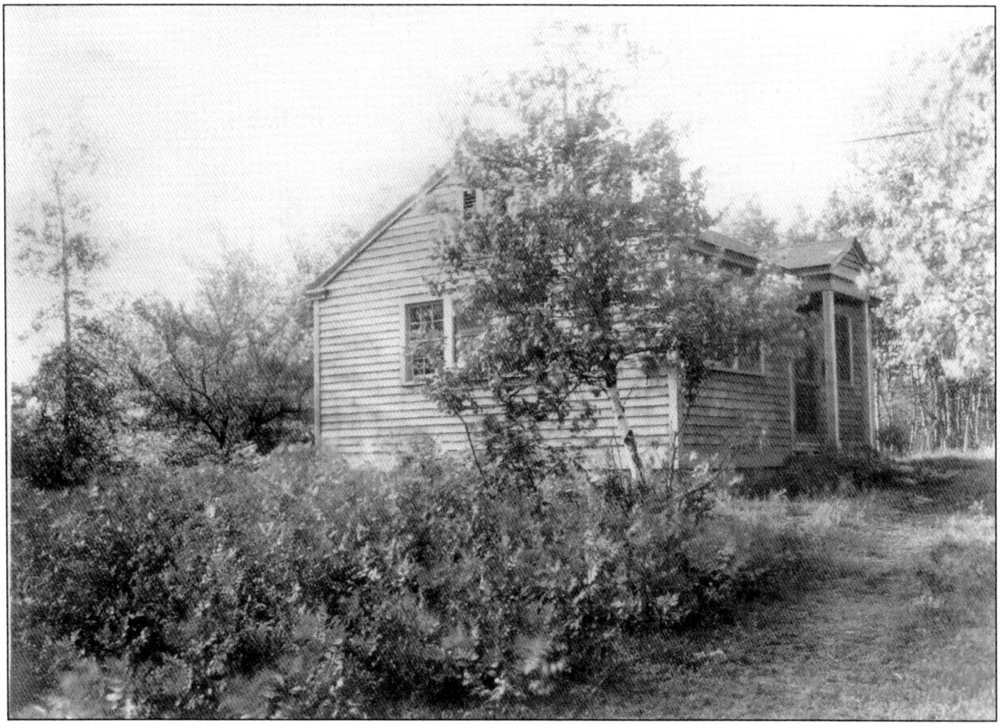

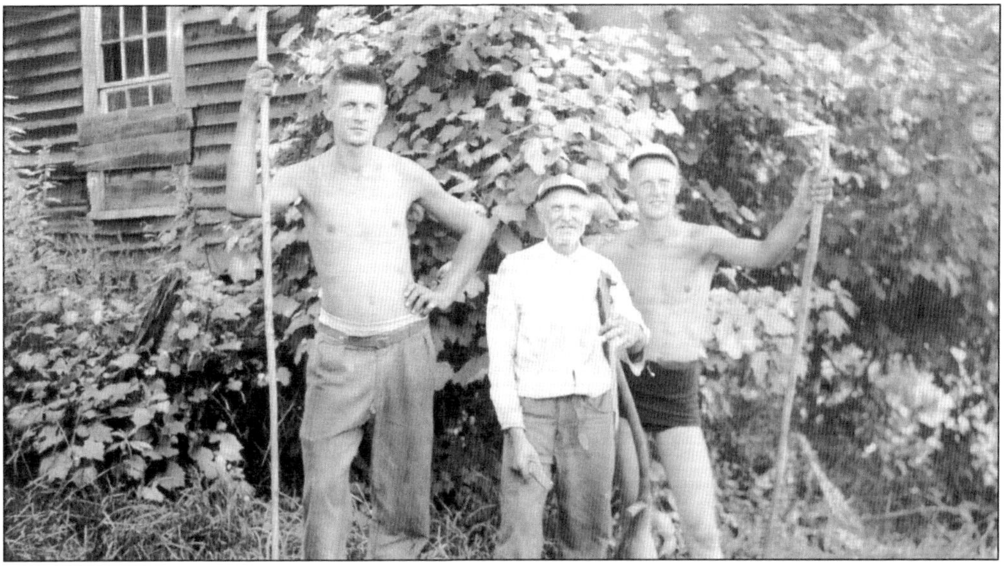

Robert Francis became close friends with the nearby Adamites family, who had sold him the land for the cabin. The parents were from Lithuania and spoke broken English. They had four sons. Shown above, from left to right, are Joe Adamites, his father Kiet, and brother Frank. At right is another photograph of Frank. In his memoir *The Trouble with Francis*, Robert Francis recalled sitting with Frank in the lantern light playing cat's-cradle. (Both courtesy of the University of Massachusetts Amherst, Special Collections.)

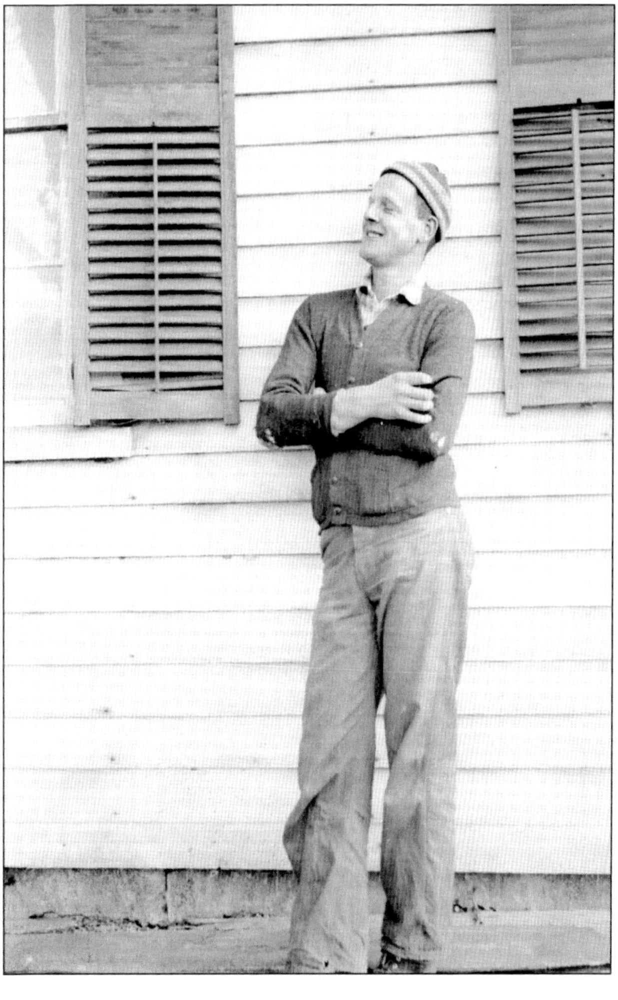

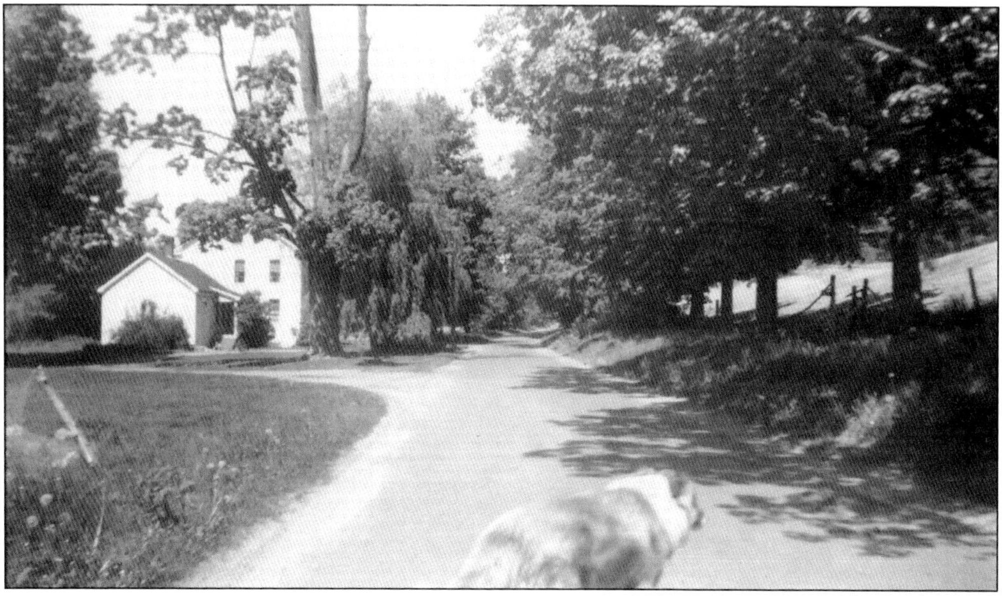

Nearby on the road were the two houses of the Battistoni family, one for the father Jim Tony (Eugenio Battistoni) and family, and the other for his son Milo and his family. The Battistoni family also had a farm of 5,000 chickens up on the hill. At 234 Market Hill Road was the Max Stosz family. Stosz was a factory worker and farmer. His birth name was Matthias Stosz, and he was born in 1912 in Segenthau, Hungary. He met Alice Mitchell of Amherst, and they married in 1934. The farm was owned by her father, Peter Mitchell, one of three he had in Amherst. Above are the house and their dog Brownie in 1954; below are their sons Max and Stanley Stosz. (Both courtesy of Pauline Lannon.)

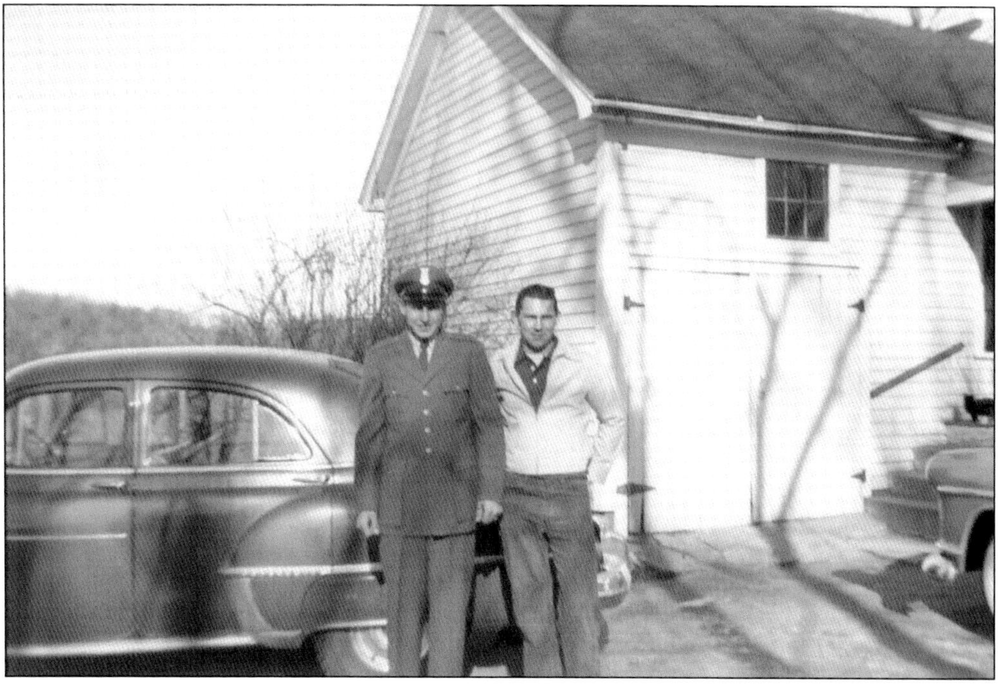

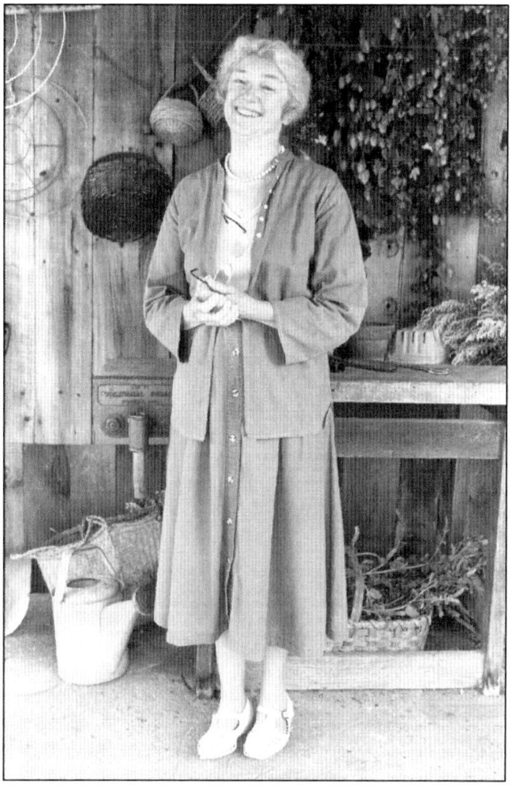

Not far from the right turn to Flat Hills Road is 460 Market Hill Road. The land there used to belong to a chicken farmer, Joe Rockwell, and later to Edward and Fay Kaynor. A portion is still occupied by Reed Kaynor, one of their sons. Fay Kaynor, shown here, was a devoted historian of Cushman and the factories along the river. She published her research in journals concerned with preservation and local history. Below is the first page of her article on saving the Keet house. (Above, courtesy of Reed Kaynor.)

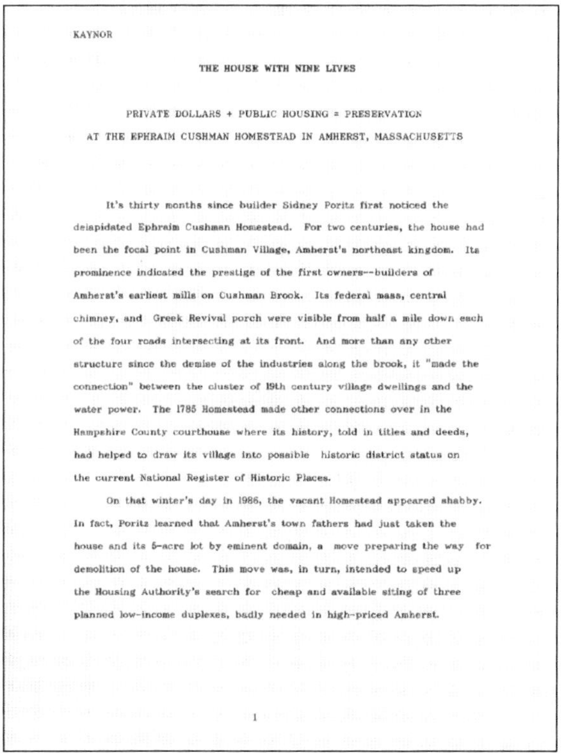

KAYNOR

THE HOUSE WITH NINE LIVES

PRIVATE DOLLARS + PUBLIC HOUSING = PRESERVATION

AT THE EPHRAIM CUSHMAN HOMESTEAD IN AMHERST, MASSACHUSETTS

It's thirty months since builder Sidney Poritz first noticed the delapidated Ephraim Cushman Homestead. For two centuries, the house had been the focal point in Cushman Village, Amherst's northeast kingdom. Its prominence indicated the prestige of the first owners--builders of Amherst's earliest mills on Cushman Brook. Its federal mass, central chimney, and Greek Revival porch were visible from half a mile down each of the four roads intersecting at its front. And more than any other structure since the demise of the industries along the brook, it "made the connection" between the cluster of 19th century village dwellings and the water power. The 1785 Homestead made other connections over in the Hampshire County courthouse where its history, told in titles and deeds, had helped to draw its village into possible historic district status on the current National Register of Historic Places.

On that winter's day in 1986, the vacant Homestead appeared shabby. In fact, Poritz learned that Amherst's town fathers had just taken the house and its 5-acre lot by eminent domain, a move preparing the way for demolition of the house. This move was, in turn, intended to speed up the Housing Authority's search for cheap and available siting of three planned low-income duplexes, badly needed in high-priced Amherst.

1

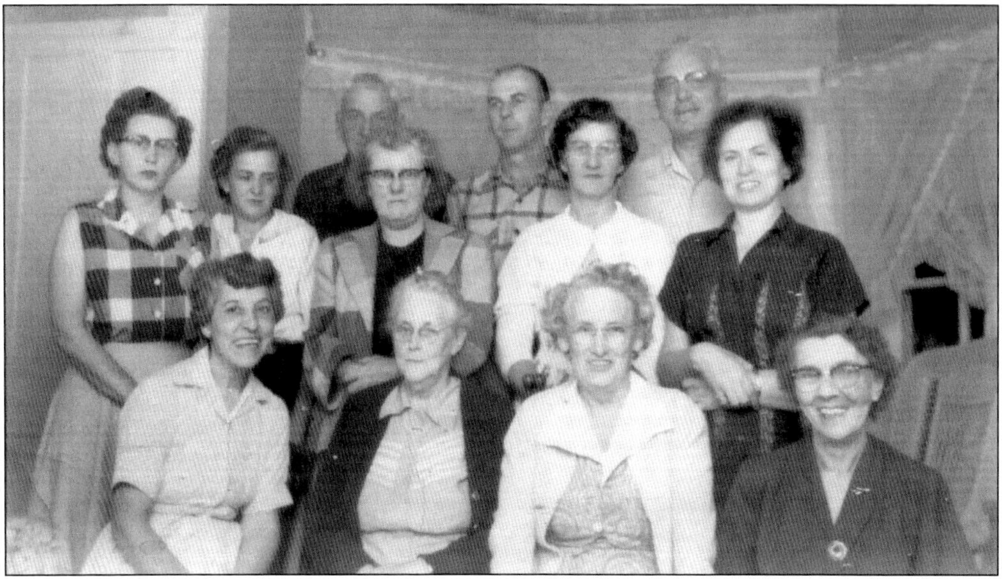

The Pratt family, originally from Shutesbury, Massachusetts, has lived since 1928 on Flat Hills Road. Above are, from left to right (first row) unidentified, Ada May Pratt, Edna Pratt, and unidentified; (second row) Gertrude Stockwell, Alice (Pratt) Booth, unidentified, Victoria Pratt (Harold's wife), and unidentified; (third row) unidentified, Harold Pratt (Victoria's husband) and unidentified. Ada Pratt had nine children. Gertude Stockwell was married to Edward C. Stockwell, a press operator in Chicopee, Massachusetts. Below are, from left to right, (first row) Jenny Pratt (Clate's daughter), Anne Pratt, and Teresa Pratt; (second row) Marie Pratt (Clate's wife), Chester Pratt, Ada May Pratt, Alice (Pratt) Booth, Clate Pratt, and Harold Pratt. Harold was a mechanic at University Motors. He and Victoria Pratt lived on Flat Hills Road. Clate (officially Clayton) and Marie Pratt lived on Henry Street, near the farm of her father, Guiseppe Sacco. Clate and Marie's house was originally an apple storage bin he moved from the land that was flooded for the Quabbin Reservoir. (Both courtesy of Lawrence Britt.)

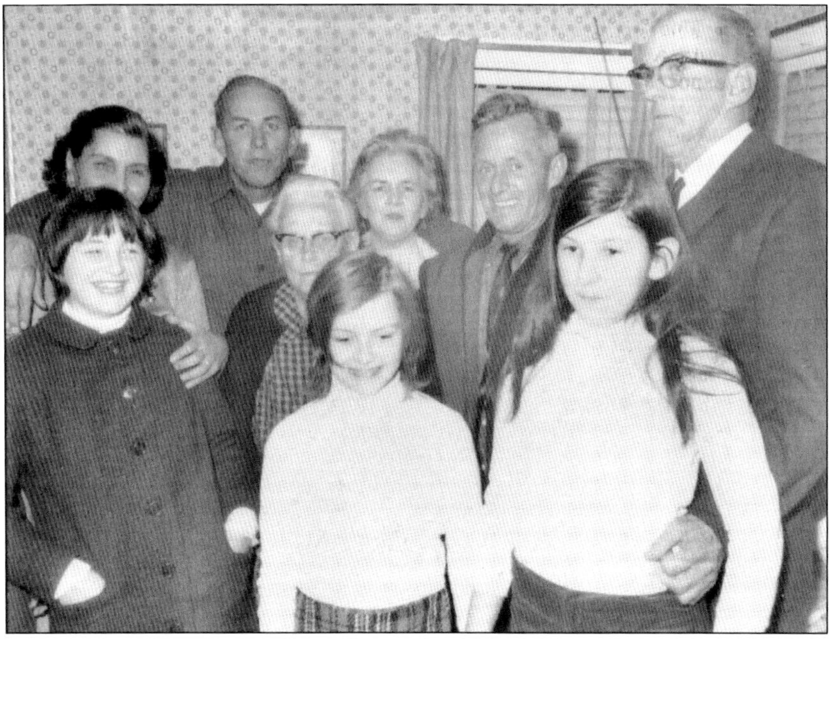

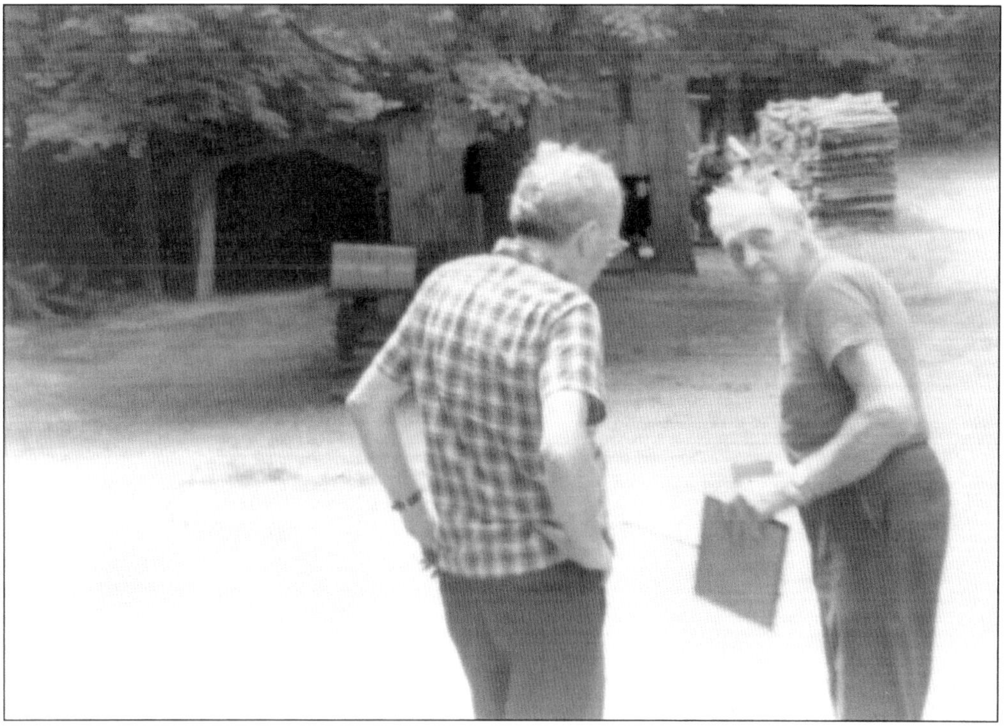

Harry Tyler and Henry Martin are shown here at Chet Pratt's house at 248 Flat Hills Road about 1972. Harry Tyler worked for Chet for 30 years, doing logging and cutting cordwood; Henry Martin did the same for many years as well. (Courtesy of Larry Britt.)

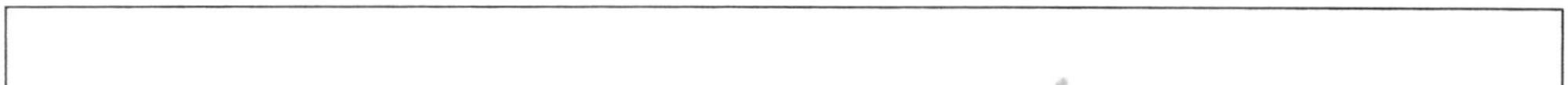

The old farm at 222 Flat Hills Road is now owned by Thomas Perron. Formerly 100 acres, the farm is now divided between the Perrons and the George Comings family. Here is their tractor and faithful dog. In 1948, the Amherst selectmen changed the name of Flat Hills Road to North East Street. Resident Sam Collins drew up a petition in protest, and among the signers were Ida Pratt, the Perrons, and the Comings. The petition was successful. (Courtesy of Thomas Perron.)

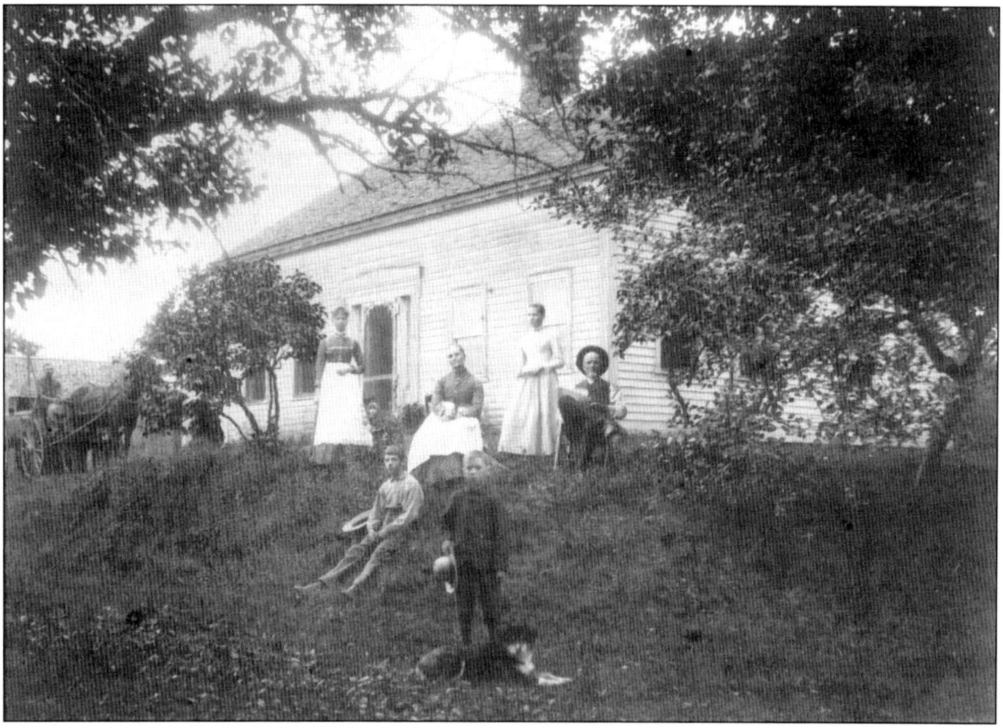

The photograph above shows the Perron house as it was in the 1800s. The one below was taken between 1885 and 1890, and the two young women are Clara A. Comings and Maud Perron. Clara Comings remained single, and, according to the 1920 census, when she was 58, lived on the family farm with her sister Stella. Living with them were four Swedish children, Edna, Fritz, Henry, and Vailette Carlson, ages six to twelve. Notice the teams of oxen and the team of horses in the photograph. The young boy on the lower right is probably training young oxen. (Both courtesy of Thomas Perron.)

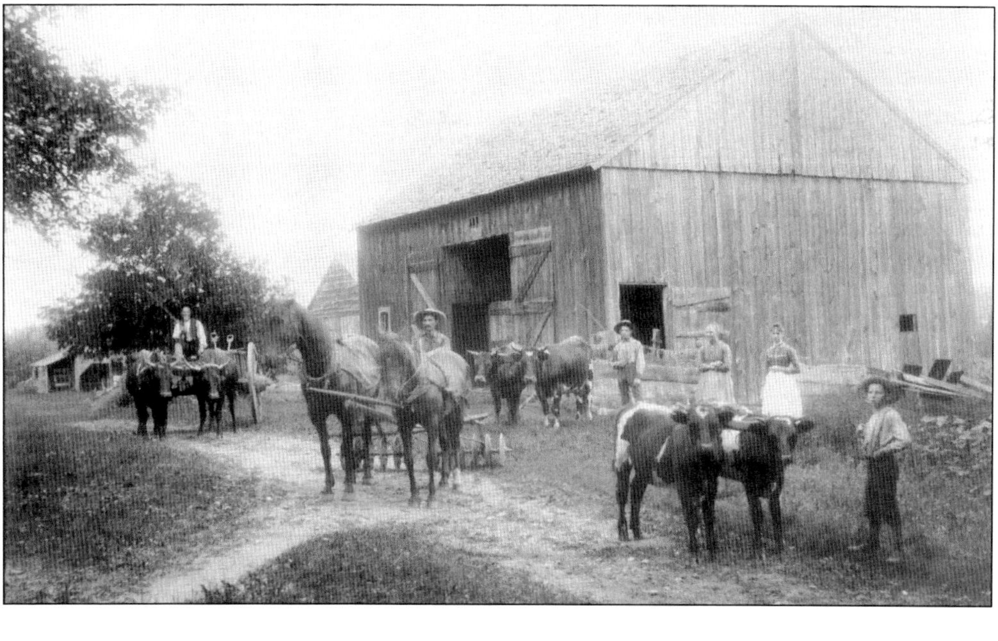

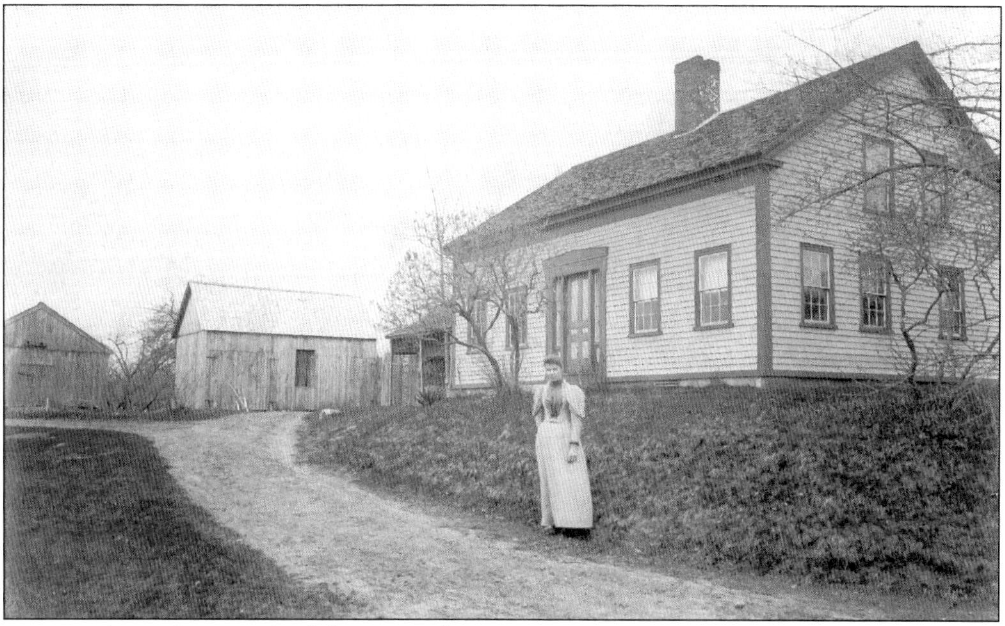

Here is a later photograph of the Perron house, taken when the leaves have gone. The house looks freshly painted with contrasting trim. The woman is unidentified. In the 1940s, the family would have visitors who liked to join in the work. The group of folks below are coming back from haying Joseph B. Wysocki's farm on North East Street. One man is propped up against the tractor's fender, and Joe is holding his hat. High-tension wires can be seen in the background. (Both courtesy of Thomas Perron.)

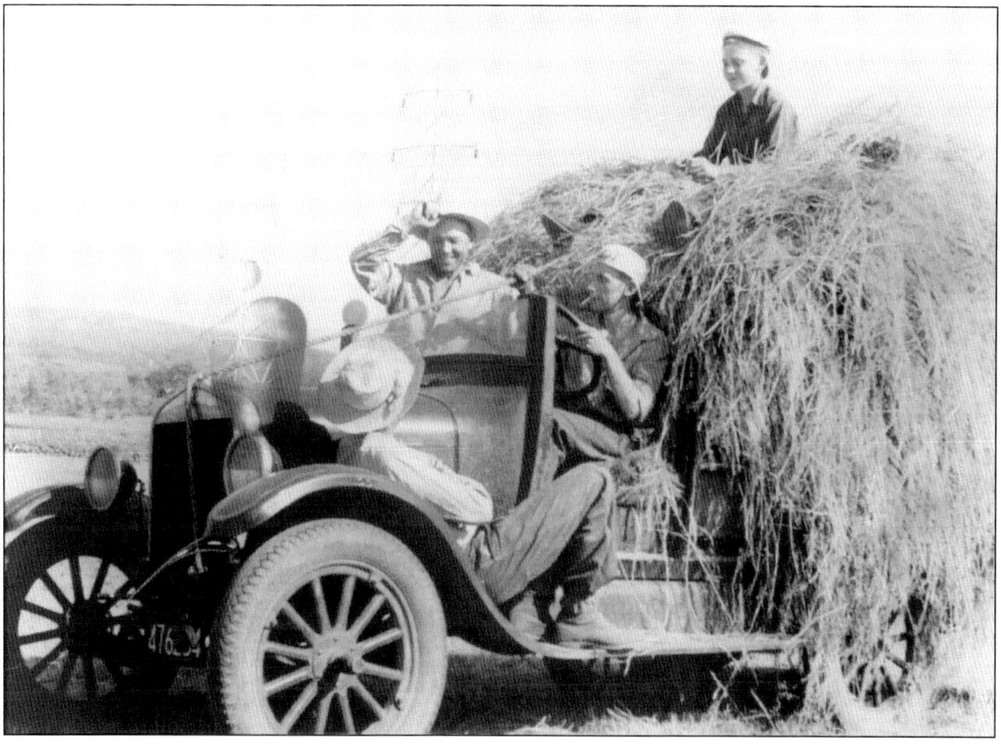

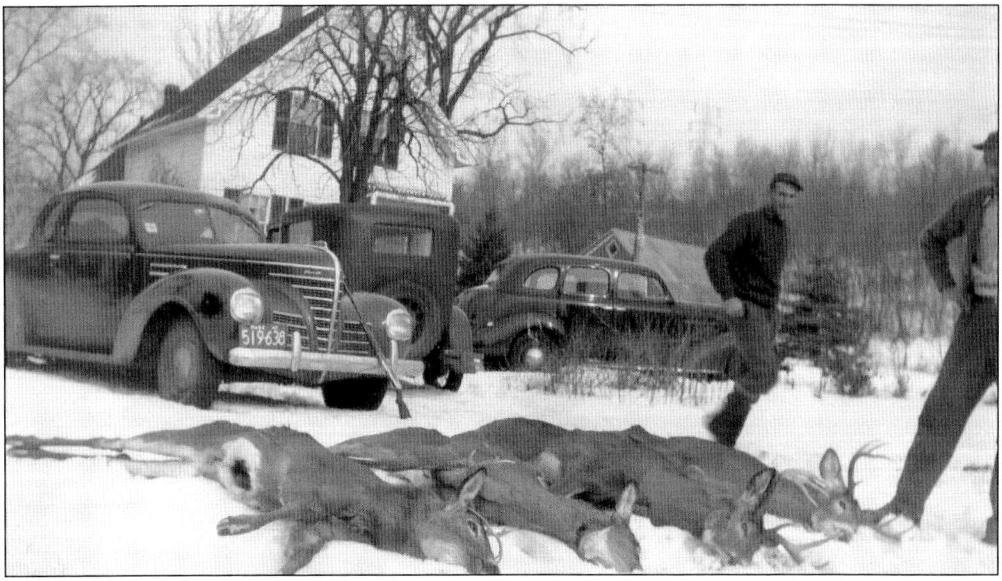

Hunting was an important way to enhance a family's supply of meat and leather along with being one way of reducing the numbers of deer and bobcats. It was also sport. In front of the Goldthwaite house on Henry Street, Herman "Dutch" Stockwell and Charles Stockwell display the results of their hunt. (Courtesy of Judith Schaefer.)

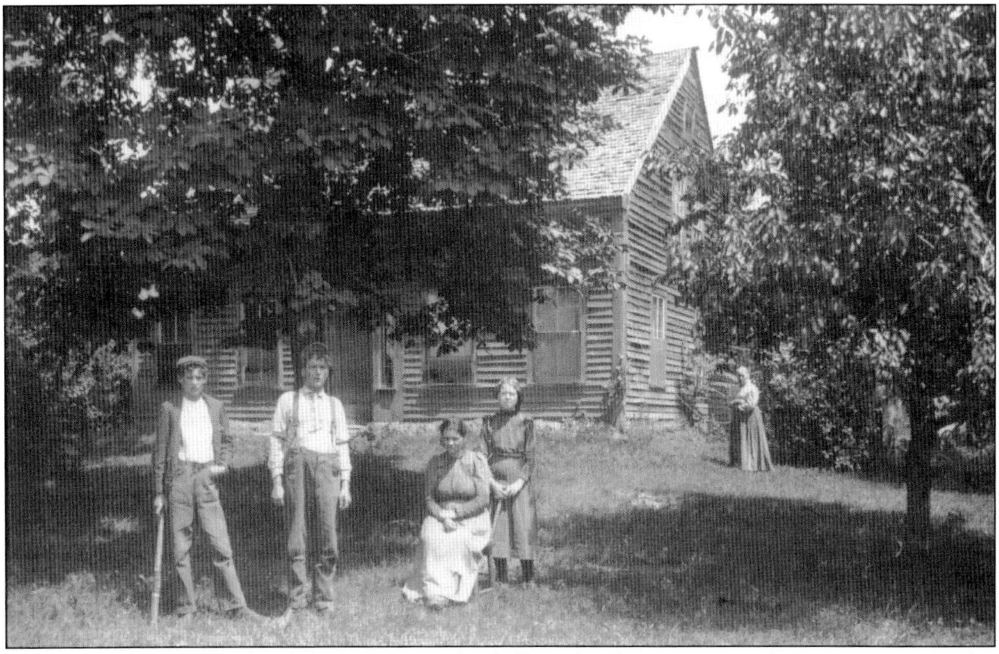

The Plantinger family lived farther down the hill in this house on North East Street. Shirley Whittemore remembers Sarah Plantinger coming to buy eggs. She would announce that her family was descended from Polish kings, but to save money she would only buy eggs that were cracked. The family shown here in the 1890s is unidentified.

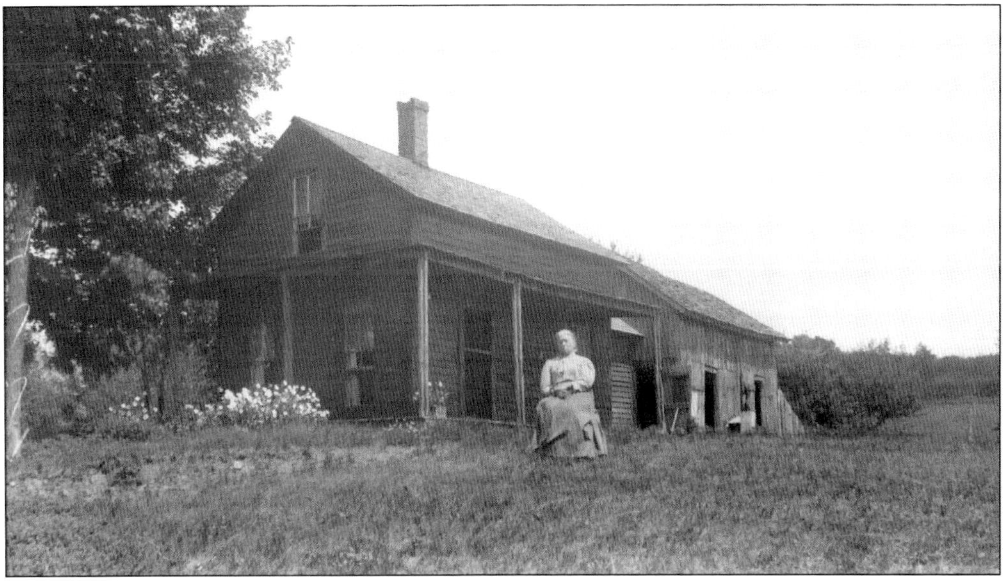

This house on North East Street, shown in the 1890s, became the home of Earl and Florence (McDonald) Robinson in the early 1940s. Florence's mother, who was born in England, had been a cook for the Charles Lindbergh family in Bridgeport, Connecticut. Earl Robinson worked in the physical plant at Amherst College, and they lived all their married life in the house, raising their family. Below are William and Myron Robinson, ages two and one. In the summer of 1948, their younger brother Sanford, age three, was playing in the family barn when the hay suddenly caught on fire. His mother shouted for help, and their neighbor, Katy Spear, dashed into the blazing barn and carried Sanford out to safety. The barn, three tons of hay, and farm equipment were a total loss. (Below, courtesy of William Robinson.)

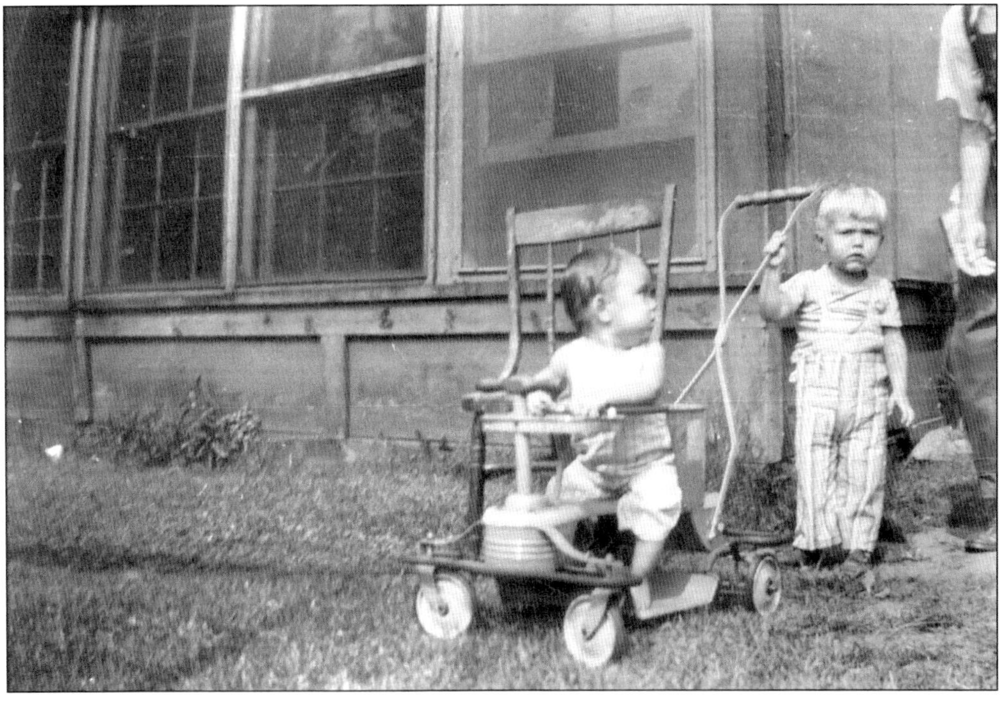

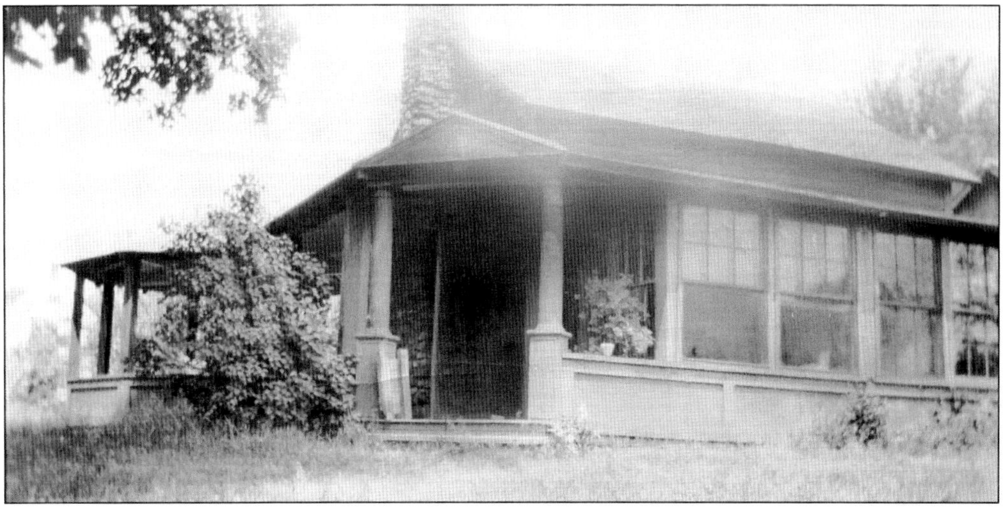

The Robinsons' house is shown above in the 1930s, remodeled from the earlier version shown on the previous page, a much more spacious porch added on to the north, and the south-facing porch enclosed. Below, in November 1972, the Robinson family gathered for Thanksgiving Day. There were seven children in the Robinson family, six boys and finally a daughter. Not all were present for Thanksgiving Day. From left to right are Sanford, Earl (father), Stephen, Florence (mother), William, Donna (William's wife), Paul, and Myron. The grandchildren are April and Matthew Sanford. Florence Robinson used to play the organ at the Grace Episcopal Church in Amherst. (Above, courtesy of Phyllis E. Longto; below, courtesy of William Robinson.)

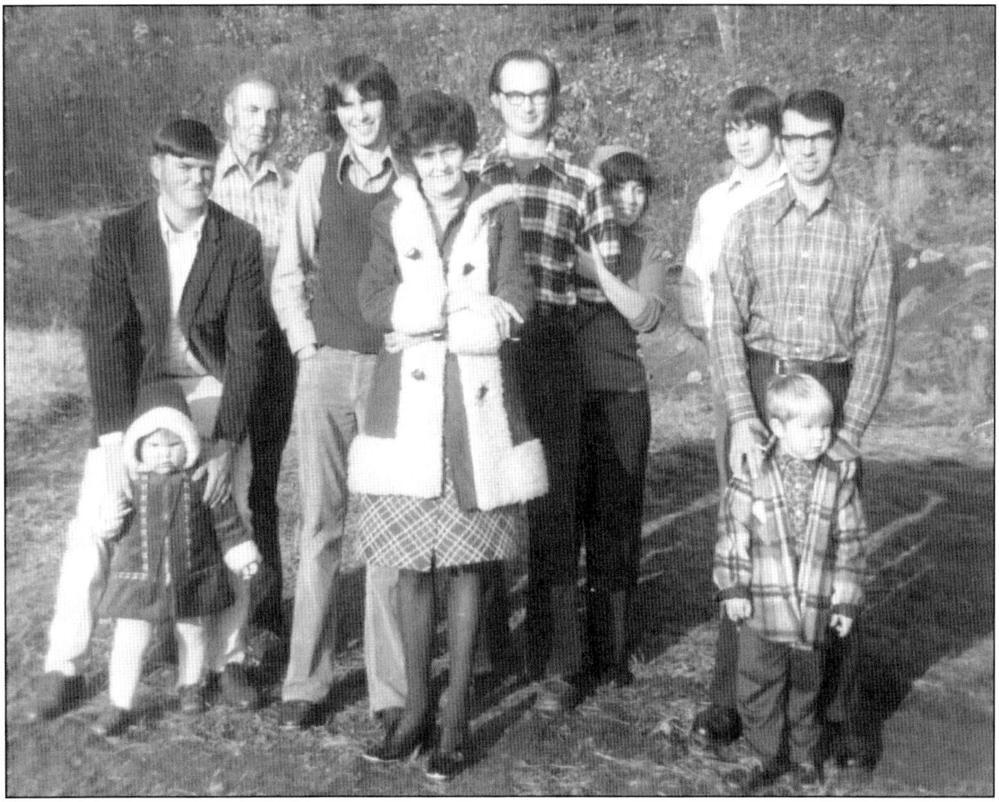

Six

East Pleasant Street, Pine Street, and North Pleasant Street

The land off the western side of East Pleasant Street has belonged for many years to the University of Massachusetts. Now occupied by dormitories, the location was called Orchard Hill, and many of the old apple and pear trees still blossom and grow. The school was founded in 1863 as the land grant Massachusetts Agricultural College, became Massachusetts State College in 1931, and the University of Massachusetts Amherst in 1947. Farther down that hill is the house of the president of the university. The house is on a site called Prexy's Hill. That area includes a parcel of old-growth forest, a place where the trees have never been logged. The rest of the land in the area has been logged, first for farming, and since the 1950s, for housing development. Development began in earnest in 1948 when the college expanded to meet the demands of veterans, with their GI Bill funds, for college education. Both Amherst College and the university increased enrollments for students and thus the size of their faculties. In 1947, as town historian James A. Smith has written, sewers were put in both in North Amherst and along East Pleasant Street all the way to Cushman. Water mains were extended, and a town inspection service was created. All this was done to permit and encourage more home-building. Along with the increase in population came a demand for better schools. The children of some college faculty often went off to private schools when they reached high school, but most people, including a good portion of faculty members, could not afford private schools. Old schools were closed, and new ones built. Meanwhile, the university expanded its enrollment from 6,500 in 1960 to 21,000 in 1970. Amherst College increased in size as well, and a new school, Hampshire College, started in 1970. East Pleasant Street, which in the 1930s was an unpaved country road, is now a busy through road.

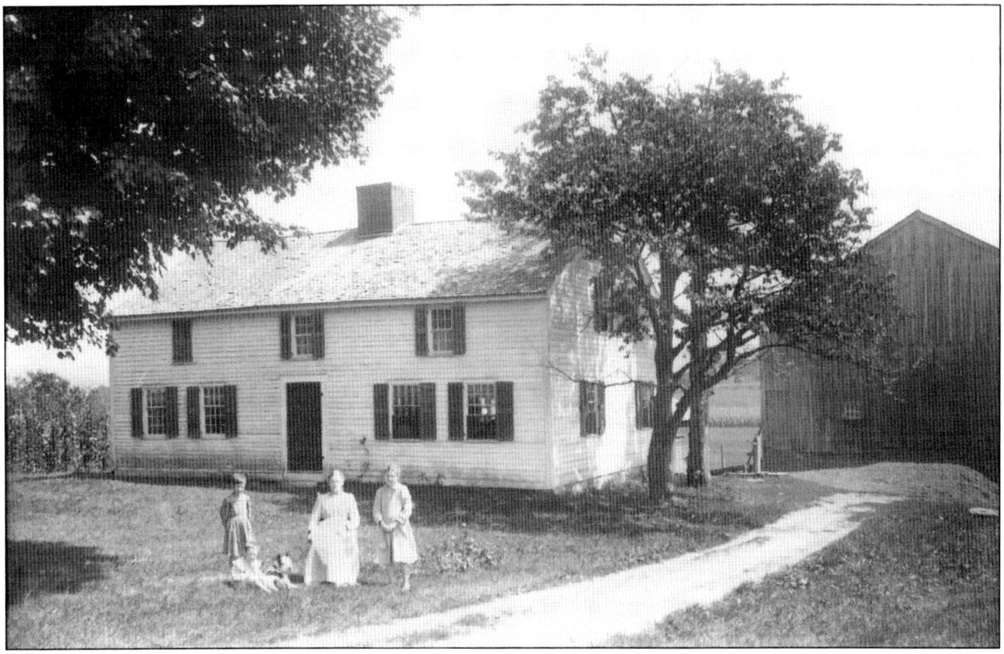

Ruth and Richard Hooke lived for many years raising their two children in this house at 437 East Pleasant Street that was built in the 1700s. It had low ceilings, narrow, steep stairs, and a center chimney with openings into three rooms. The house is pictured above in a Howes Brothers photograph from the 1890s. A mother sits comfortably in a chair with her children and dog around her. They are dressed for summer. The well is visible toward the back, and the barn presents an imposing solidity set off by a tiny window. Below is the same house on a wintry day in the 1980s. (Below, courtesy of Ruth Hooke.)

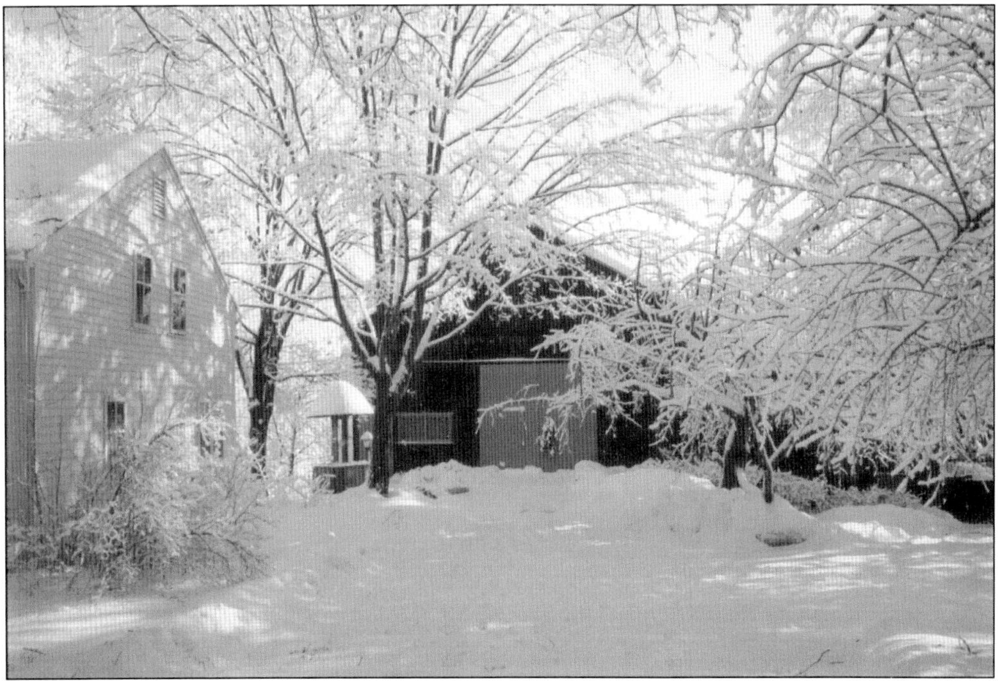

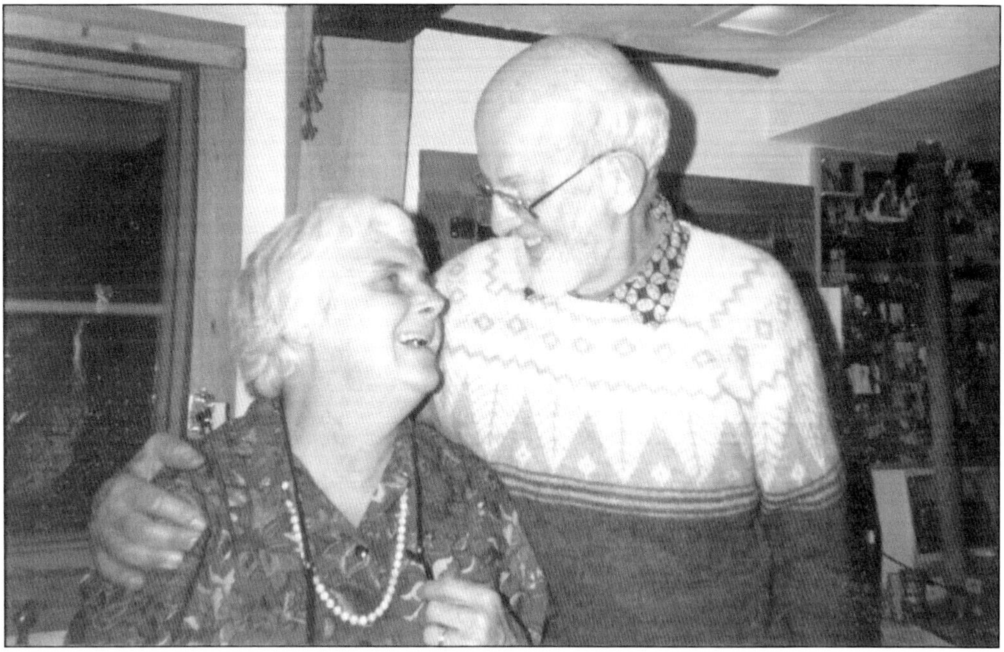

The Hookes loved having friends over for potluck dinners and singing on Friday evenings. Richard Hooke played a variety of instruments, including the viola da gamba, and their daughter played a small accordion. Above are Ruth and Richard at one of their evenings. Richard Hooke was a skilled and imaginative artist and craftsman, and his old barn was his studio. He worked on his whirligigs and paintings there and also ran a school called the Dancing Possum to teach woodworking to children. Here, this class of girls and boys is getting ready to launch the sailboats they made. (Both courtesy of Ruth Hooke.)

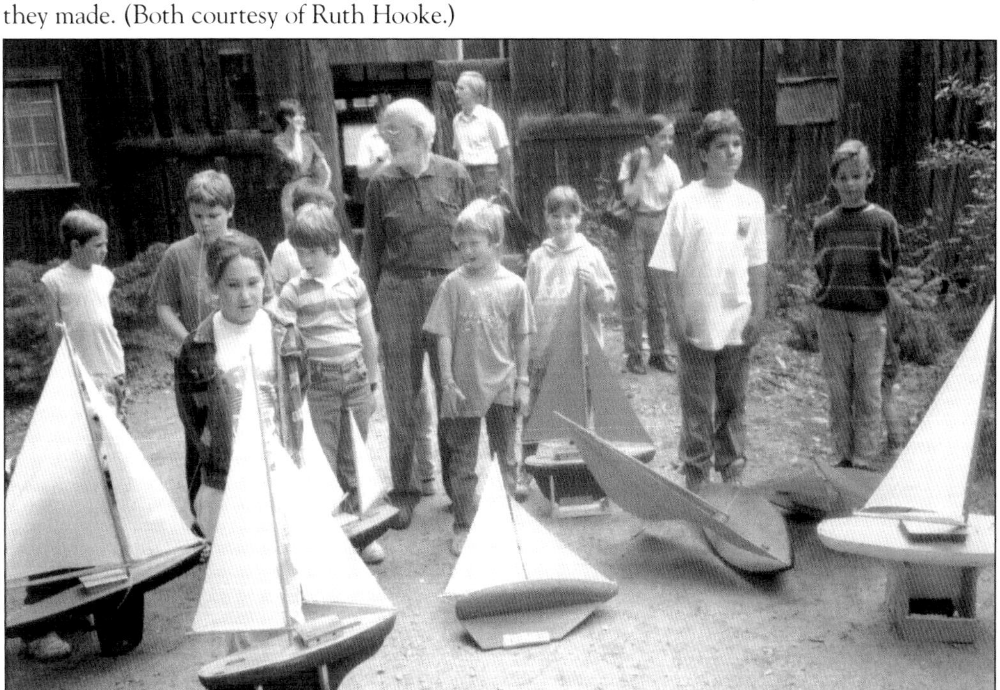

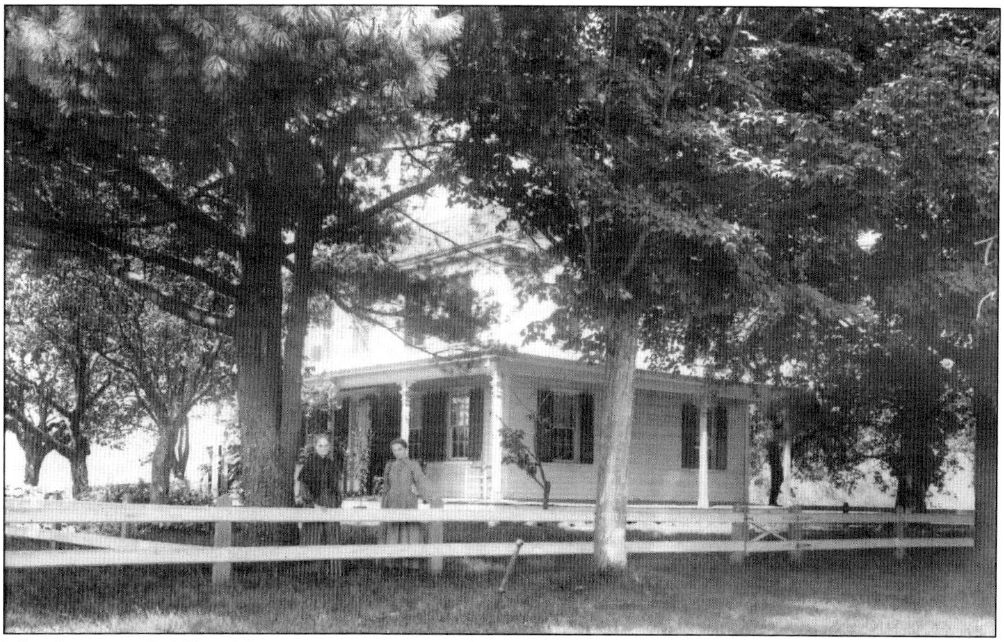

This house at 512 East Pleasant Street is now demolished. It used to sit on top of a hill overlooking an apple orchard, but now the university owns the land. Eastward and well off the street are two large, low-income housing projects and a fraternity park. One house is a university office. There is also the police station for the university and a large concrete fire station for the town.

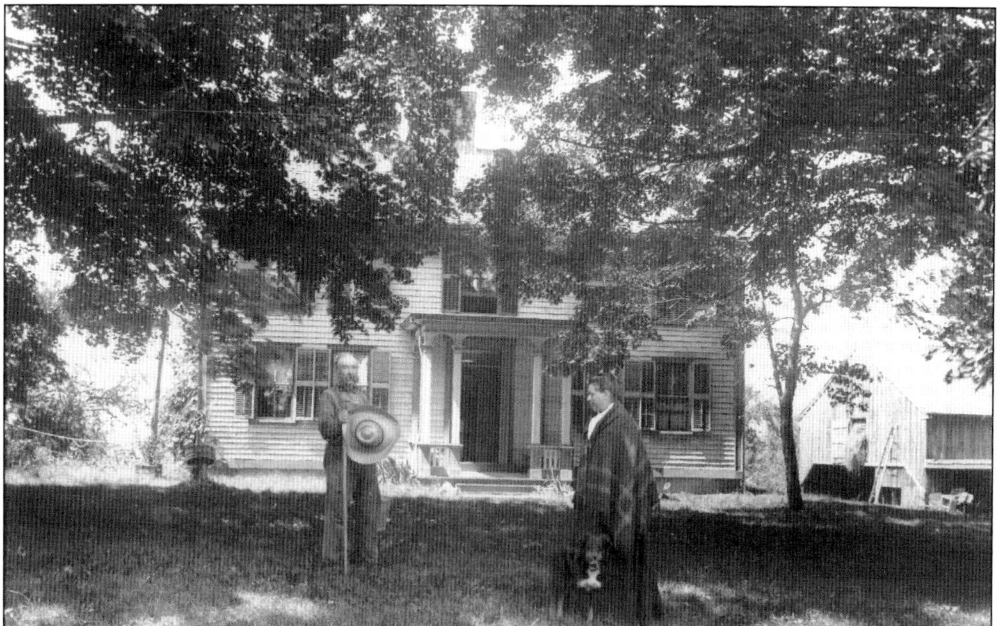

610 East Pleasant Street is the address of this stately home. The names of the man with a straw hat, the woman with a blanket, and her dog with its mouth full are not known. The house now belongs to Merle and Billie Howes, stalwarts in town affairs who maintain lovely grounds.

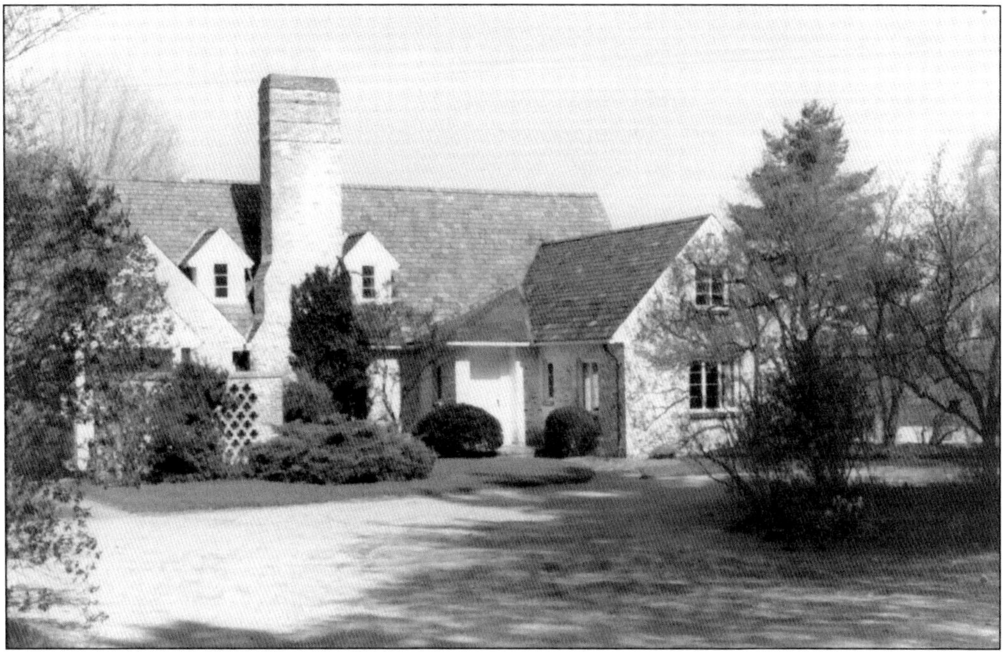

This house at 535 East Pleasant Street is now the Massachusetts Center for Interdisciplinary Renaissance Studies, which is devoted to collecting materials about the European renaissance, and sponsoring plays, games, and workshops for academics and the general public. It is under the auspices of the university and directed by Prof. Arthur F. Kinney. Here are two views in different seasons. The property used to belong to Winthrop and Janet Dakin, who built the house in 1948 and willed it to the University of Massachusetts. It has magnificent views in back of the valley and hills to the west, and the formal gardens consist of brick and crushed stone walks and a central pool bordered by clipped boxwood hedges.

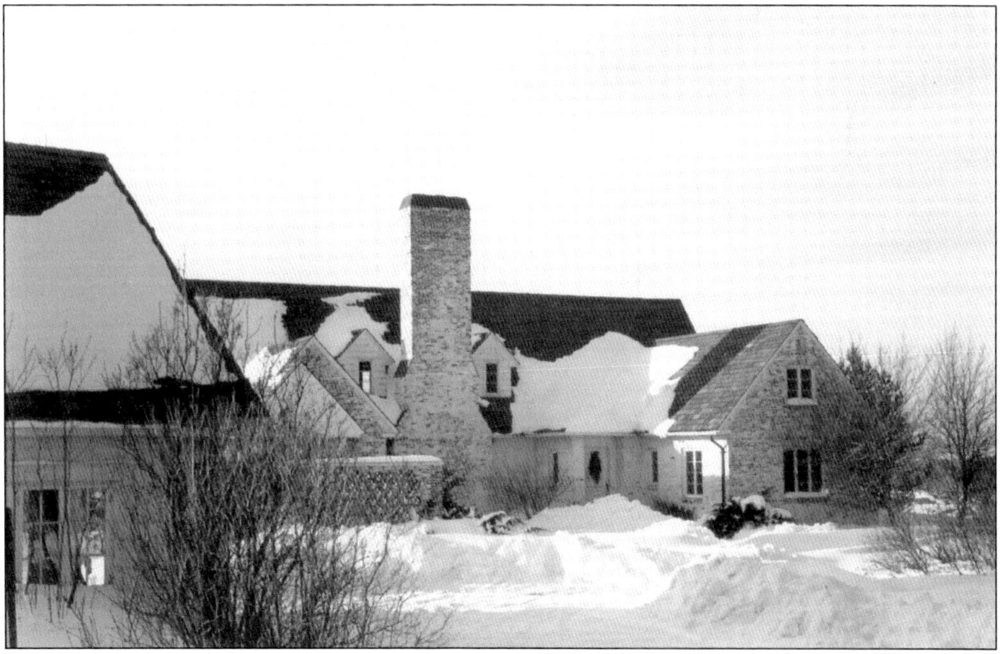

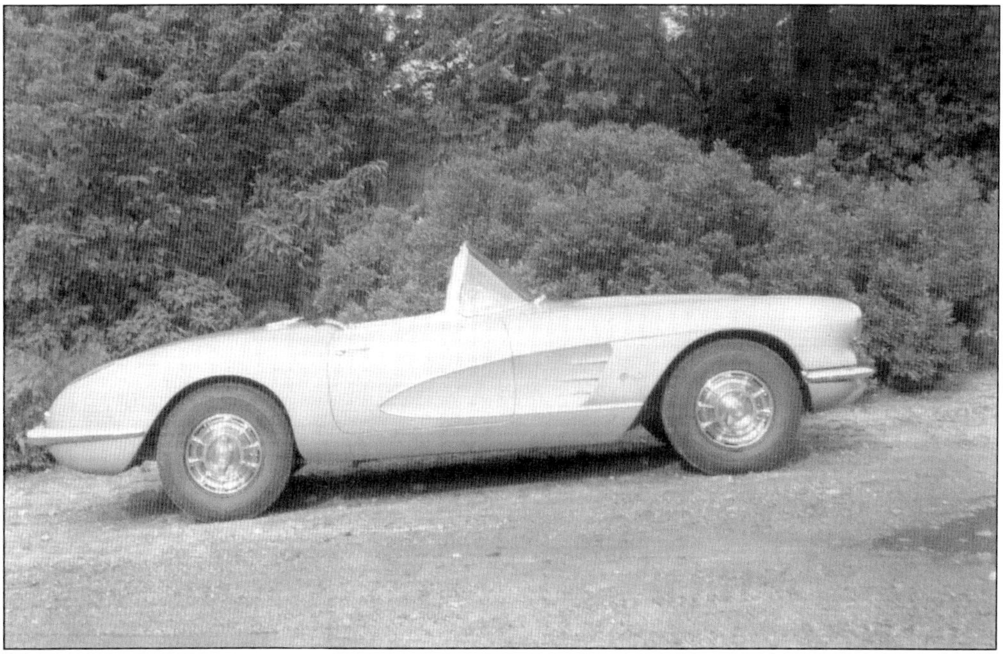

The Dakins were wealthy and well traveled. Janet Dakin was devoted to her horses, Winthrop Dakin to his cars, one of which, a Corvette, is pictured above. Winthrop "Toby" Dakin (1906–1982) had a law office in Northampton. He met Janet Wilder while she was teaching zoology at Mount Holyoke College just before World War II. They married in 1941 and became involved in the war effort. He was chief of the international law branch in the judge advocate general's office in Washington, D.C. The couple did not have children. He served as a town meeting moderator and was one of the original trustees of Hampshire College in Amherst.

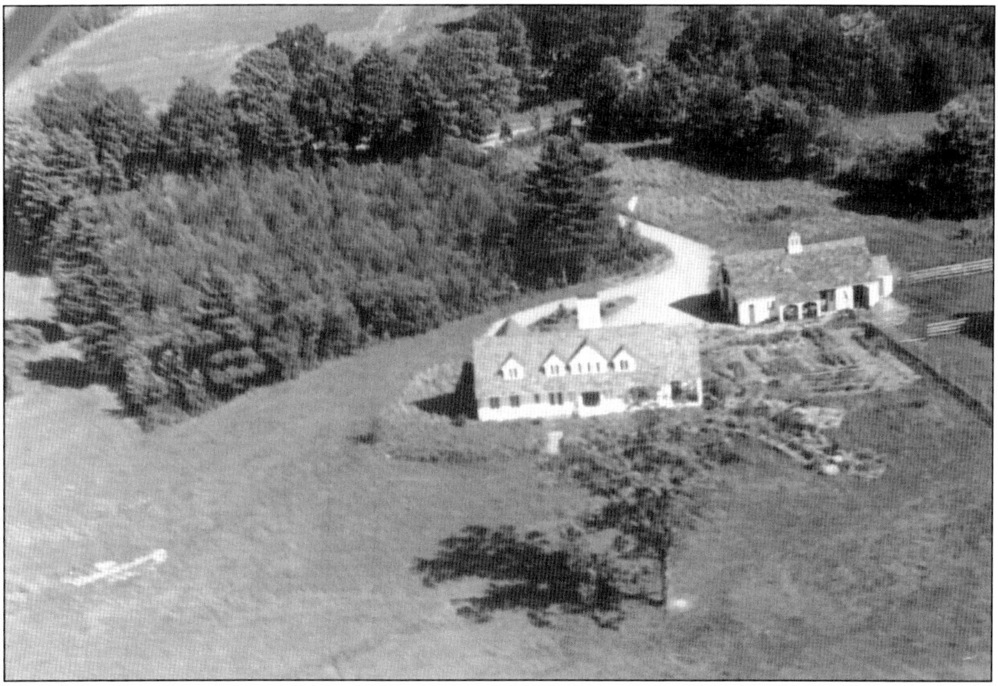

Janet Frances Wilder (1910–1984) was born in Berkeley, California. Her brother was the playwright Thornton Wilder. She was active with Morgan horse societies and worked for the preservation of open land for wildlife and for recreational and educational purposes. She was a charter member of the Amherst Conservation Commission from 1962 to 1974, which worked to preserve the Holyoke Range. In 1970, she founded and served as executive director of the Kestrel Trust, a private land trust that acquired land in neighboring communities for conservation purposes. The Dakins gave a large collection of their papers to the Jones Library in Amherst along with photograph albums documenting their many travels around the world. The photograph of her at right was taken in December 1940; the one of Winthrop below was taken in 1943.

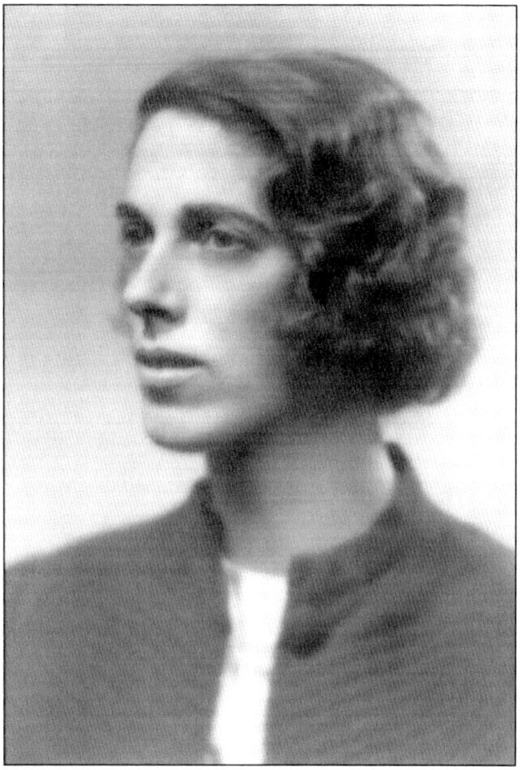

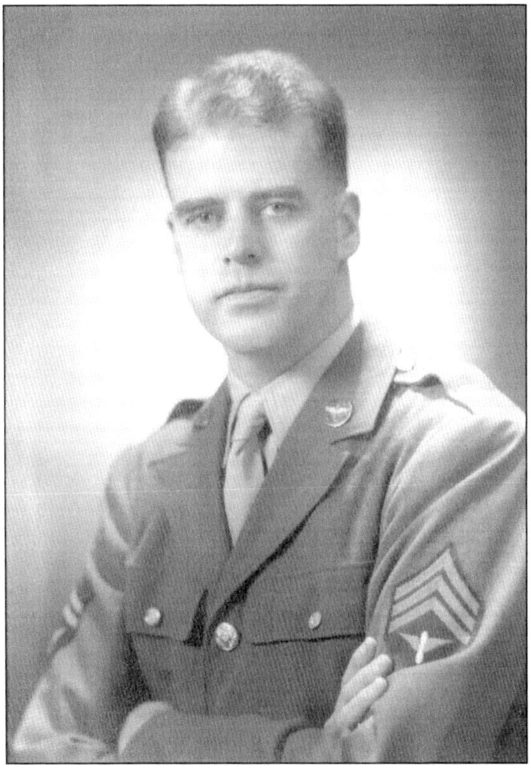

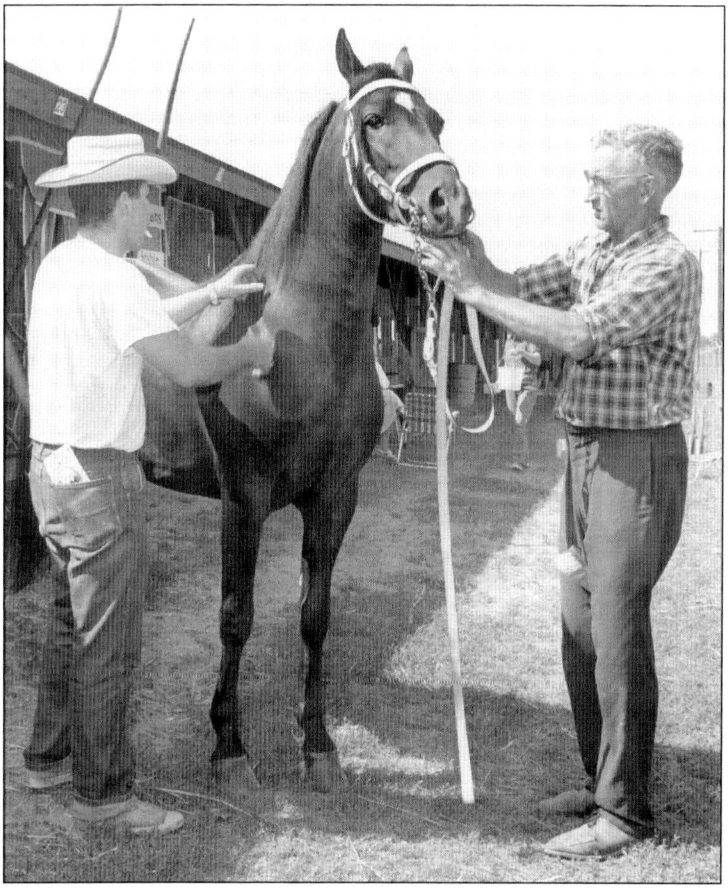

To the north, Richard Nelson's farm was located at 676 East Pleasant Street. Nelson, on the right in the photograph at left, was the director of the equine center at the university. In 1955, he sponsored the first annual Tally-Ho 4-H Riding Club's field day festival there. That group has been meeting at different locations in Amherst ever since. Linda Goodall, 13, below at left, did her riding bareback. Marjorie Rockwell, 16, right, from Cushman, talks with Linda and Susan Hummel while waiting for her event.

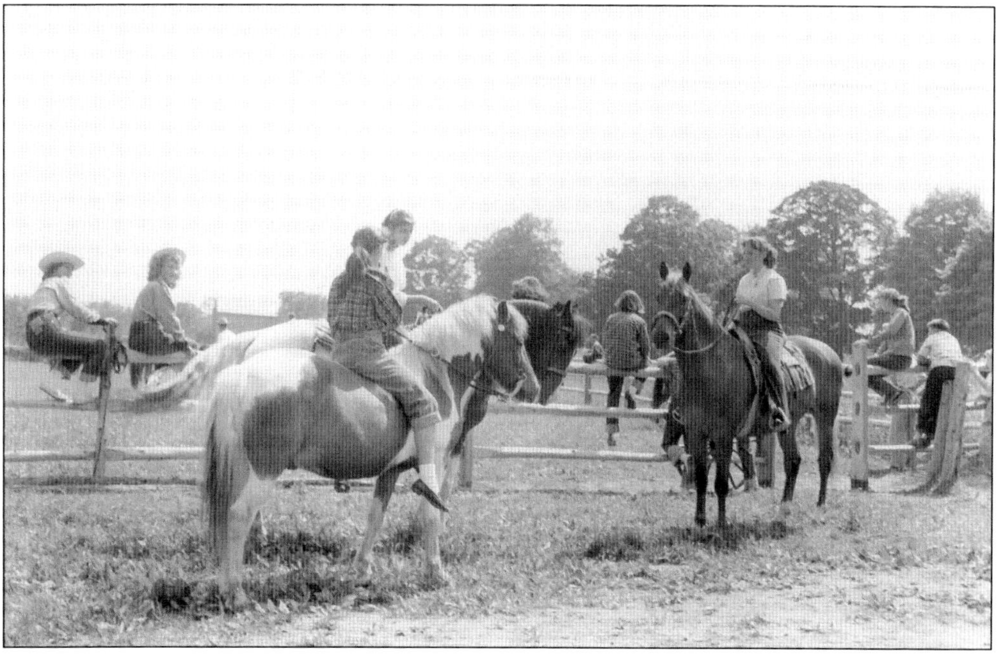

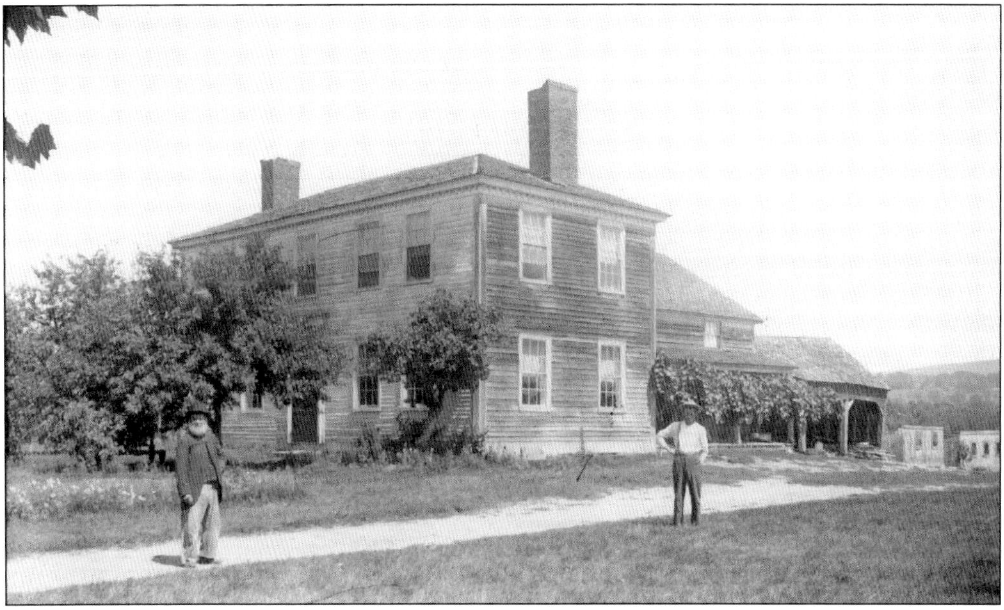

According to a note with this photograph, this was the Ebenezer Matoon house owned by Ellen M. Humphrey in 1900. Later, Alice Clarke Mullen lived with her sister there, raised chickens, and did some rebuilding. In the 1960s, it was the home of John and Virginia Callahan. Below, this house across the street at 868 East Pleasant was the home of Ellis Chandler Harlow who owned the Jerseydale Farms and pioneered in breeding Jersey cows. Though the house is still there, a housing development called Grandview Heights, built in 1965, put close to 100 houses on the farmland. The realtor held a naming contest and many of the streets acquired names like Van Meter, Hartman, and Harlow, honoring prominent local people. The section of the house on the right was moved some distance away and is now a separate dwelling.

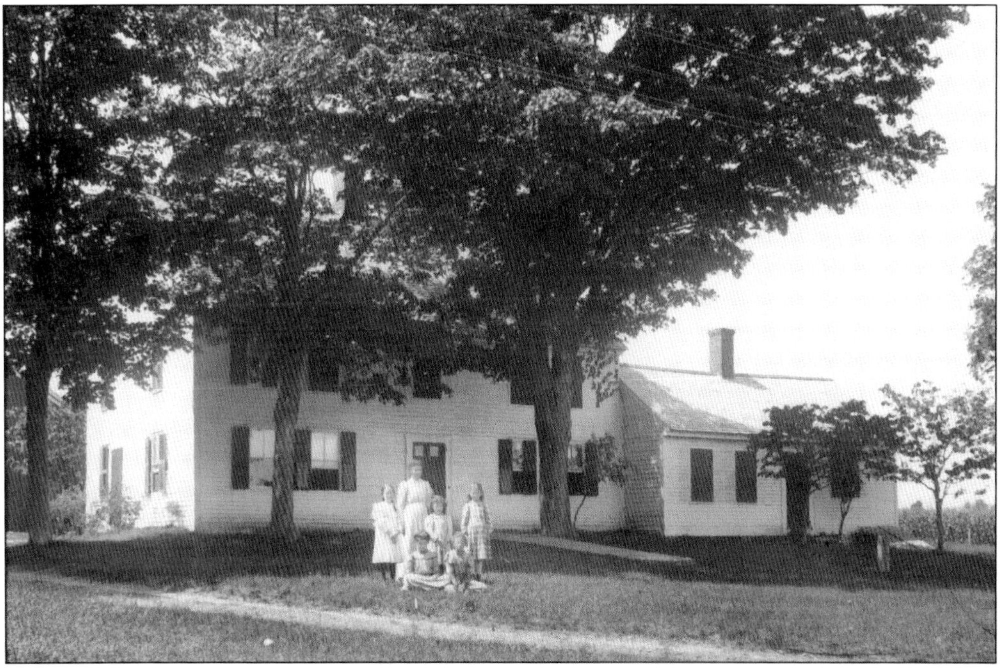

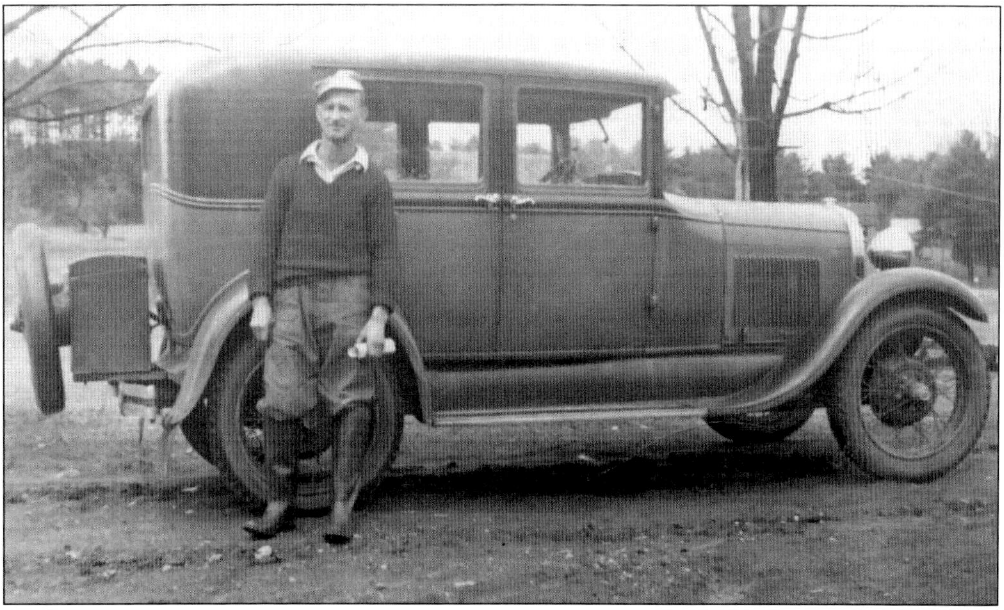

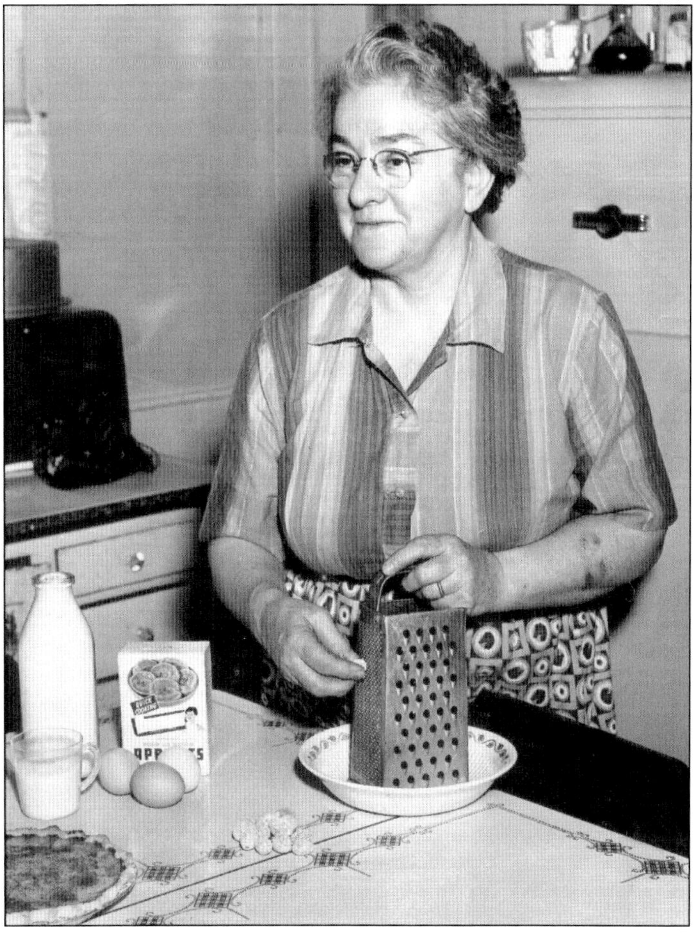

Frank and Emma Bowen lived for several years on East Pleasant Street starting in 1928, when Frank worked on Mr. Harlow's big farm. The pay was $20 a week plus a house and all the milk the family of six needed. Frank Bowen's job was to clear the farmland of trees to make a pasture. On January 27, 1939, he was hitching two horse-drawn wagons together when a horse pulled on a chain Bowen was carrying. The chain coiled around his hand, crushing all the bones. A surgeon saved his hand, but he had to stop working, and his wife, at left, went to work at a store in Cushman. Later, Fred Ruder Sr., a veterinarian, hired him to help with the animals and tend their large gardens. (Both courtesy of Isabelle Callahan.)

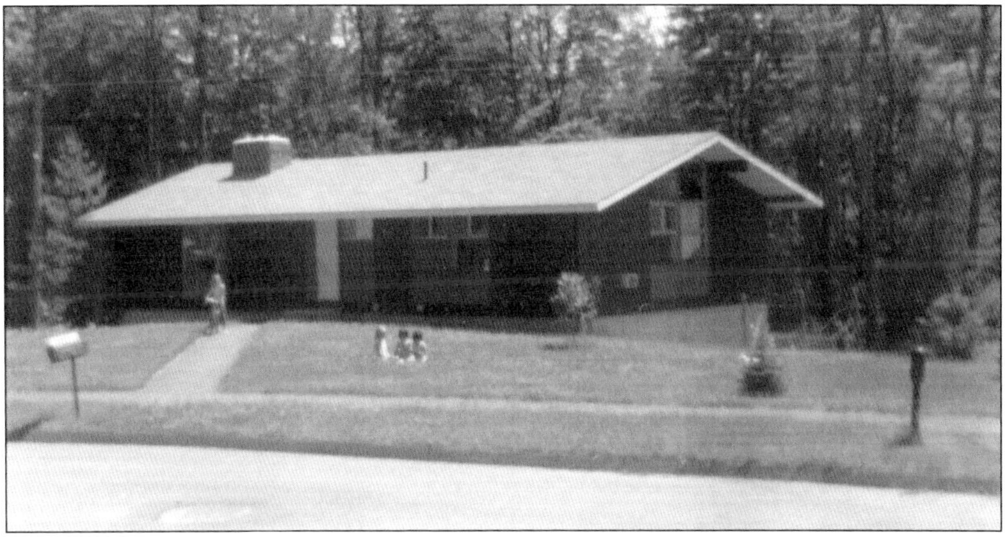

On the east side of East Pleasant Street the developer Donald Grant put in houses on a field where Frank Bowen had pulled stumps many years earlier. Toward the back of the development, a few families put in so-called modern houses designed by the Tech-Built company. A big truck would deliver the preassembled sides and ends of the houses, and a builder could assemble the pieces in a day or two. Shown above in 1967 is a Tech-Built house at 105 Blackberry Lane; below, Jon and Lucy Barber pose with their neighbor's Tech-Built in the background. (Courtesy of Patricia Holland.)

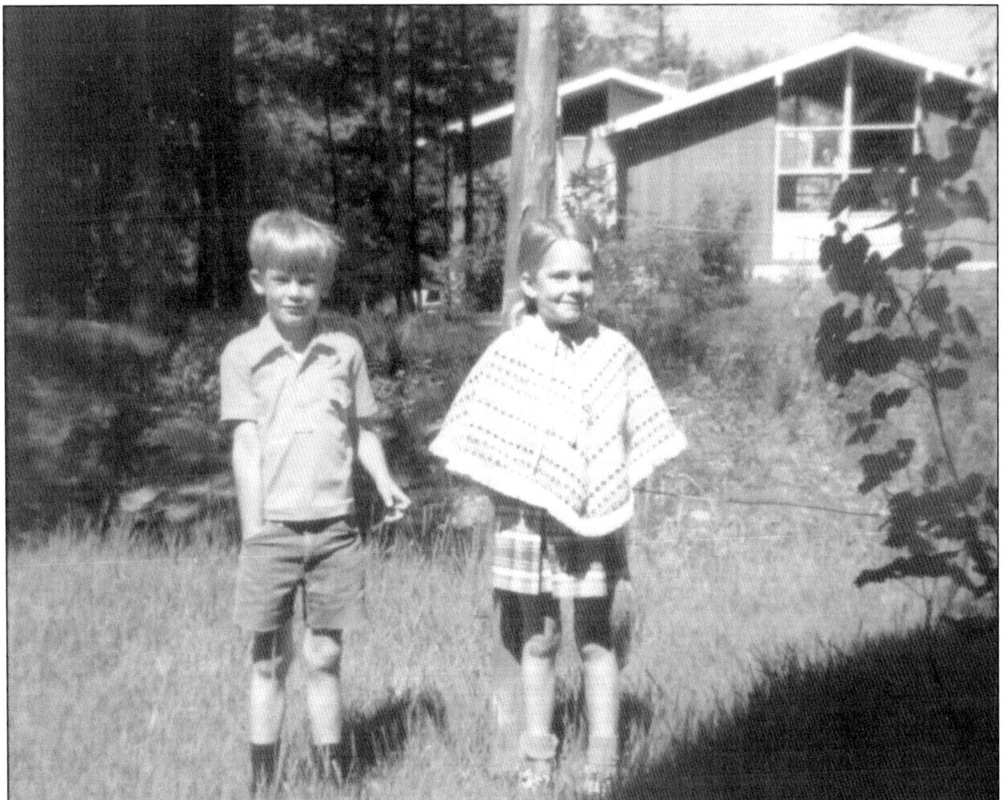

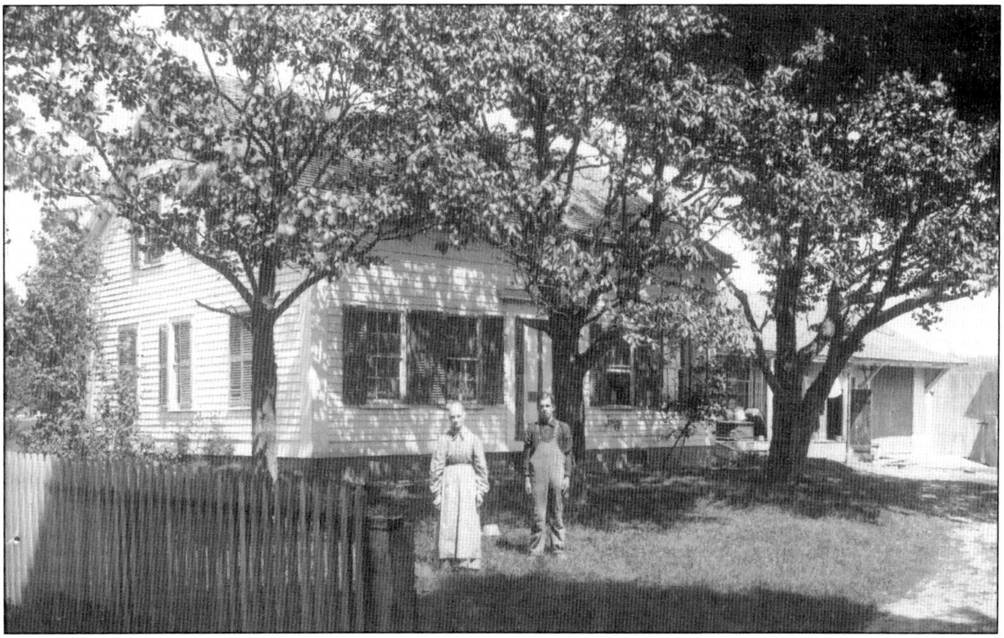

Here is an 1890s view of a house at 869 East Pleasant Street, currently empty and in need of repair. In 1957, John and Annette Quinlan lived here. He worked with the local highway department and she was a nurse working in Leeds, Massachusetts, probably at the veterans' hospital there.

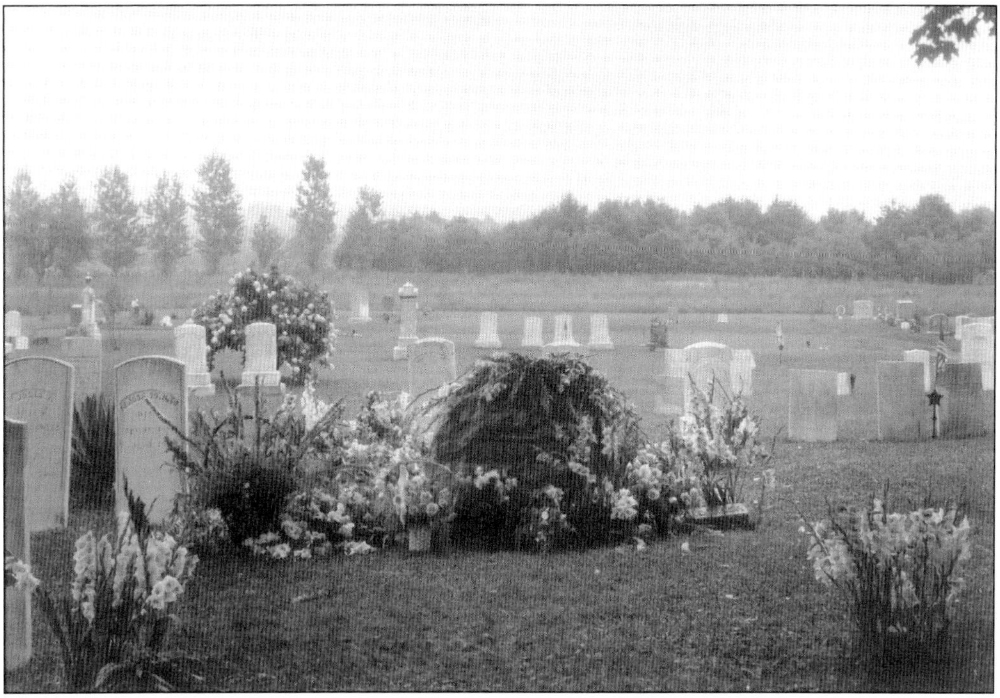

This photograph shows the graves of Enoch and Julia B. Cowles in the North Amherst Cemetery. Rev. George Cooke commented on the cemetery in 1883, "There was nothing about it suggestive of sentiments appropriate to a resting place of loved ones, on the other hand its bleak, forbidding aspect added a repulsive feature to the repulsiveness of death itself."

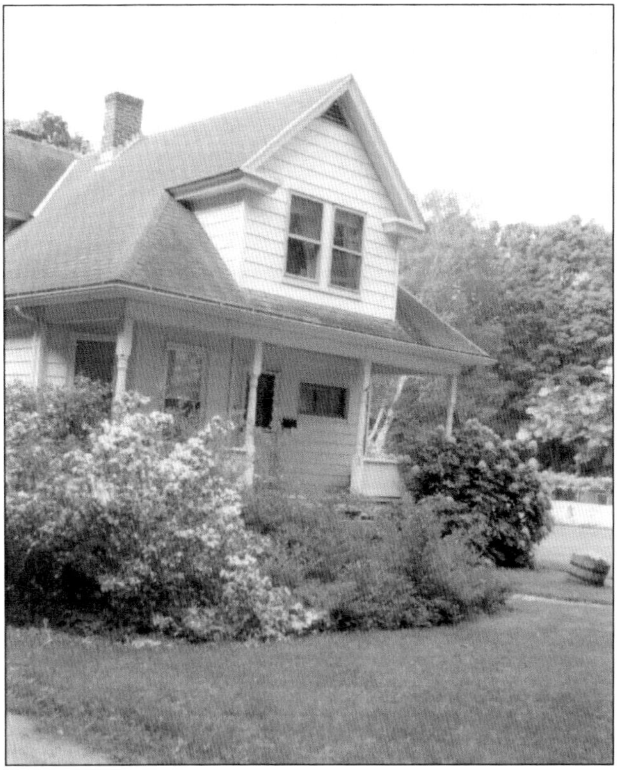

Towards the end of East Pleasant Street, Joe Doktor had a bomb shelter in his house on the southwest corner of the intersection with Pine Street. At the end is the farmhouse for the Ostrowski farm. Other buildings on the property burned in 1955, and now there is a housing development there. Left down Pine Street toward North Amherst Center is 107 Pine Street, where a house was built in 1912. (Courtesy of Edna Ball.)

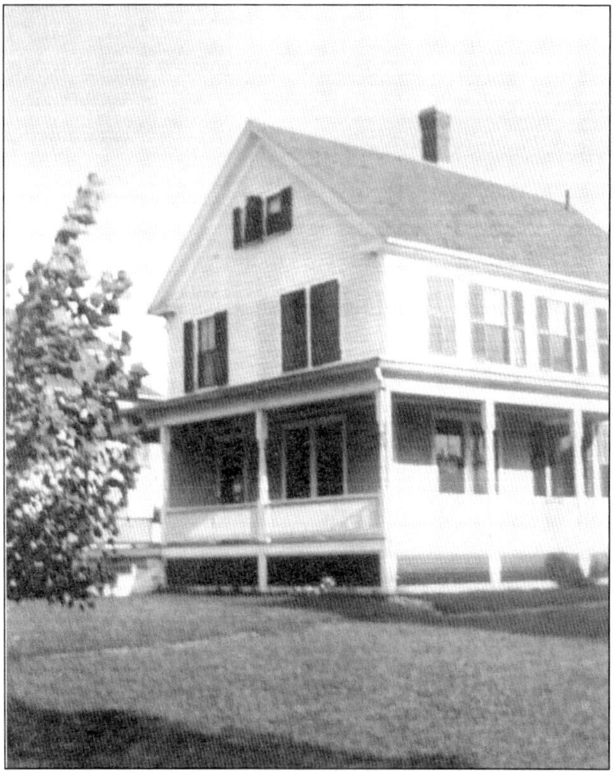

At 33 Pine Street is the house of Lucia Church, pictured here around 1914. Built about 1900, it is a vernacular Victorian with a high foundation and wraparound porch similar, though not identical, to its neighbors. Shirley Whittemore, who later ran the Cushman store, lived here in 1940.

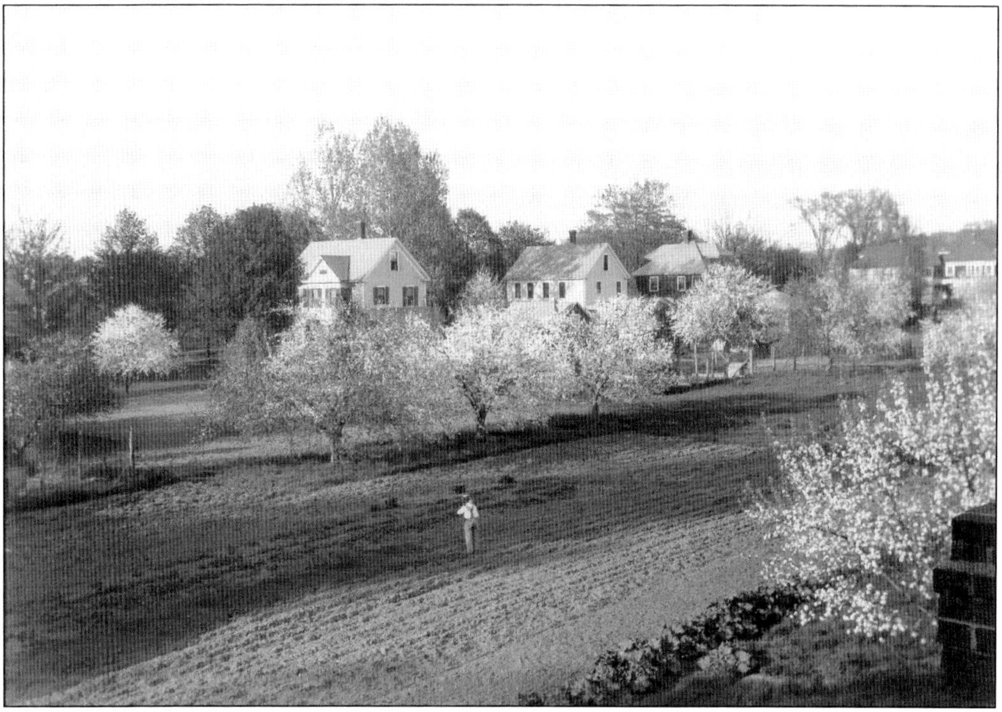

The photograph above shows the row of houses on Pine Street from the rear. Edgar Scott, the photographer, titled it "Apple Blossoms, May 10, 1930." He lived at the Old Ladies' Home on North Pleasant Street and took this photograph from the third floor. Below is a photograph of the same location in winter. From left to right, the houses belong to Carl and Clara Billings, Cora Grover and her sister Lucia Church, James and Maud Brown, William Loomis, Walter and Cornelia Hatch, George and Addie Ball, and Ed and Dorothy Hagen.

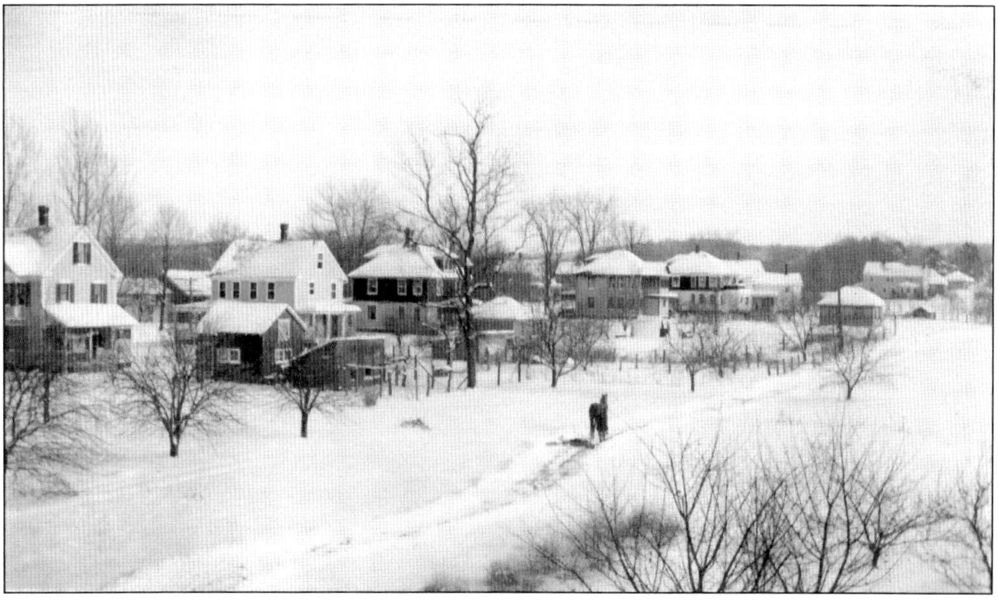

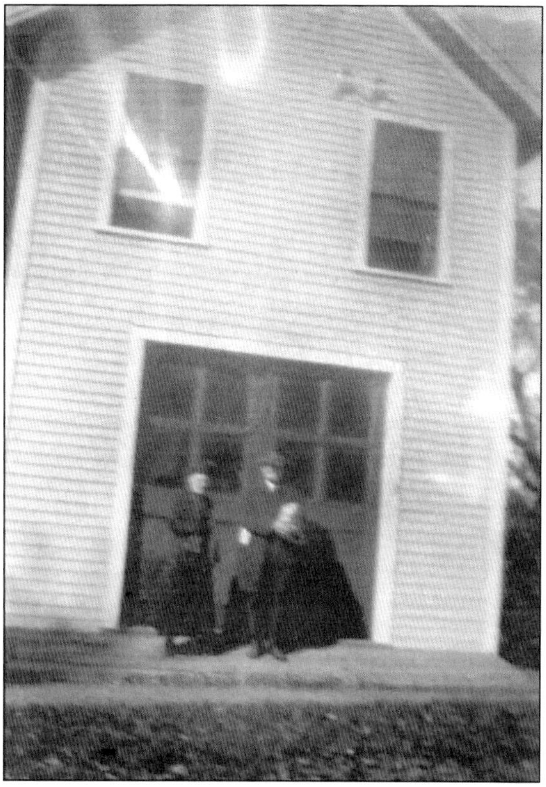

The North Fire Station, now turned into a dwelling, is a very plain building with a three-story hose tower. The firemen were volunteers who lived in homes nearby. Three stories were needed so the hose could be hung up to dry. The building was last used as a fire station in 1971; in 1974, a big new fire station opened on East Pleasant Street. The house next down the street at 10 Pine Street, just behind the church, belonged to Dr. Theron Temple during the mid- to late 1800s. Built about 1835, it had four entrances, probably to accommodate his practice as well as his family. Below is a group of North Amherst girls in the mid-1800s. Marcia Bates is in the second row, first on the left.

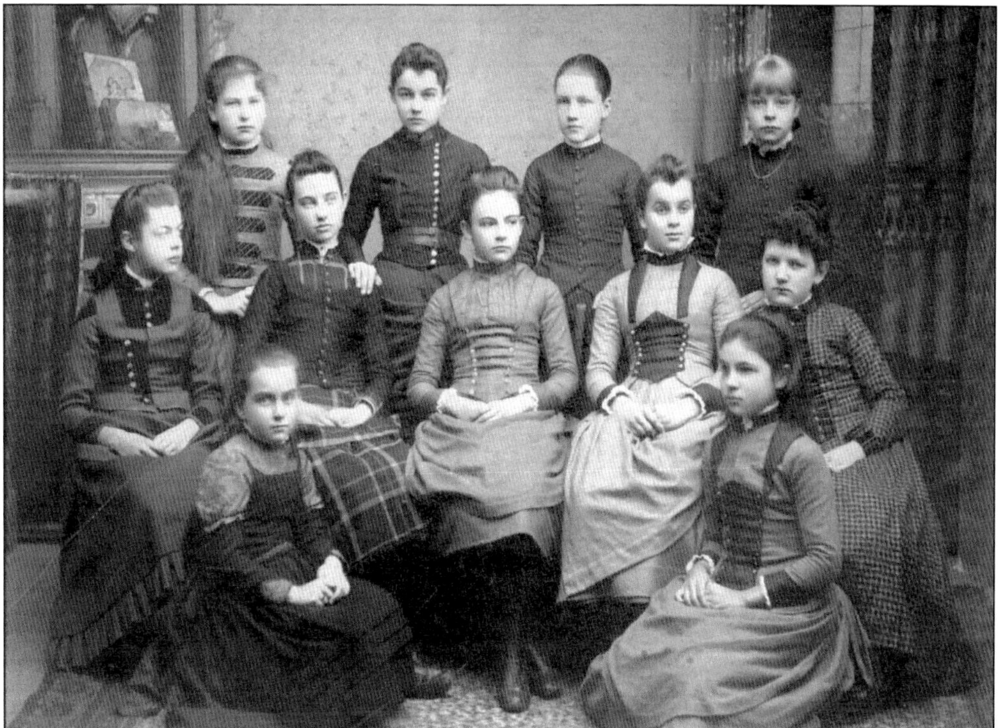

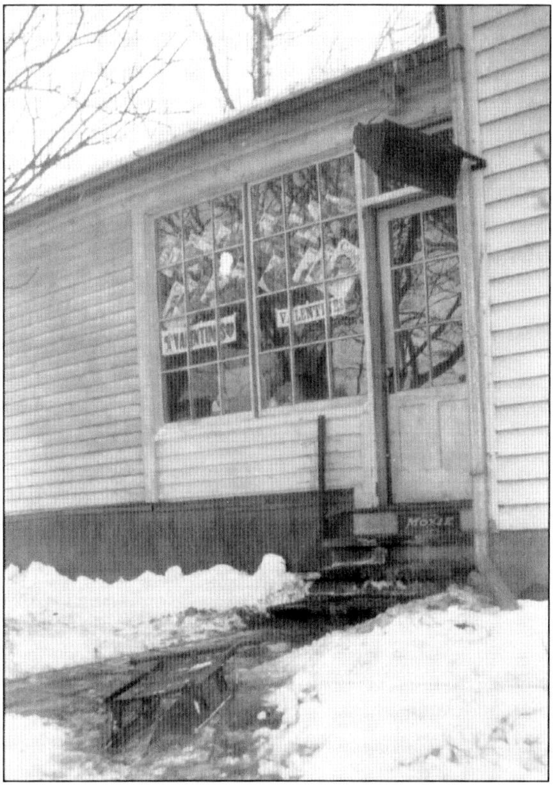

Nearing the center of North Amherst, there used to be a store run by the Bates family on the south side of Pine Street. The following was inscribed on the back of the photograph at left: "Store as it used to look when it had its beginnings in the back of the Bates Inn." It used to be an ell on the back of the inn that fronted on North Pleasant Street. Note all the Valentine's Day cards on display in the window and the sled on the walkway. Below, the store became part of a separate house behind the Bates Inn.

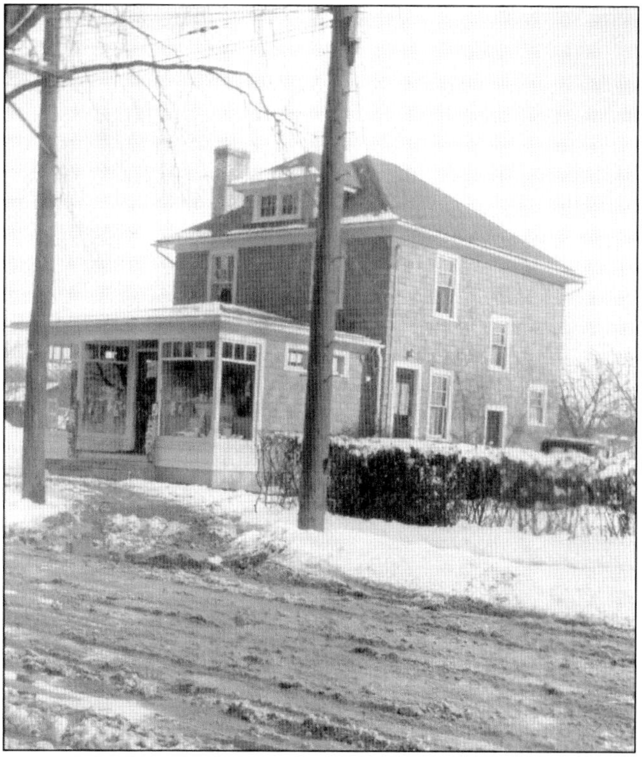

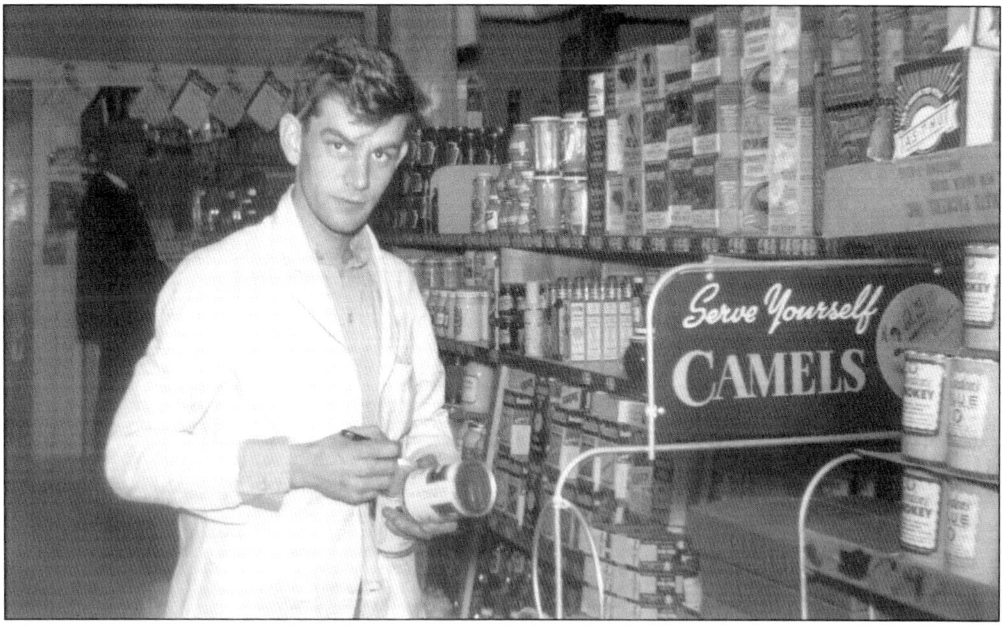

Above is a young man at work in the Bates store, perhaps marking the prices. Below is a photograph of the store's van, a 1952 Ford panel truck, with the phone number 655 on it. A few years later, Amherst telephones all had the exchange Alpine 3 plus four numbers; a decade later that became 253, and soon, additional exchanges were added. Isabel Callahan remembers four stores from the early 1960s: Stanwood King's, the old Dickinson store, the Bates store on Pine Street, and Ottinger's on North Pleasant Street, which also included the post office.

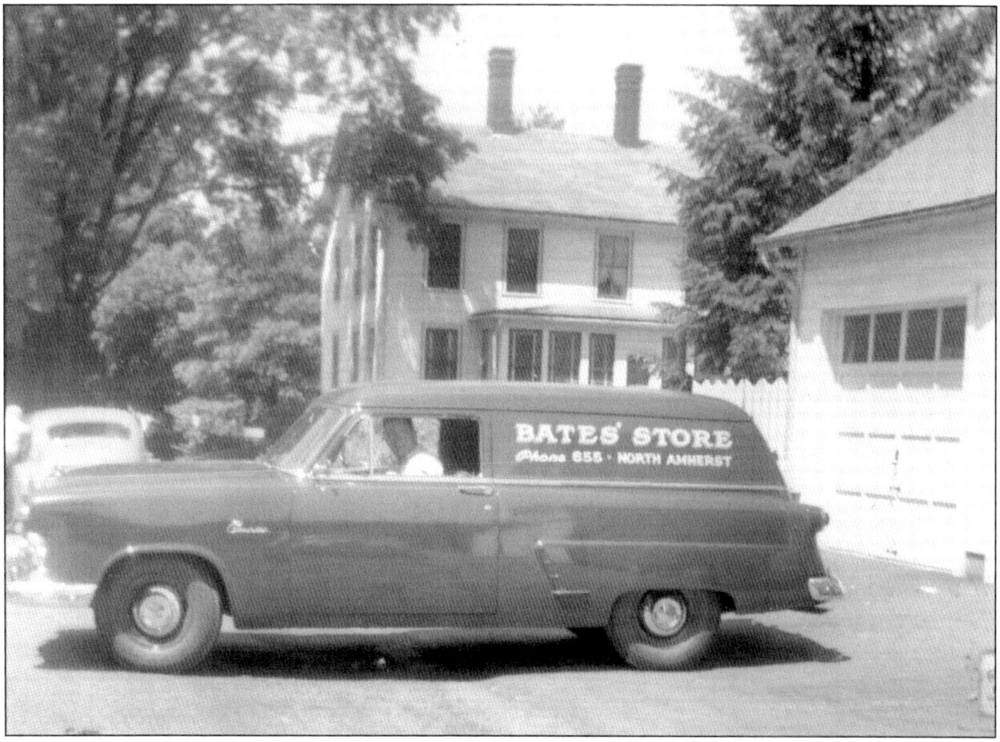

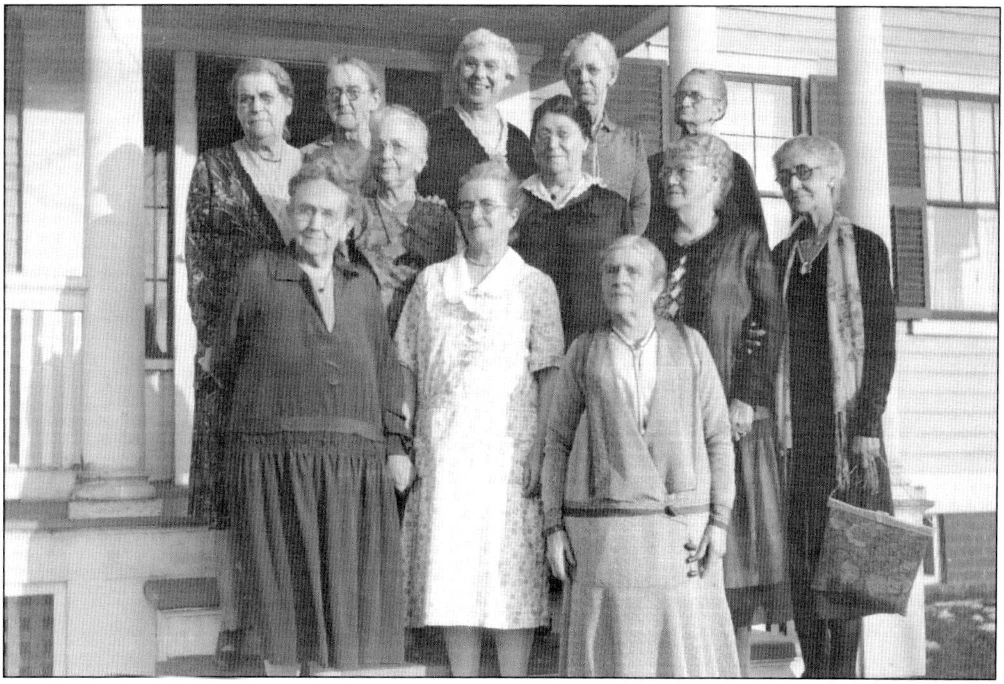

On the back of the photograph above is written: "The Birthday Club, North Amherst, all, now over 72, age, had annual dinner—without a skip—for past 32 years—all were married in North Amherst—all but Mrs. Cushman lived all the years after marriage in North Amherst." The photograph was dated December 31, 1929, though the clothing suggests a warmer time of year. It was probably taken at the Bates Inn in the center of North Amherst. Below is the view down North Pleasant Street with the trolley tracks, and on the left, the shop building that held the post office and a general store. A Japanese and Korean restaurant is there now. Just beyond that building is a house set right on the sidewalk—the Old Ladies' Home.

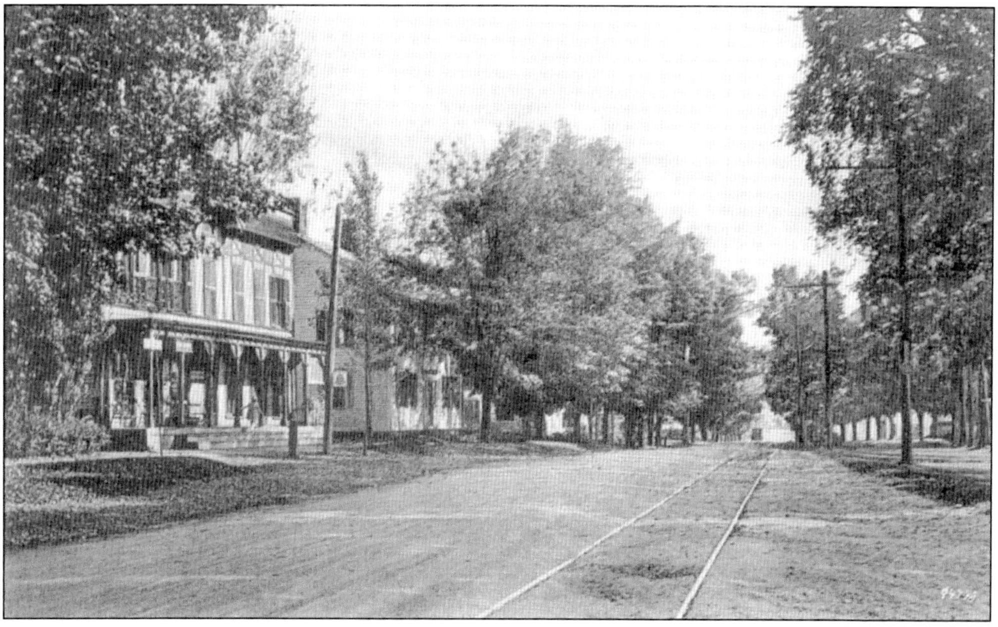

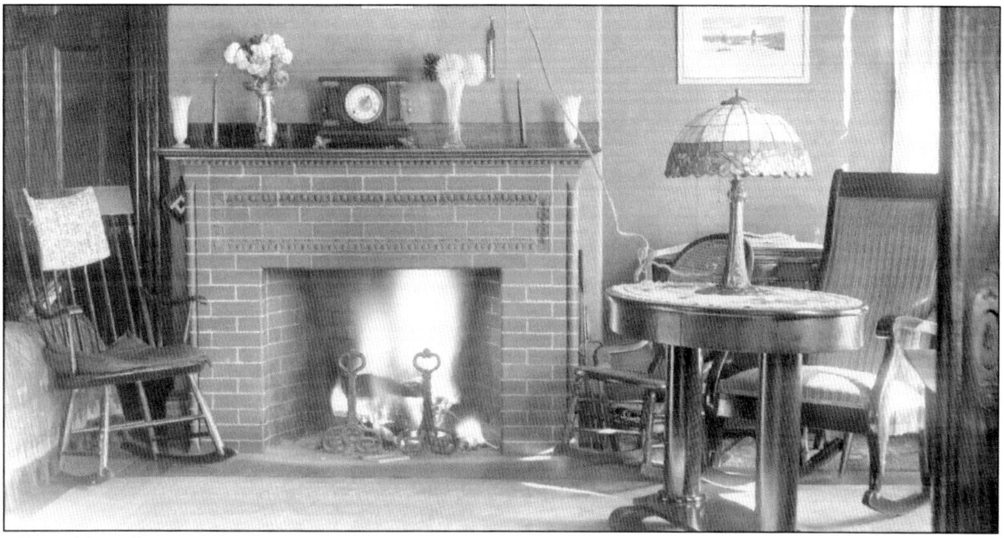

The Old Ladies' Home was formerly the home of Ellen Fisher, who in her will, designated it for the Old Ladies' Home. She died in 1906. In 1970, the house was moved to Hobart Lane to be a private residence. A new building set far back from the busy road was built. This was the ladies' living room about 1935. Below is a close-up view of the post office and A. Cloud general store. John Stetson is in the wheelchair. Rev. George Cooke recalled the post office as "an institution answering all the ordinary purposes of an Intelligence Office.— A resort of gossips and boys who had their projects to discuss.— And of loafers of older growth whose loud talk and laughter were the most striking symptoms of vitality in the week-day aspect of the parish."

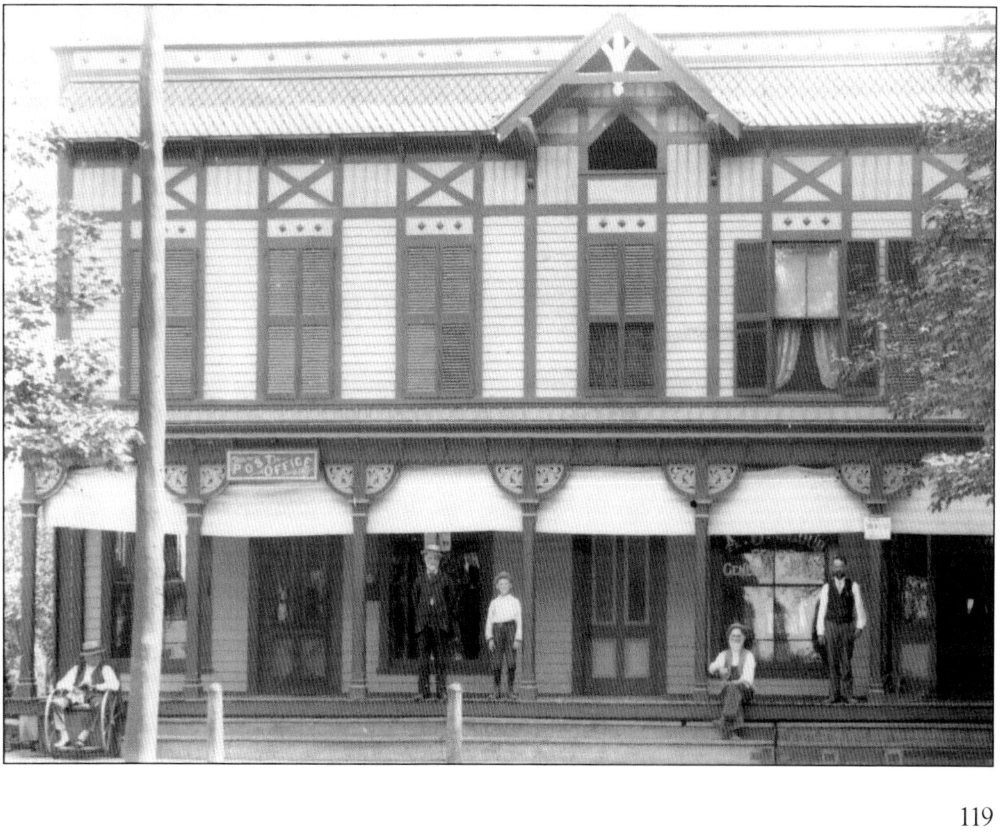

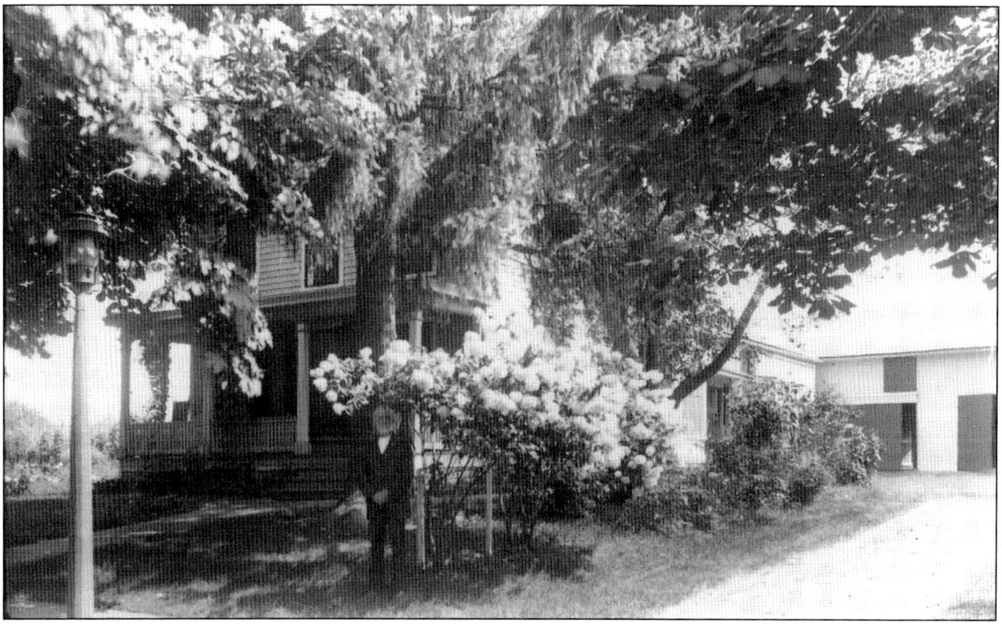

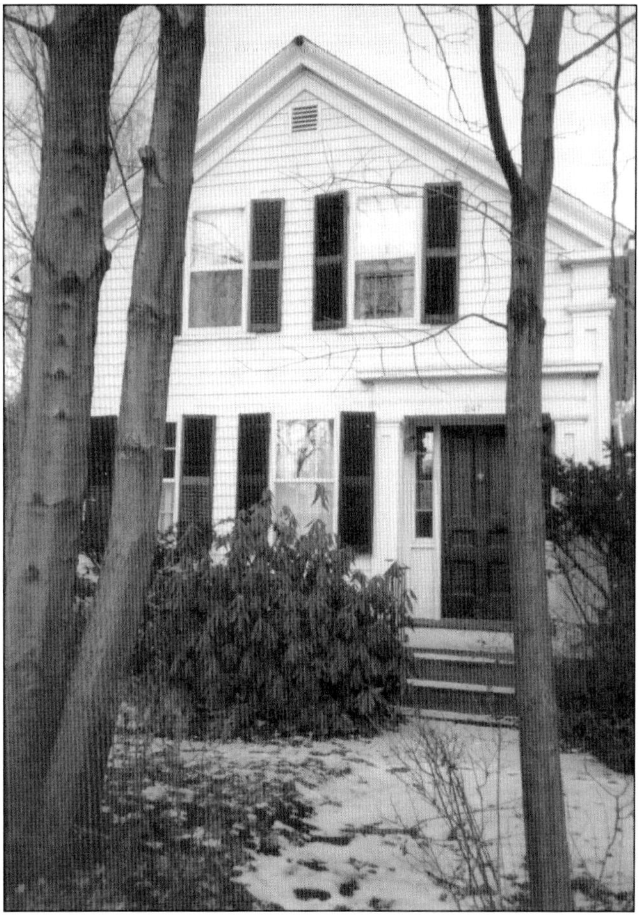

Continuing down the street, the house above is at 1157 North Pleasant Street, pictured in the 1890s. It was built around 1863 by John Russell, a farmer, and is a side-gabled house with a full veranda. In 1957, university professor Lawrence E. Briggs lived there with his family, and in 2009, engineer Edward L. Valerio and his family lived there. Farther on, at left, is the house at 1147 North Pleasant Street. It was built in 1835 and has a recessed doorway with four-pane sidelights. Julia L. Pushee, a widow, lived there in 1957. (Courtesy of Robert Winne.)

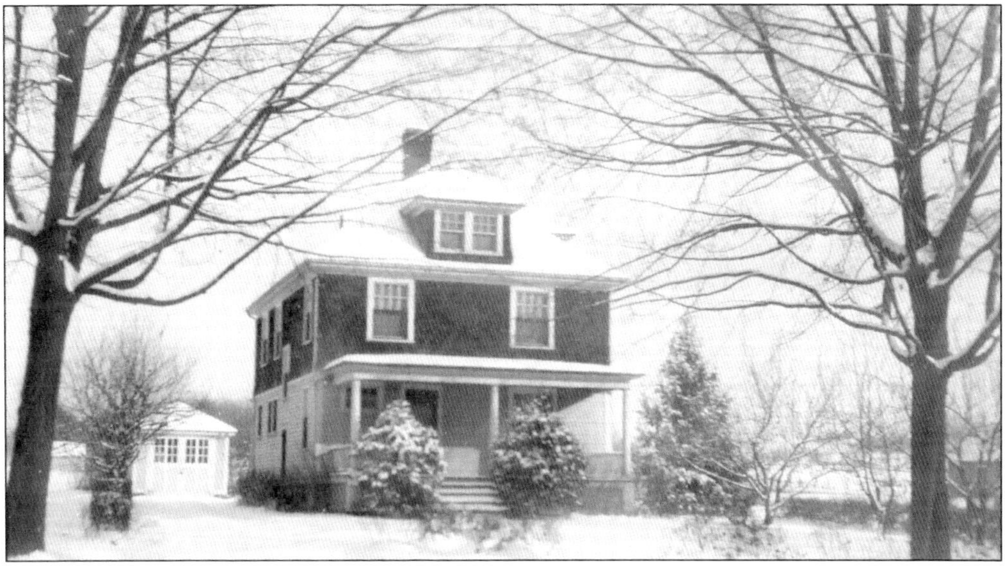

Next on the left is the house on the corner of Fisher Street at 1133 North Pleasant Street, built in 1910 with four bedrooms. In 1957, Robert and Claire Watson lived there. He was a chef at the university. Fisher Street was named for Rev. George E. Fisher, whose portrait appears on page 32. The photograph below shows a bridge over a small brook, taken from behind the Gustin home on the corner of Harris and Fisher Streets. The bridge led to the farm next door.

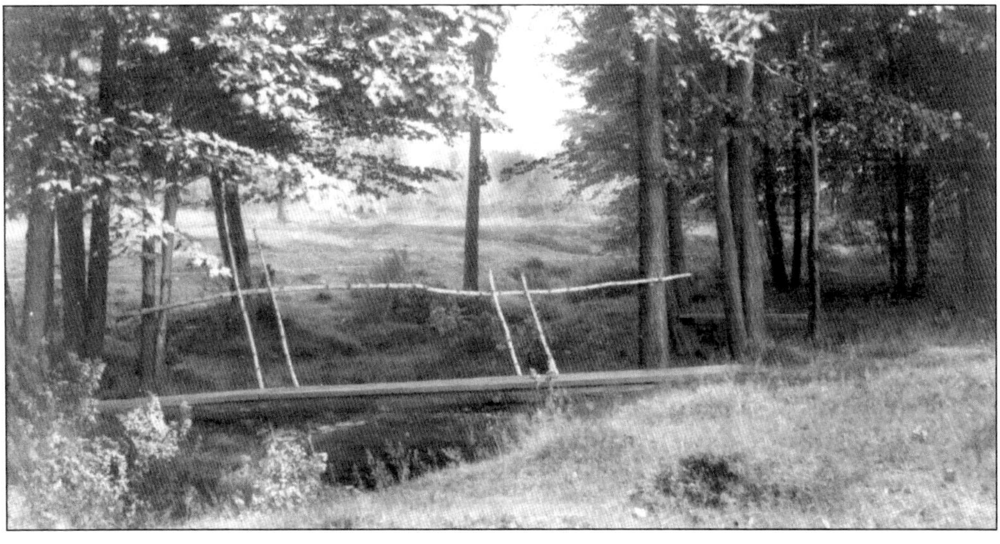

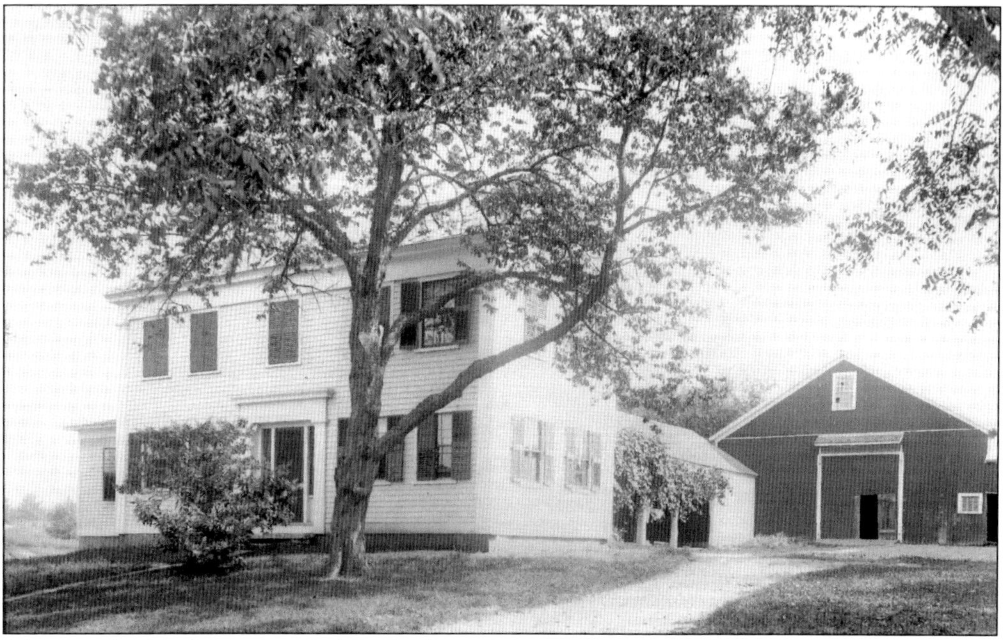

Above is the farmhouse at 1089 North Pleasant Street as it was in the 1890s. Since 2005, it has belonged to the North Amherst Community Farm, a nonprofit group that raised money from the state, the town, and local people to buy the farm, put the land in conservation, and save it from a housing development. Two farmers rent the land, calling it Simple Gifts Farm. They raise vegetables organically. They also have chickens, pigs, sheep, and cattle. They sell shares to local people and encourage them to visit the place whenever they like. The farm is within a one-mile radius of 10,000 people. Below is the farm's neighboring farmhouse to the south as it was in the 1890s. Mary and Leon Barkowski lived at 1069 North Pleasant Street. Their daughter was a nurse at Amherst College.

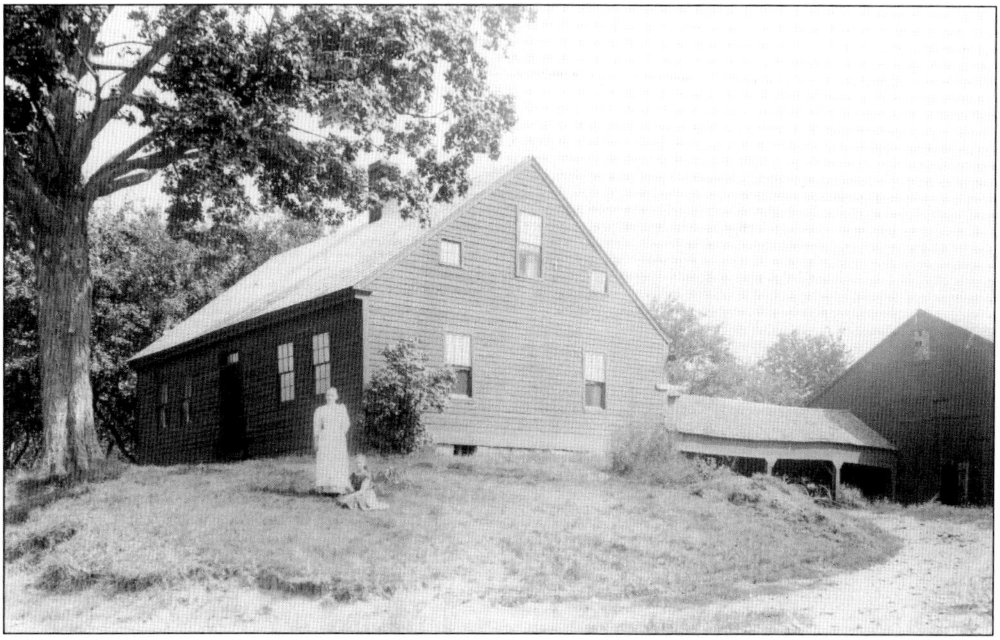

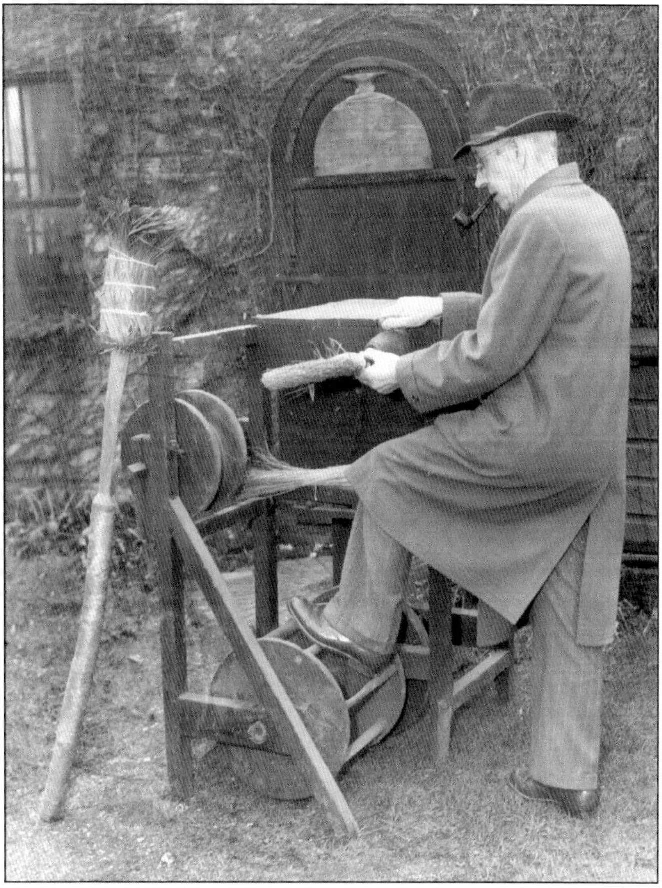

Robert Newlon lived at 1039 North Pleasant Street, where he had an antique shop called The Old Barn. According to a story in the *Daily Hampshire Gazette* of April 18, 1953, he is demonstrating how a broom-making machine works. Below is an 1890s photograph of 1013 North Pleasant Street. The house sits close to the street there still. In 1957, it was occupied by Robert C. Ames, who worked in investment services, and his family, and by Hans C. Duus, a professor, and his family.

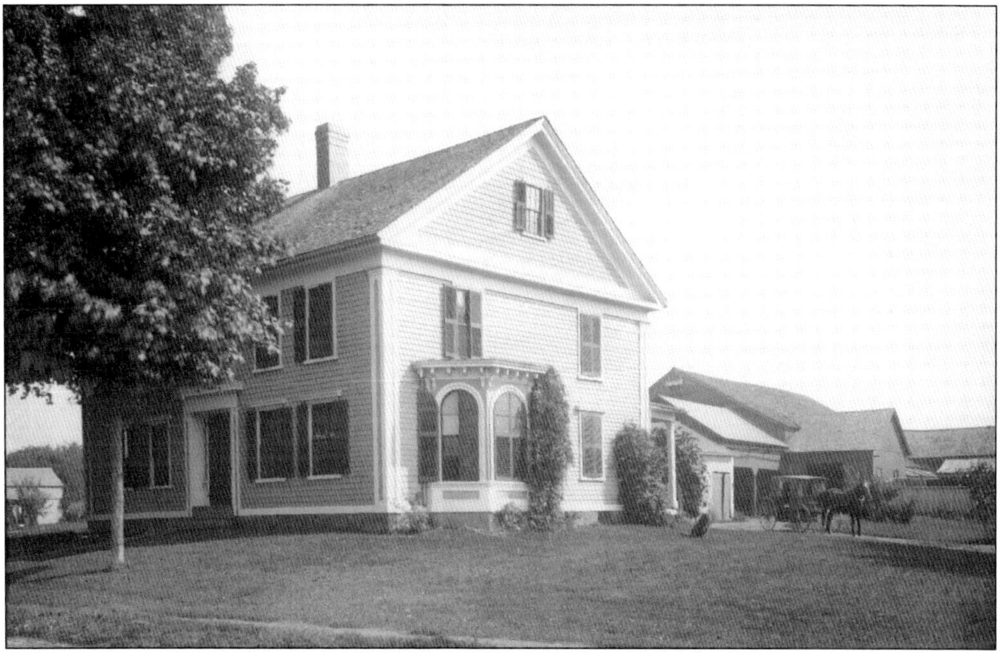

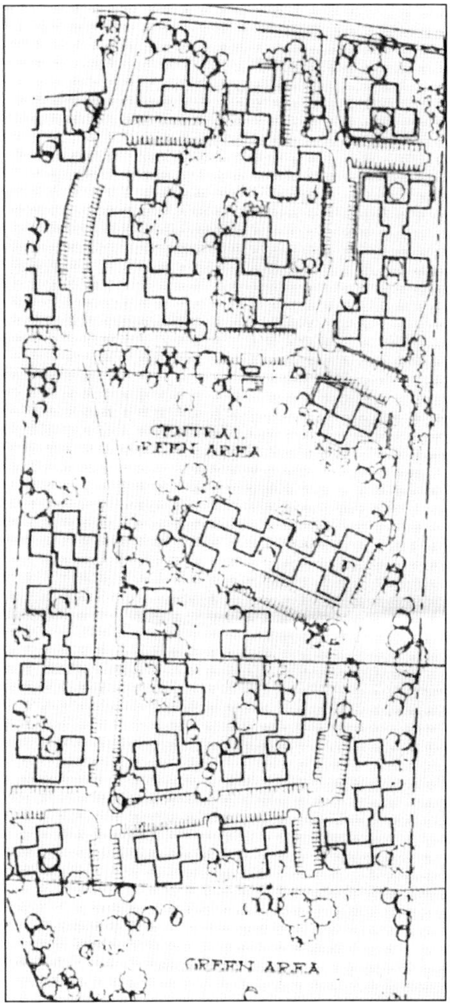

In 1968, Stephen Puffer decided to build apartment houses that would not look like blocks of apartments. He bought land on the west side of North Pleasant Street and with his architects came up with the scheme pictured at left. North Pleasant Street is shown at the top of the drawing. Puffton Village opened in 1970. The high rents angered many people. In the photograph below, Amherst police chief Don Maia makes an appearance at a protest in 1976.

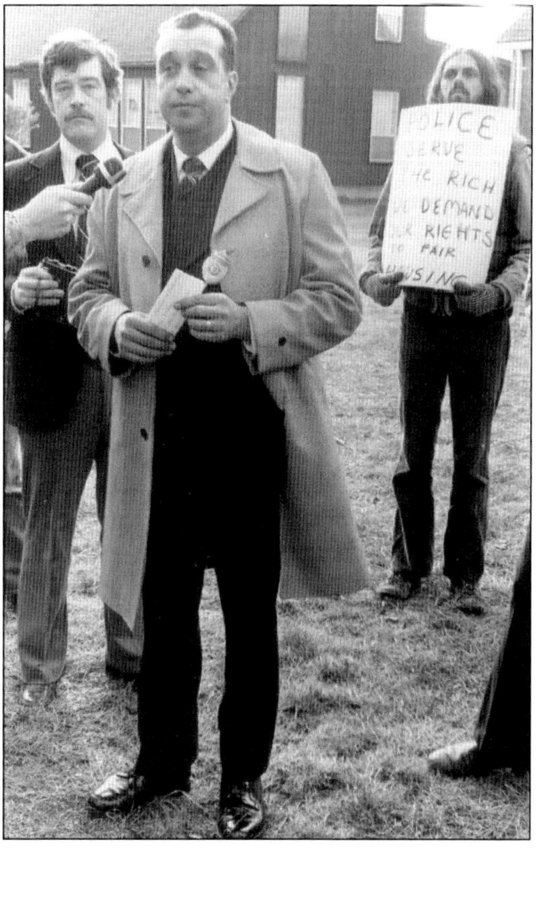

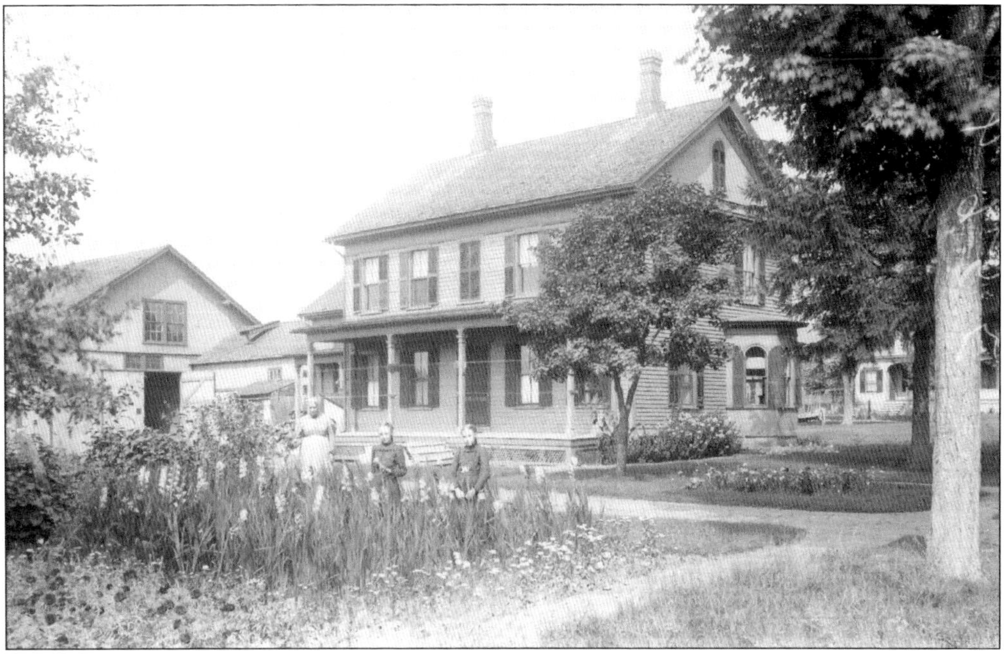

The house at 1106 North Pleasant Street, above, and the house at 1136, below, appear here in the 1890s. The house below belonged to Doctor Fish from the 1830s through the 1870s. George Cooke often met him at the bedside of ill patients, and had this to say: "Dr. Fish had small eyes, a round red face, a short neck, wore high collars to his coats, and when sitting, especially when driving seemed to have retreated for hibernating. His general education was not superior, yet for professional and indeed broad common sense judgment, he was really excellent." He was also impressed with Doctor Fish's skills with a horse, including his treatment of them.

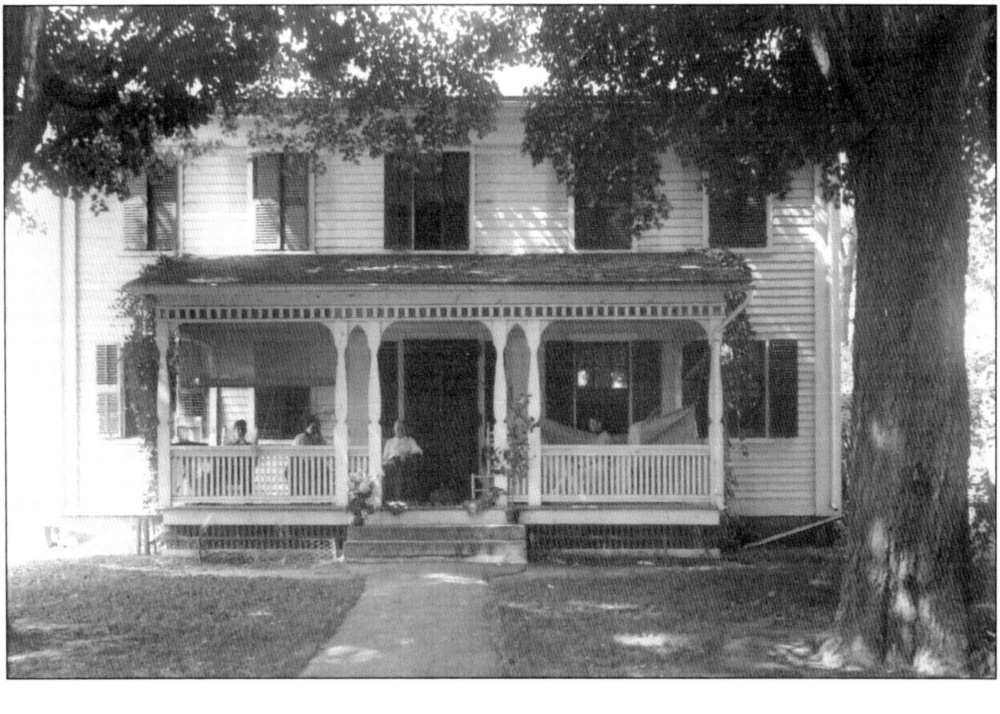

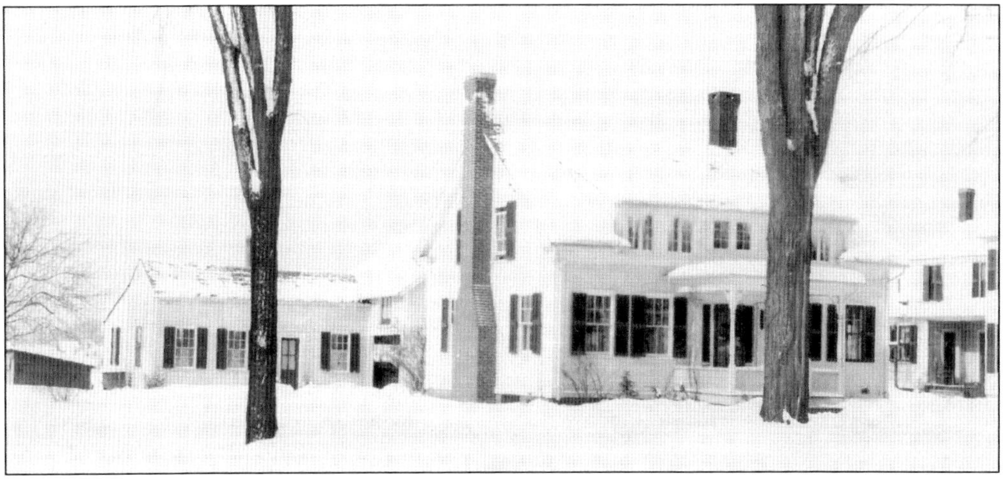

The house at 1146 North Pleasant Street (above) is a side-gabled, center hall plan house. The veranda was added in the late 1800s. The photographs of this and the house below were taken in the 1890s. George Cooke wrote that he designed the Greek Revival house below at 1170 North Pleasant Street on the back of an envelope. It was built as the church parsonage in 1840. William Kellogg sold the land for $81, and the house was built for $1,409.99. This photograph shows a pleasant tent in the yard to the left of the house. In the 1970s, the house belonged to Garret and Mary Mathews.

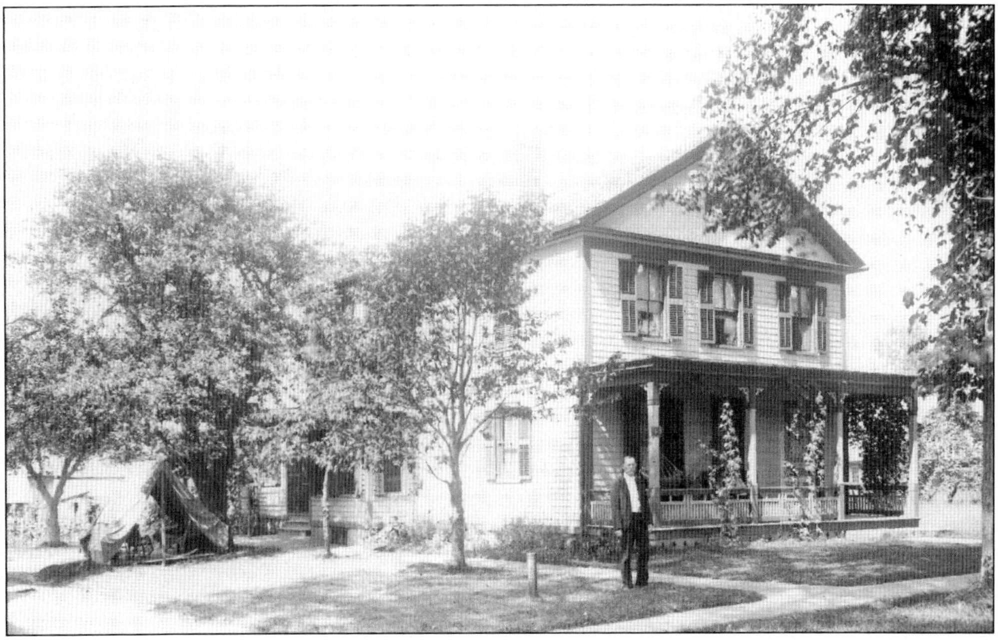

Further Reading

Here are suggestions for further reading. All of these sources are available at Amherst's public library, the Jones Library, Special Collections:

Essays on Amherst's History. Amherst, MA: Vista Trust, 1978.

Acker, April, Cindy Mathews, James Mathews, and Abby Acker. *Cushman Village: The Eighth Wonder of the World.*

Callahan, Isabelle M. "My Eighty-Two Years in Amherst." Unpublished typescript, Sept. 4, 2011, plus addition, 2012.

Carpenter, Edward Wilton and Charles Frederick Morehouse. *History of the Town of Amherst, Massachusetts*. Amherst, MA: Press of Carpenter & Morehouse, 1896. Available for free on Google Books.

Cooke, George. *Reminiscences of the North Parish, Amherst, Massachusetts. from Oct. 1838 to March 1852, Former Pastor (AE, 72) now 1883, living in Winchester, Massachusetts. Scribblings at random, Topographically arranged, in the form of a letter-at-large to the Rev. Geo. H. Johnson present pastor*. Unpublished manuscript.

Essays on Amherst's History. Amherst, MA: Vista Trust, 1978.

Folsom, Ethel King. "From Shutesbury to the Connecticut." Unpublished typescript, September 1938.

Rand, Frank Prentice. *The Village of Amherst: A Landmark of Light*. Amherst, MA: Amherst Historical Society, 1958.